Participatory Pluralism

Participatory Pluralism

POLITICAL PARTICIPATION AND INFLUENCE
IN THE UNITED STATES AND SWEDEN

Marvin E. Olsen

Nelson-Hall nh Chicago

LIBRARY OF CONGRESS CATALOGING IN PUBLICATION DATA

Olsen, Marvin Elliott.
  Participatory pluralism.

  Includes bibliographical references and index.
  1. Political participation – United States.
2. Political participation – Sweden. 3. Pluralism
(Social sciences) – United States. 4. Pluralism
(Social sciences) – Sweden. I. Title.
JK1764.045   323'.042'0973   82-2263
ISBN 0-88229-711-2   AACR2

Copyright ©1982 by Marvin Elliott Olsen

All rights reserved. No part of this book may be reproduced in any form without permission in writing from the publisher, except by a reviewer who wishes to quote brief passages in connection with a review written for broadcast or for inclusion in a magazine or newspaper. For information address Nelson-Hall Inc., Publishers, 111 North Canal Street, Chicago, Illinois 60606.

Manufactured in the United States of America

10 9 8 7 6 5 4 3 2 1

The paper in this book is pH neutral (acid-free).

Contents

Preface

For several years I have been grappling with the question of how to expand democratic political processes in modern societies so as to maximize the ability of citizens to affect governmental policies and decisions. More pointedly, how can "power to the people" be achieved in contemporary societies?

This book brings together three strands of that endeavor. First is a theoretical concern with the sociopolitical processes and structures necessary to promote political participation and exertion of influence, which are often labeled either "participatory democracy" or "sociopolitical pluralism", although these concepts have different meanings. The second strand is an empirical concern with the ways in which individuals participate in political activities and the factors that encourage such activity. Third is another empirical concern with the role of private-interest organizations as influence mediators between the public and the government.

There is both unity and diversity in this volume. The unity is theoretical, provided by the broad perspectives of participatory democracy and sociopolitical pluralism, as well as my synthesis of them as "participatory pluralism." The diversity is empirical, in that several different research studies are reported here — differing in the problems investigated, the countries from which the data were taken, and the methodologies and styles of analysis employed. In effect, these studies can be viewed as efforts to empirically test various aspects of participatory democracy and sociopolitical pluralism theories. Some of this research has previously been published in professional journals, but the two major studies reported in chapters 4 and 10 have not been published.

Each of the main themes of this book has been strongly influenced by an earlier work in that area, to which I gratefully acknowledge my intellectual debt: for the theory of participatory democracy, Carole Pateman, *Participation and Democratic Theory* (London: Cambridge University Press, 1970); for the theory of sociopolitical pluralism, Robert A. Nisbet, *Community and Power* (New York: Oxford University Press, 1962); for individual political participation, Sidney Verba and Norman H. Nie, *Participation in America* (New York: Harper and Row, 1972); and for interest-group politics, David B. Truman, *The Governmental Process* (New York: Alfred A. Knopf, 1951).

I am also deeply indebted to many people for help in conducting the empirical studies reported in this book.

For the research conducted in Indianapolis, Indiana, a large portion of the costs of collecting and analyzing the data was financed by a research grant from the National Science Foundation. Most of the interviewing and all of the coding for these studies were done by the following graduate students in the 1968 Indianapolis Area Project of the Institute of Social Research at Indiana University: Clifford Copeland, Judy Corder, Steven Denner, Lois Downey, Keith Fernsler, Jack Franklin, Steven Gates, Joan Harms, Curdina Hill, Michaell Houston, Judith Ann Lewis, Phyllis Mansfield, Dianne Manske, Gale Mull, Richard Polikoff, Joseph Scott, Donald Simet, Larry Smith, Joan Splinter, Maria Teriumniks, Clarence Turner, Hari Uttley, Nancy Wendlandt, Tom Whitsitt, Susan Wisely, and Martin Zusman. Invaluable as both supervisors of these students and as my colleagues and critics were three advanced graduate students who served as IAP research assistants that year: Kenneth Brown, Elizabeth Mullins, and William Philliber. Betsy Gethers and Cynthia Griffin both worked innumerable hours on the initial index construction and data calculations. I especially want to express my deep appreciation to Lois Downey, Mary Anna Hovey, James Huber, and Daniel Maguire, each of whom labored many months performing the endless computer runs and other data analyses for this research.

For the studies conducted in Sweden, collection of the data was financed by research grants from the International Development Research Center and the West European Studies Program at Indiana University. The Sociology Department at Uppsala University in Sweden gave me an academic "home" for the year during which that research was conducted. Professor

Nils Elvander of the Political Science Department at Uppsala University kindly provided me with considerable background information and advice in planning the research. Interviews for the survey in Gävle were conducted by students in the Sociology Department at Uppsala University and supervised by Dr. Jürgen Hartmann of that department. For the study of organizational influence procedures, I am indebted to all the Swedish organizational and governmental leaders who gave so generously of their time for the interviews, and for their willingness to be interviewed in English. I am also very grateful to Dr. Lennart Lundqvist of the National Swedish Institute for Building Research in Gävle, Sweden, for his many helpful suggestions for improving that portion of the manuscript.

Finally, I want to gratefully thank Carol Gorski for her detailed and painstaking editing of the manuscript.

To live in a civil society is the first step toward civilization; such a society comes about only through political activity.

Robert J. Pranger
The Eclipse of Citizenship

1. Political Powerlessness as Reality*

Why are the times so dark?
Men know each other not at all,
But governments quite clearly change
From bad to worse.

Days dead and gone were more worth while.
Now what holds sway? Deep gloom and boredom,
Justice and law nowhere to be found.
I know no more where I belong.
                                        —Eustache Deschamps

A sense of political powerlessness is certainly not unique to our era, as seen in the writings of the fifteenth-century French poet Deschamps. Many commentators on modern social life nevertheless view estrangement from power and politics as a fundamental and pervasive characteristic of all urban-industrial-bureaucratic societies: "Rarely before have men experienced such mass resignation before the forces of society, such a sense of distance from the sources of power, such defeatism in the face of an explosive world situation" (Keniston, 1960).

*Reprinted by permission from Marvin E. Olsen, "Political Powerlessness as Reality" in Theories of *Alienation,* edited by R. Felix Geyer and David R. Schweitzer (Leiden, The Netherlands: Martinus Nijhoff Social Sciences Division, 1976), pp. 245–54. Portions of the original article are omitted here.

Since the 1950s, the concept of political alienation has come increasingly into vogue as an explanation of all sorts of political phenomena, and political sociologists have explored its effects in such diverse areas as public opinion, voting turnout, community referendums, protest legitimacy, political socialization, extremist politics, and party involvement. An impressive array of scholarly research has demonstrated that political alienation does have observable—but often rather small—effects on all kinds of political attitudes and behavior. Moreover, these effects appear to be at least partially independent of socioeconomic status, although they tend to become nonsignificant after participation in interest associations has been taken into account (Erbe, 1964).

My purpose here is not to review or criticize this heritage of social-psychological research, however. Rather, my twin goals here are to (a) call into question the basic conception of political alienation that has underlain almost all of this research and argue that we have been looking at the problem from a seriously biased perspective; and (b) suggest several courses of action that might significantly alter the position of individuals in relation to the political system, and hence reduce political powerlessness in modern societies.

As originally conceived by Marx, alienation is inherent in capitalistic societies as workers become separated from the products of their labor and are forced by their social conditions to view themselves and others as impersonal objects.

> Thus alienated labor turns the *species life of man* . . . into an alien being and into a *means* for his *individual existence*. It alienates from man his own body, external nature, his mental life, and his *human* life. A direct consequence of the alienation of man from the product of his labor, from his life activity and from his species life, is that man is alienated from other men . . . [Marx, 1963: 103]

For Marx and his followers (Fromm, 1961), therefore, alienation is an objective social condition produced by the nature of modern capitalistic—or industrial (Dahrendorf, 1959)—society.

As American sociologists "rediscovered" Marx in the 1950s, however, they applied the prevailing social psychological orientation of that time to his concept of alienation. Instead of an objective condition existing in society, alienation became a subjective attitude within the individual.

Writing at the end of that decade, Bell (1959) carefully distinguished between these two meanings of alienation:

> The idea of alienation as derived from Marx and employed by intellectuals today, has a double meaning which can best be distinguished as *estrangement* and *reification*. The first is essentially a sociopsychological condition in which the individual experiences a sense of distance, or a divorce from his society or community. . . . The second . . . implies that an individual is treated as an object and turned into a thing and loses his identity in the process. . . . The two shades of meaning of estrangement and depersonalization are sociologically quite distinct.

Most subsequent researchers have chosen to treat alienation as a subjective attitude, largely or totally ignoring Marx's argument that dehumanization is created by the conditions of modern society. This tendency may have partly been caused by a general resistance to Marxist political philosophies among American social scientists at that time, although two other likely contributing factors were (a) the dominant tendency in American sociology during that period to interpret many social phenomena in psychological terms; and (b) the fact that scales were available to measure subjective estrangement, but not object reification, which clearly influenced the direction of subsequent research.

Students of political behavior, consequently, have typically conceptualized political alienation as a subjective sense of powerlessness or futility toward the political system (Seeman, 1959; Thompson and Horton, 1960; McDill and Ridley, 1962; Litt, 1963; Olsen, 1965). In the words of Murray Levine (1960), "The alienated voter who feels powerless believes that his vote or any other political action he may take has no influence on the course of political events." Similarly, I have in the past described political alienation as taking two contrasting forms, one of which I called "attitudes of incapability," which occur when the individual feels incapable of participating effectively in the political system because of its basic nature (Olsen, 1969).

While it is certainly true that—for a variety of reasons—some people tend to feel powerless politically while others do not, such attitudes unfortunately tell us little about the actual conditions existing in a society. Since objective reality and subjective attitudes are often not perfectly aligned, individuals who do exercise considerable influence within the political system may nevertheless feel politically powerless—which might be justified on the argument that no one really controls the political system of modern societies, but which is not true in comparison with other people. Conversely, individuals who are totally incapable of exerting any effective political influence may nevertheless experience no subjective sense of political powerlessness—which may be due either to ignorance or to "false consciousness" in the Marxian sense.

My thesis in this essay is that it is time for social scientists to again "rediscover" Marx's idea of alienation, but this time retain his original conception of it as an objective social condition rather than a subjective personal attitude. In particular, I argue that large portions of the population in all modern societies are in reality largely or totally powerless in relation to the political system. Political powerlessness is an objective fact of contemporary social existence, not merely a subjective view of the world. To the extent that individuals become aware of this condition of mass powerlessness, they may experience feelings of incapability toward politics, but political powerlessness is social reality in modern societies.

To clarify this distinction between objective conditions and subjective attitudes, I propose that we reserve the term *political powerlessness* for objective situations in which the nature of the political system prevents individuals from exercising significant influence on governmental decisions, policies, and actions. Let us then use the term *political alienation* for the subjective feeling that one cannot affect politics.

Before carrying this argument further, let me digress to answer two initial questions that are likely to be levied at this thesis. First, are you not implying that political powerlessness is a serious social problem in modern societies? What grounds are there for this stance, when it is obviously impossible for all citizens in a society such as the United States to participate directly in governmental affairs? My answer is that, although the amount of influence any individual can exert on the national government is severely limited under even the best conditions, political democracy nevertheless rests on the assumption that citizens can collectively, if not individually, ultimately control the government. When the people are powerless, however, that control is absent, and most people are unable to exert any significant political influence at all, no matter how much effort they expend. Powerlessness is clearly never total among all citizens in a society, for at least some must govern, but my argument is that the vast majority of the population in the contemporary United States and other modern societies is objectively powerless, both individually and collectively.

The last statement leads directly into the second anticipated question: Are you suggesting that there has been a historical trend toward political powerlessness, so that people living today exert less political influence than did citizens a hundred years ago? No, I am not suggesting that there has been a decline over the past fifty or one hundred or two hundred years in the amount of political power wielded by the mass of citizens. If anything, there may have been a slight increase in absolute terms. My point, rather, is that, with rising educational levels and mass communications, there is at the present time a steadily growing awareness by increasing numbers of people that they are in fact politically powerless, coupled with widespread belief that the situation should be otherwise. Hence the answer to this second question is that people today are powerless relative to what they think they should be in an ideal democracy.

Thus far there has been virtually no empirical research on this topic of mass political powerlessness in modern societies; hence I cannot offer any statistical data to substantiate my thesis. I must therefore caution the reader to view this as a speculative theoretical argument, not a verified empirical generalization. Nevertheless, at least five lines of observation and reasoning lead to my proposition, as sketched in the following paragraphs.

1. *Mass enfranchisement is virtually meaningless as a form of political participation in modern societies.* Classical democratic theory rests on the assumption that all citizens of a society are essentially equal in both their concern with public issues and their competence to make political decisions, which leads to the proposition that all citizens should exercise the same amount of influence through the ballot—"one man, one vote." Formulated as a reaction against the gross inequalities of European feudal society, classical democratic theory offered a radically new conception of how power should be distributed and used in a society. The democratic ideal of political power resting collectively in the hands of all citizens, who entrust it periodically through mass elections to public officials who are empowered to act on behalf of the people, has been the impetus for one of the most far-reaching shifts in political philosophy in the history of mankind. This vision of political equality for all has become the central ideological theme of most political struggle throughout the world in the twentieth century, and its acceptance as a political ideal is precisely why more and more people are today experiencing their political powerlessness as an undesirable or intolerable condition.

In actual practice, however, voting for national political leaders—I exempt local elections from this argument—has become little more than a public ritual through which people discharge their minimal political responsibilities and grant legitimacy to the existing political system. Many well-documented facts can be marshaled to support this contention. Large proportions of the people in even the most highly developed societies know almost nothing about their political system or any current political issues. They express little or no interest in politics, rarely discuss any political topics with others, avoid political news in the mass media, and have no party preference. On election day, people may go to the polls out of a sense of citizen duty, but research (Verba and Nie, 1972; Olsen, 1973) has demonstrated that close to half the adult population in the United States is not competent or concerned enough to participate meaningfully in national elections.

Even if people are politically competent and concerned, however, the political party system is usually quite effective in severely limiting the amount of influence they can exercise through the polls. First of all, this system allows them to vote only for candidates, not on specific substantive issues; nor is the winning candidate obliged to support the positions that he or she espoused in the campaign. Second, a two-party system forces both parties (if they wish to win the election) to pick candidates who stand as near the political center as possible, in order to attract the large mass of undecided and unconcerned voters. The frequent result is "Tweedledee-Tweedledum" elections in which opposing candidates are politically indistinguishable. Alternatively, in multiparty systems, one party commonly becomes so strong relative to the others that no meaningful choice remains; one can vote one's principles or prejudices if one wishes, but doing so will not likely affect the outcome of the election. And third, as we have clearly seen in recent years, election outcomes can be heavily influenced, if not predetermined, by the amount of money spent in campaigns. This obviously benefits whichever party can attract (or coerce) the most financial support, and reduces elections to gigantic advertising campaigns.

Indeed, if one wished to be slightly cynical, it might convincingly be argued that popular enfranchisement is only a mechanism devised by the ruling classes of modern societies for pacifying the masses by encouraging them to believe that they are ultimately controlling the government, thus masking their actual powerlessness and keeping them committed to the existing political system. Rather than resist democratic ideology, these sophisticated elites have realized that, by accepting universal suffrage—while maintaining effective control of the political system through manipulation of the parties, financial resources, mass media, personal relationships, etc.—they can have a political system with legitimacy, support, and stability and still retain their dominant positions. Their political power is thus less obvious than in monarchies or dictatorships, but it may be even more effective precisely because it is more subtle. The masses of citizens, meanwhile, remain pacified and docile, but relatively powerless.

2. The second line of reasoning leading to my thesis of mass powerlessness concerns other forms of political participation. As Robert Pranger (1968:30) has argued, "representative democracy . . . consistently encourages low-quality citizen action by making a fetish out of only one form of political participation—voting." There are many other alternative forms of political participation, however, and perhaps if we could shuck the voting fetish we might discover more effective means of exerting influence on government. Rather than relying solely on voting, the concerned citizen might join a political club or organization, attend public meetings, write letters to political leaders, do volunteer work for a political party, circulate a petition, or join a demonstration.

These possibilities do exist, but the problem is that relatively few people ever take advantage of them. In the United States, for instance, no more than one-fourth of the adult population has even once done any of these things (Verba and Nie, 1972:31), and the proportion who do them on a regular basis is minute. *Most people therefore reinforce their political powerlessness through failure to engage in any forms of political participation other than voting.*

Even if these alternative forms of political participation were much more extensively utilized, however, it is doubtful whether most citizens would gain appreciably greater leverage over their governments. These procedures are certainly useful as upward communication channels, enabling political leaders to become more accurately informed about the needs, interests, and wishes of their constituents. By and large, however, such procedures bring little effective pressure to bear on political leaders and usually exert only factual or moral persuasion. If the leaders are genuinely concerned with serving the public interest and are in general agreement with the majority of citizens concerning political values and goals, such persuasive tactics may be sufficient. But any time fundamental conflicts arise—whether based on class, ethnic, ideological, or any other factors—most of these alternative forms of political participation become relatively useless for exerting meaningful influence on government (Verba and Nie, 1972:299–333). They lack the political clout necessary to significantly affect established political policies or entrenched power elites. This argument is clearly more applicable at the national than at the local level, but under no conditions do these alternative forms of political participation appear to erase the problem of mass political powerlessness.

3. Voting and other traditional forms of political participation may be somewhat more effective as influence channels on the local than on the national level, but their utility is rapidly declining as contemporary societies become increasingly metropolitanized. This trend refers to the emergence of huge metropolitan complexes consisting of a central city, surrounding suburbs, dependent satellite communities, and adjacent areas of "rurban" settlement. With a total population of perhaps a million or more persons, a metropolitan area is economically and culturally a single entity but is commonly divided into 50 or even 100 autonomous political units and numerous functional subsystems ranging from education to sewerage.

For fifty years, sociologists have been writing about the loss of individual identity and social relationships that can occur in urban settings, but much less attention has been given to the concurrent loss of opportunities for exerting influence on local government. In contrast to a small town or even a moderate-sized city, the sheer scope of the metropolitan area makes it almost impossible for most residents to have any direct interaction with political leaders. Furthermore, the organizational complexity of a large metropolis virtually defies any attempt at rational political participation or leadership (Sayre and Kaufman, 1960), and elections are often tightly controlled by a powerful political machine. Even the ethnic and other neighborhoods within the city that have traditionally given urban dwellers some sense of local belonging and involvement are rapidly disappearing, while out in the suburbs housing and commercial developments expand and merge to the point where no separate identifiable communities remain. Finally, local government becomes even more remote from the citizens to the extent that functional activities are organized and administered on a metropolitanwide basis by centralized and politically autonomous boards of professionals. *The individual resident of a contemporary metropolitan complex is therefore quite realistic in believing that he or she has no significant effect on the shape or activities of the community.* The metropolitan resident is essentially powerless locally as well as nationally and is quite aware of this situation.

4. The picture is no different if one turns instead to such realms of social life as work or interest organizations. These and many other

activities of daily living commonly occur within large bureaucratic organizations, the central structural feature of which is a vertical hierarchy of authority. Max Weber's classical bureaucratic model, which underlies most contemporary formal organizations, assumes that hierarchial structure provides the most efficient way of organizing and operating complex organizations. In the name of functional efficiency, therefore, hierarchial authority pervades the organizations in which most people live large portions of their daily lives.

Since most members of any large organization will necessarily occupy positions near the bottom of the authority hierarchy, they will inevitably find themselves relatively or totally powerless in relation to their organizations. The flow of communications, commands, and controls will be largely or entirely downward from the top of the structure to the masses of members at the bottom. Although sophisticated executives may solicit opinions or complaints from the members, there is rarely an expectation, among either members or executives, that people at the bottom of the structure will (or should) be able to exert meaningful influence on organizational decisions or policies. Ralf Dahrendorf's (1959) conception of modern societies—as polarized around two classes defined in terms of occupying or not occupying positions of authority in bureaucratic organizations—is certainly oversimplified, but it nevertheless points out the critical importance of bureaucratic authority, mass powerlessness, and resulting potential class conflict in all realms of social life. Participatory democracy is hardly an ideal, let alone an avowed goal or operating practice, in most contemporary bureaucratic organizations. And almost all attempts thus far to provide organizational members with opportunities for exerting more influence—from human relations management to workers' councils—have proved to be either hypocritical farces or functional disasters (Pateman, 1970).

Moreover, when a structure of hierarchical authority is compounded by other features commonly found in industrial, business, and many other organizations—such as (a) minute role specialization and specification that deprive actors of any opportunity for autonomy or creativity in their roles, and (b) pervasive procedural rules and control mechanisms that ensure rigid conformity to established standards—the ordinary member of such an organization is left not only powerless in relation to organizational decisions, but also a mere mechanical cog in a vast, complex, automated social process. No wonder he or she feels politically alienated, as writers from Marx to Mills (1956) have repeatedly insisted.

The crucial point, again, is that the ordinary member of a large bureaucratic organization is in reality powerless to affect that organization in any significant way.

5. Finally, from a more abstract but encompassing perspective, *numerous observers and critics of modern societies have argued that a general tendency toward increasing power centralization is evident everywhere— but especially on the national level.* In the process of power centralization, the ability to exercise influence or control over any particular set of social activities or organizations becomes concentrated in the hands of a relatively small number of actors, commonly termed elites. This process can be caused by numerous factors, including creation of social patterns and rules in areas where none previously existed, formalization of previously informal authority relationships, growing functional dominance of one position or activity over others dependent on it, or outright imposition of force. Whatever its causes, however, the process of power centralization obviously decreases the amount of influence that the masses of nonelites can exercise in that setting, leaving them increasingly powerless.

On the national level in the United States, C. Wright Mills (1956) pointed over twenty years ago to the extent of power centralization occurring in business and industry, government, and the military. To this list today might also be added communication, transportation, labor unions, science, and several other realms of activity. Numerous critics have questioned Mills's thesis that the elites in these various functional realms are coalescing to form a single, unified "power elite," and the more common model today consists of multiple sets of "strategic elites" (Keller, 1963), each wielding dominant power within a limited sphere of functional activity. From the perspective of the ordinary citizen, however, the process of power centralization leaves him or her effectively powerless long before it reaches its final state of complete unification. This fact is demonstrated by numerous daily experiences, from the frustration of trying to correct a mistake made by the automated billing service of a national retail organization to the realization that all three national television networks are slanting the news in the same way. As a result, individuals quickly become thoroughly aware of the extent to which their social world is shaped and controlled by actors who are remote, unknown, and completely immutable by ordinary people.

As one encounters such experiences time and time again in the course of daily living, the fact of one's relative powerlessness becomes inescapable. Consequently, when asked how they view themselves in relation to society, the political system, or any other realm of considerable power centralization, individuals are understandably likely to answer "powerless to affect what goes on here." The social scientist may then label such persons as "alienated" and devise elaborate social-psychological models in an attempt to explain what is in fact straightforward social reality. Most members of modern societies are relatively powerless, and attitudes of alienation merely reflect reality. As eloquently expressed by Martin Oppenheimer (1971:271):

> The history of industrialized, urbanized society is the history of man's increasing alienation from decision-making processes. As society has moved from village life to city, from closely-integrated primary groups in which one's relationship to all aspects of life was well understood and well regulated, to a life in which individuals are no longer the captives of tradition, freedom has become possible. Yet freedom from tradition has not become freedom to decide the course of one's life, because modern life is organized, bureaucratic, and increasingly centralized. The institutions which have freed Western Man from "the idiocy of rural life" have at the same time subjected him to organizational structures farther and farther removed from his immediate control. The factory, the school, government, religion, the media, and even the arts are more and more subject to bureaucratic processes, and less and less open to communication from, much less control by, those who work in them and are subject to them, except on the highest levels of the "power structure."

In summary, I am suggesting that large segments of the population in all modern nations are in reality powerless to significantly affect the political decisions, policies, and actions of their societies. This condition exists despite mass enfranchisement and other forms of popular political participation, and despite the insistence on "citizen rule" in the ideology of democracy.

Given this fact of contemporary political powerlessness, standing in stark contradiction to the democratic ideal of equalizing and maximizing citizens' opportunities for exerting influence on government, how might political reality be altered to bring it closer to democratic ideology? The empirical studies reported in subsequent chapters of this book, conducted in both the United States and Sweden, were all intended to explore various aspects of this problem. The final chapter then draws on this research to propose a theoretical design for political systems in contemporary societies that is intended to increase the ability of all citizens to exert meaning-ful political influence and thus escape their current condition of political powerlessness. Before turning to those studies, however, we shall in the next chapter examine the two currently prevailing theoretical models for increasing political participation and influence: participatory democracy and sociopolitical pluralism.

2. Participatory Democracy and Sociopolitical Pluralism

Two "ideal-type" political cultures may be envisaged: One that gives citizens primary responsibility for governing themselves directly—a "politics of participation"—and one that grants the most important governmental responsibilities for making authoritative decisions to a select few acting in behalf of, or in spite of, the citizen body—a "politics of power." . . . The politics of power divides into two kinds of leadership: those who act "in behalf of"—a "politics of representation"—and those who act "in spite of"—a "politics of oligarchy." In either case, however, the few govern and the many are governed, a situation which is the most salient feature in any form of power politics. [Robert Pranger, 1968:12]

Pranger's polarity of "politics of power" versus "politics of participation" is oversimplified, since the purpose of participation is to exercise power, but it dramatically emphasizes a fundamental feature of all modern societies: a few rule the many. As a result—as argued in the preceding chapter—the masses of citizens are relatively powerless to influence political decision making.

Inequality is certainly not new in human existence. With the possible exception of the most primitive tribes, all societies have evidenced numerous forms of organized inequality: economic, political, social, legal, racial, and sexual. Much human history is a record of steadily increasing inequality in all these realms, to the point where small sets of elites have dominated, controlled, and exploited the masses of people (Lenski, 1966).

13

14

A countertrend has slowly but incessantly been gaining strength in modern societies during the past two hundred years, however—a development that Herbert Gans (1968) calls the "Equality Revolution." This trend has been most evident in the economic realm, as more and more people have struggled to attain adequate incomes and standards of living. In most Western societies, large segments of the population have substantially improved their economic lot during the twentieth century, although this has generally resulted from rapid rates of economic growth rather than extensive redistribution of existing wealth (Miller and Roby, 1970).

In the political arena, early efforts to establish elected parliaments and gain universal suffrage (Moore, 1966)—efforts that continue today in many parts of the world—have taken on new dimensions as citizens demand an increasingly larger voice in political decision making and governmental processes (Leggett, 1973). In the legal realm, we have witnessed a continual struggle to expand the sphere of protected civil rights—from freedom of speech and trial by jury to sexual activities and protection from child abuse—and to extend these rights to all persons (Marshall, 1964). In complex bureaucratic organizations, workers, students, clients, and other participants are increasingly questioning and challenging traditional hierarchical authority patterns (Bottomore, 1964; Thayer, 1973). And most recently, ethnic minorities, women, and other disadvantaged peoples have insistently joined the Equality Revolution (Killian, 1968; Howard, 1974). Total equality is far from being attained in any of these realms, but the struggle continues, expands, and grows in strength.

Political Power and Equality

Underlying all manifestations of inequality in human social life is the process of power exertion (Dahrendorf, 1959; Lenski, 1966). Let us therefore briefly examine the ideas of social and political power and then explore three different conceptions of political equality.

Social and Political Power

In its broadest meaning, social power is the ability to shape the process of social organization through time, despite resistance (Olsen, 1978). Social power can be exercised by either individuals or organizations, but it always occurs within dynamic social relationships and is never a static possession of any single social actor. Power exertion can vary from highly problematic influence attempts to fully deterministic control procedures, and it can assume such specific forms as persuasion, authority, force, and coercion.

Thus individuals and organizations acquire and utilize resources to exert influence or control on others in pursuit of their goals. Structured patterns of inequality emerge whenever this power exertion becomes seriously unbalanced or unchecked. The exercise of social power is a morally neutral social process that can be utilized to attain all manner of goals, but inequality and exploitation are exceedingly common outcomes of unrestrained power exertion.

We speak of political power when the process of power exertion is directed toward political or governmental decision making. Politics is only one of many arenas for the exercise of power in contemporary societies, but as governments assume increasingly dominant roles in modern societies (Galbraith, 1973), the ability to influence governmental policies and programs rapidly becomes the crucial key to affecting the entire process of power exertion and patterned inequality. Our focus in this book, consequently, is on political participation and influence exertion, but this concern is set within the broader context of the Equality Revolution. Our purpose here is to investigate ways of achieving greater political equality in modern societies by expanding the ability of citizens to participate in and influence political decision making.

Political Equality

As an ideal, achieving greater political equality is highly appealing to many people for many reasons. But as a practical goal, what does it entail? First of all, since power is always exercised in interactions among actors and cannot be possessed by any single actor, it is never possible simply to divide the existing "power pie" into equal shares and distribute them among all actors. The resources from which power is derived might conceivably be distributed in such a manner, but not the dynamic interactive process of power exertion.

Our common tendency to think of social or political equality in terms of equal shares often results in—and reinforces—the uncritical assumption that the total amount of power in any social setting remains constant through time. In that kind of "zero-sum game" situation, any one actor gains only at the expense of others. Real social life more nearly resembles a "variable-sum game," however, in which social relationships are constantly changing. Consequently, the total amount of power being exerted is usually either increasing or decreasing through time.

In modern societies, many patterns of social organization are growing in size and complexity, thus expanding the scope and intensity of power processes. In such a growth situation, it is possible for all participants to increase their ability to exert social or political power without simultaneously depriving any other actors of this ability. Moreover, it is also possible in a growth situation to move toward greater power equality by distributing excess resources and power-wielding abilities to relatively powerless actors without arousing active resistance from elites who feel that their status is being threatened. Conversely, however, growth conditions can also mask movement toward greater inequality. As long as nonelites believe that their conditions are slowly improving, they may not realize that elites are increasing their resources and power-wielding abilities at a disproportionately faster rate. In any growth situation, therefore, we must ask not only, How much new power is being generated? but also, Who is benefiting from these changes?

A second factor to be considered when seeking greater political equality is our conceptualization of "power equalization." Are we striving for equal opportunities or equal outcomes? With an equal opportunities approach, we would attempt to give all actors (either individuals or organizations) approximately similar amounts of resources, and to structure the political system to permit and encourage everyone to participate as fully as they wished. All participants would not necessarily wield equal political power, however, since some would undoubtedly choose to be more active than others, and some would be more successful than others in their efforts to exert political power. In short, with this approach opportunities for exerting power are equalized as far as possible, but the eventual political outcomes are left unrestrained and will undoubtedly evidence at least some inequality.

With an equal outcomes approach, in contrast, we would attempt to ensure that all actors exercised approximately similar (though not necessarily identical) amounts of political power. As a result, they would presumably be able to attain relatively similar results and benefits in the political arena. In short, with this approach, power outcomes as well as opportunities would be equalized as much as possible. In addition to being extremely difficult to attain and enforce, however, this form of political equality would largely eliminate volition of action, since all power exertion would have to be regulated or controlled by the society.

Both the equal opportunities and equal outcomes conceptions of political equality thus have serious drawbacks in the eyes of many critics. The former approach permits considerable inequality in actual conditions, while the latter approach severely restricts freedom of action. It is possible, however, to synthesize these approaches into a third conception of political equality that avoids both of their objectionable features. Its goal is political equity, or fairness, rather than strict equality. To determine whether equitable political opportunities are being provided to all actors, we must have continual feedback from the outcomes of political activities. Without attempting to attain total equality of outcomes, we can establish acceptable ranges of outcomes to serve as guidelines for this feedback. As long as existing conditions remain within these acceptable ranges, we can assume that relatively equitable opportunities exist and that the resulting outcomes are relatively fair to most people. If conditions exceed these acceptable limits, however, we can take corrective actions to redistribute political resources in a more equitable manner. In short, we can aim for political equity based on a fair distribution of political opportunities and acceptable ranges of political outcomes.

Two Theories of Political Equity

Two bodies of sociopolitical theory have been developed by social scientists and political activists in recent years as strategies for promoting greater political equity in modern societies. Both are usually presented as alternatives to traditional representative democratic theory.

One of these new theories is the idea of participatory democracy. Its major proponents have been Peter Bachrach (1967), Carole Pateman (1970), Terrence Cook and Patrick Morgan (1971), and C. George Benello and Dimitrios Roussopoulos (1971), as well as many advocates of "new left" politics. The central idea of this thesis is to promote the fullest possible participation by all individuals in public decision making, leading ultimately to full citizen control of the entire political process.

The second theory is sociopolitical pluralism. Although its roots lie in the eighteenth-century writings of Alexis de Tocqueville (1961), its major contemporary proponents have been Arthur Bentley (1908), David Truman (1951), Robert Dahl (1956), William Kornhauser (1959), and Robert Nisbet (1962). This thesis argues that citizens can exert significant influence on political decision making only when they act collectively within voluntary interest associations.

Both of these current theories are oriented toward the same goals of achieving greater citizen influence in politics and preventing over-concentration of political power in government. They differ sharply in their approaches to these goals, however. Participatory democracy stresses direct citizen involvement, while sociopolitical pluralism emphasizes collective action through organizations. The remaining two sections of this chapter discuss these contemporary theories of political equity in greater detail. The final chapter of the book will propose a synthesis of these two complementary theories, under the label of "participatory pluralism."

Participatory Democracy

Traditional democratic theory rests on the assumption that all citizens are—or should become—essentially equal in both their concern with public issues and their competence to make decisions concerning these issues. Consequently, all citizens should participate equally in public decision making and should exercise relatively equal amounts of influence in the political system. "One man, one vote" became the rallying cry of this political movement in the eighteenth and nineteenth centuries, and its principal goal was the election of all governmental leaders through popular voting. Borrowing heavily from laissez-faire economic theory, early proponents of this political philosophy argued that the "invisible hand" of collective balancing operates in the political as well as the economic marketplace, so that in the long run the best interests of the total political community are served when all citizens participate in the political process and the majority rules.

Formulated as a reaction against the gross inequalities of European feudal society, with its extreme concentration of power in the hands of small numbers of land-holding nobles who preserved their social privileges behind rigid and almost impervious class barriers, democratic theory offered a radically different conception of how power should be distributed and used in society. The democratic ideal of political power resting collectively in the hands of all citizens, who entrust it periodically through mass elections to officials who are empowered and trusted to act on behalf of the people, has provided the impetus for one of the most far-reaching shifts in political philosophy in human history.

Democracy and Voting

Traditional democratic theory allows citizens to participate in collective decision making primarily through elections in which they choose public officials but do not directly decide policy issues. With the advent of public polling in the 1930s, citizens acquired a means of expressing their opinions on current issues, but these preferences are never binding on government officials. The introduction of the public referendum did give citizens a direct role in public policy decisions, but only on a very limited basis.

With these narrow exceptions, democratic theory has traditionally encouraged "low quality citizen action by making a fetish out of only one form of political participation—voting" (Pranger 1968:30). This theory viewed elections as a vital but also sufficient procedure for ensuring citizen control of the government, and until quite recently the idea of citizen participation was restricted to vote casting. In Carole Pateman's words:

> Elections are crucial to the democratic method, for it is primarily through elections that the majority can exercise control over their leaders. Responsiveness of leaders to nonelite demands, or "control" over leaders, is ensured primarily through the sanction of loss of office at elections. . . . "Political equality" in the theory refers to universal suffrage and to the existence of equality of opportunity of access to channels of influence over leaders. . . . "Participation," so far as the majority is concerned, is participation in the choice of decision makers. [1970:14]*

This emphasis on voting in traditional democratic theory severely restricts the political influence of citizens in two vital ways:

First, as numerous studies have discovered (Almond and Verba, 1963; Berry, 1970; Verba and Nie, 1972), a large proportion (often a majority) of the citizens in modern societies are not interested in political affairs, are uninformed, and rarely or never vote. Among those who are interested and do vote, the most important factors in determining their choices are (a) the political stance of their parents, and (b) their own socioeconomic status. Neither of these factors involves the rational decision making presumed by democratic theory. As a result, elections often become merely a process for legitimizing the system, rotating the faces (but not the policies) of leaders, and perhaps pacifying the citizens by convincing them that they are sharing in decision making and thus keeping them from challenging the existing system and power structure.

Second, we also know from much research that elections frequently have little effect on political policy formation and administration at both the local (Banfield, 1961; Dahl, 1961) and national (Domhoff, 1970; Miliband, 1969) levels. Although these studies differ on numerous

---

*Reprinted by permission of Cambridge University Press from *Participation and Democratic Theory* (Cambridge: Cambridge University Press, 1970).

specific points and conclusions, they all agree that political decision making is a multidimensional process, in which elections are only one—and often a minor—factor. This thesis is summarized by Emmette Redford (1969:44) in his analysis of contemporary "administrative states" in this manner: "The attainment of the democratic ideal in the world of administration depends much less on majority votes than on the inclusiveness of the representation of interests in the interaction process among the decision makers."

Elitist Democracy

As social scientists became increasingly aware during the 1950s and 1960s of the limitations of traditional democratic theory, they gradually developed an alternative conception of democracy that presumably was closer to empirical reality. In essence, this "elitist theory" conceives of democracy as a procedure for electing governmental leaders, and maintains that a political system is democratic as long as there is competition among political leaders (Dahl and Lindblom, 1953; Bachrach, 1967). As first expressed by Joseph Schumpeter (1943:269), "the democratic method is that institutional arrangement for arriving at political decisions in which individuals acquire the power to decide by means of a competitive struggle for the people's vote." More recently, Emmette Redford (1969:200) argued that, in contemporary "administrative states,"

> workable democracy is achieved in public affairs through the interaction of leaders of different types in strategic positions of influence, who are forced by the interaction process, the complexity of interests involved in a decision-making situation, and the access of nonleaders to their positions, to give attention to all the interests in the society.

This elitist conception of democracy accepts the observed fact that many citizens are politically apathetic and inactive, while small sets of elites control most of the major political decisions. It insists, however, that democracy prevails as long as the elites take the wishes and interests of the public into consideration and act on their behalf—even if only to protect their own positions of power (Redford, 1969:200). As described by critic Jack Walker:

> At the heart of the elitist theory is a clear presumption of the average citizen's inadequacies. As a consequence, democratic systems must rely

on the wisdom, loyalty, and skill of their political leaders, not on the population at large. The political system is divided into two groups: the *elite*, or the "political entrepreneurs," who possess ideological commitments and manipulative skills; and the *citizens at large*, the masses, or the "apolitical clay" of the system, a much larger class of passive, inert followers who have little knowledge of public affairs and even less interest. The factor that distinguishes democratic and authoritarian systems, according to this view, is the provision for limited, peaceful competition among members of the elite for the formal positions of leadership within the system. . . .

Democracy is thus conceived primarily in procedural terms; it is seen as a method of making decisions which insures efficiency in administration and policy making, and yet requires some measure of responsiveness to popular opinion on the part of the ruling elites. . . . The political leaders, in an effort to gain support at the polls, will shape public policy to fit the citizens' desires. By anticipating public reaction the elite grants the citizenry a form of indirect access to public policy making, without the creation of any kind of formal institution and even in the absence of any direct communication. [1966:286–88]

A further feature of this thesis, stressed by Bernard Berelson, et al. (1954:312–13) and Giovanni Sartori (1962), is that democracy is in fact protected and maintained by low levels of citizen participation. If too many people become involved in politics—especially persons with little knowledge of political issues or understanding of the political system—they may generate conflicts and tensions that the system cannot handle. Hence citizen apathy and limited public involvement play a valuable role in maintaining the stability of the political system as a whole.

Quite clearly, the elitist theory of democracy has little concern with promoting widespread citizen participation in political affairs, and it advocates minimal levels of citizen involvement. This transference of democratic theory from a radical into a conservative doctrine that glorifies political stability and distrusts active citizen participation was explicitly noted by Jack Walker, one of the foremost critics of the elitist theory:

The contemporary version of democratic theory has . . . lost much of the vital force, the radical thrust of the classical theory. The elitist theorists, in trying to develop a theory which takes account of the way the political system actually operates, have changed the principal orienting values of democracy. The heart of the classical theory was its justification of broad participation in the public affairs of the community; the aim was the production of citizens who were capable enough and responsible enough to play this role. The classical theory was not meant to describe any existing system of government; it was an outline, a set of pre-scriptions for the ideal polity which men should strive to create. The elitist theorists, in their quest for realism, have changed this distinctive prescriptive element in democratic theory; they have substituted stability and efficiency as the prime goals of democracy. [1966]

Origins of Participatory Democracy

As extensively documented by Carole Pateman (1970), the intellectual roots of participatory democracy lie in the classical writings of Jean Jacques Rousseau and John Stuart Mill, so that this is in no sense is a new idea. She notes that:

> Rousseau's entire political theory hinges on the individual participation of each citizen in political decision making. . . . The only policy that will be acceptable to all is the one where any benefits and burdens are equally shared; the participatory process ensures that political equality is made effective in the decision-making assembly. . . . Rousseau's ideal system is designed to develop responsible, individual social and political action through the effect of the participatory process. . . . The individual's ac-tual, as well as his sense of, freedom is increased through participation in decision making because it gives him a very real degree of *control* over the course of his life and the structure of his environment.
>
> Mill argues that it is no use having universal suffrage and participa-tion in national government if the individual has not been prepared for this participation at [the] local level; it is at this level that he learns how to govern himself. . . . Perhaps the most interesting aspect of Mill's theory is an expansion of the hypothesis about the educative effect of participation to cover a whole new area of social life—industry. In his later work, Mill came to see industry as another area where the individ-ual could gain experience in the management of collective affairs, just as he could in local government. [1970:22–35]*

Both Rousseau and Mill believed fervently in the necessity of citizen participation for political democracy. Rousseau sought to justify this assumption on the grounds that participation performs a vital educational effect, teaching people to be informed, interested, and involved citizens who have a sense of control over their own lives and concern for the

---

*Reprinted by permission of Cambridge University Press from *Participation and Democratic Theory* (Cambridge: Cambridge University Press, 1970).

broader community. As these qualities develop throughout the population, they will in turn strengthen the democratic processes and institutions that promote citizen participation, in a continual cycle of self-reinforcement. Mill added the observation that the major educational effect of participation in collective decision making occurs in local government and in the work place, where the individual can have direct influence on these decisions, practice participatory skills on a regular basis, and perhaps even serve on a governing body of some kind. He rejected Rousseau's ideal of political equality for all, however, arguing instead that people's political influence should be differentially weighted according to their political knowledge and sophistication.

Pateman's principal reason for examining these two political theorists at considerable length is to make clear that democratic theory has always stressed citizen participation in public decision making, so that the concept of participatory democracy which emerged in the 1960s was basically just a rediscovery of traditional democratic philosophy. Nevertheless, the 1960s did contribute in at least three important ways to the reemergence of the ideal of participatory democracy. (1) The social and political turmoil of that decade, swirling around the twin themes of racism and poverty, awakened in many people a concern for public issues outside their own immediate lives, and demonstrated that through collective action ordinary citizens can influence governmental policy and programs. (2) The organized social movements that developed during that decade—from community organization programs to environmental protection campaigns—were primarily grass-roots efforts that drew most of their support from ordinary citizens, and in the process introduced them to political action. (3) Among social scientists, a new generation of young scholars rejected the elitist theory of democracy because of its conservative ideology, and sought to reconceptualize democracy in terms of widespread citizen involvement with "power to the people."

One outcome of the convergence of these forces during the 1960s was the idea of participatory democracy, with its insistence on full political involvement and equality among all citizens. As both a criticism of existing political processes and a vision of future possibilities, it has become a pervasive theme in the political culture of the United States and other Western societies.

Principles of Participatory Democracy

The theory of participatory democracy retains two basic tenets of classical political liberalism: (1) the individual rather than the organized group or community is the fundamental political actor; and (2) most people can act rationally, and in the long run political issues are best solved through the rational (if self-interested) choices of individuals (Ricci, 1971:10–11). At the same time, participatory democracy flatly rejects the third basic tenet of traditional liberalism, which holds that the personal and collective interests of individuals are adequately expressed and represented through the electoral process. Popular election of governmental officials is only one way—and often not a very effective way—in which people can participate in and influence public issues. Participatory democracy seeks to maximize both the opportunities for and the outcomes of citizen involvement in collective decision making.

Let us examine the basic conceptions of participatory democracy expressed by several recent writers to discover what it means to them.

- Peter Bachrach:
  The issue is whether democracy can diffuse power sufficiently throughout society to inculcate among people of all walks of life a justifiable feeling that they have the power to participate in decisions which affect themselves and the common life of the community, especially the immediate community, in which they work and spend most of their waking hours and energy.

  For many individuals political issues and elections appear either trivial or remote and beyond the reach of their influence. Of a different magnitude are issues which directly affect them in their place of work, issues which are comparatively trivial, yet are overlaid with tensions and emotions that only infuriate and try men's souls. It is here . . . that the ugliness of man's domination of man is fully revealed, and it is here, consequently, that democracy must be established and put to use. [1967:92, 103]

- Carole Pateman:
  The existence of representative institutions at [the] national level is not sufficient for democracy; for maximum participation by all the people at that level socialisation, or 'social training,' for democracy must take place in other spheres in order that the necessary individual attitudes and psychological qualities can be developed. This development takes place through the process of participation itself. The major function of participation in the theory of participatory democracy is therefore an educative one, . . . including both the psychological aspect and the gaining of practice in democratic skills and procedures.

Therefore, for a democratic polity to exist it is necessary for a participatory society to exist, i.e., a society where all political systems have been democratised and socialisation through participation can take place in all areas. The most important area is industry; most individuals spend a great deal of their lifetime at work and the business of the work place provides an education in the management of collective affairs that it is difficult to parallel elsewhere. The second aspect of the theory of participatory democracy is that spheres such as industry should be seen as political systems in their own right, offering areas of participation additional to the national level. If individuals are to exercise the maximum amount of control over their own lives and environment then authority structures in these areas must be so organised that they can participate in decision making. [1970:42–43]

- Terrence E. Cook and Patrick M. Morgan:
Participatory democracy connotes two broad features in patterns of decision-making: (1) *decentralization or dispersion of authoritative decision-making*, whereby the authority to make certain decisions is to be displaced downward from remote points near the top of administrative hierarchies or outward from central geographical locations, thus bringing authority closer to the people affected by it; and (2) *direct involvement of amateurs in the making of decisions* . . . so that they move beyond participation in the form of merely influencing officials to actually being authoritative decision-makers. . . . In other words, participatory democracy connotes decentralization of power for direct involvement of amateurs in authoritative decision-making. [1971:4]

- C. George Benello and Dimitrios Roussopoulos:
Participatory democracy seeks to reintroduce the concept of democracy from the ground up, which means introducing democratic processes into the major organizations of society, public and private. . . . In a participatory democracy, decision-making is the process whereby people propose, discuss, decide, plan, and implement those decisions that affect their lives. This requires that the decision-making process be continuous and significant, direct rather than through representatives, and organized around issues instead of personalities. . . . A movement that builds participatory democracy from the base is committed to the full dissemination of power, whether political, bureaucratic, or corporate, to those affected by it. It also involves the creation of organizational forms whereby shared power can be used for the good of all. [1971:4–8]

Five central features of participatory democracy can be distilled from these statements:

1. All individuals must have full opportunity to participate as extensively as they wish in all collective decision making that pertains to them.

2. Participation in collective decision making must not be limited to voting, but should include a wide variety of activities requiring varying degrees of commitment and involvement.

3. Responsibility for collective decision making is to be widely dispersed, so that it is not limited to officials and/or experts but includes all persons who will be affected by those decisions.

4. Participation in collective decision making must not be limited to the political system, but should extend throughout all realms of social life, especially work organizations.

5. Participation in collective decision making within nonpolitical spheres of life will teach individuals political skills and norms and will motivate them to become involved in larger political issues.

These five principles can be combined into the following definition: In a participatory democracy, collective decision making is highly decentralized throughout all sectors of society, so that all individuals learn participatory skills and can effectively participate in various ways in the making of all decisions that affect them. Particularly crucial in this conception of participatory democracy is the insistence that full democratization of decision making within all local and private organizations is a necessary prerequisite for political democracy at the national level. In Pateman's (1970:35) words: "For the operation of a democratic polity at the national level, the necessary qualities in individuals can only be developed through the democratization of authority structures in all political systems."

In recent years, the idea of participatory democracy has invaded numerous areas of social life, including industry (Blumberg, 1969), neighborhoods (O'Brien, 1975), and race relations (Altschuler, 1970). Perhaps most evident, however, has been the rapid expansion of relatively formalized programs for promoting citizen participation in community programs and government (Cahn and Passett, 1971; Lind, 1975).

In practice, citizen participation programs have taken many forms, such as (a) public meetings at which officials describe proposed plans or programs and ask for questions and comments from the audience; (b) hearings sponsored by governmental agencies at which "intervenors" can respond to proposed policies or projects in a quasi-legal manner; (c) workshops at which citizens, planners, and public officials jointly discuss and develop action programs; (d) citizen advisory councils that meet regularly with officials to formulate public policies for specified issues; and (e) citizen control boards that exercise final decision-making powers in various areas. With the exception of citizen control boards, however, all of these procedures allow citizens to exercise only reactive, suggestive, or advisory roles, not actual decision making, which has led some critics to describe most citizen participation programs as "pseudo participation" (Walker, 1975). If participatory democracy is to be fully realized, there is clearly a pressing need to devise and implement additional procedures for involving citizens in public decision making.

Problems of Participatory Democracy

Because we have so little experience putting the ideas of participatory democracy into practice, it is quite easy to point out numerous potential probelms inherent in this political theory. Some of the more obvious of these problems are briefly mentioned in the following paragraphs:

1. Do people want to be involved in collective decision making? "Participatory democracy would inevitably involve a very large part of the ordinary citizen's time, both for participation and to prepare adequately for it. There is no overwhelming evidence that most people want to devote this much time and effort to politics; for many, nothing would destroy enthusiasm for participatory democracy as much as a little experience with it" (Cook and Morgan, 1971:33).

2. Will participatory skills and attitudes learned in small settings such as the home or the work place necessarily promote participation in larger community and societal affairs? Pateman (1970) argues that involvement in decision making at work will teach individuals to participate in politics, but the available evidence on this linkage is not wholly convincing. A sense of personal efficacy is not equivalent to a sense of political efficacy, as she assumes. Pateman's total reliance on an educational process to transform work participation into political participation is the weakest link in her theoretical chain. It completely overlooks the possibility that this linkage might be considerably strengthened by either (a) providing external inducements or pressures to promote political involvement; or (b) establishing formal procedures that would bridge the present gulf between work place and government.

3. What resources, in addition to the ballot, can individuals use to exert influence on decision makers or other citizens? If we rule out money and prestige as political resources because of the problems of inequality asso-

ciated with them, what other resources can the ordinary citizen draw on? Are personal interest and effort sufficient, or must the concerned individual acquire special knowledge or interaction skills in order to extend his or her political influence beyond the ballot box?

4. What procedures can be established to facilitate individual participation in collective decision making? Citizen participation programs have experimented with a wide variety of communication and decision-making techniques, as mentioned above, but these have generally failed to attract more then a tiny proportion of the population.

5. How can organizations of all kinds be structurally decentralized so as to make decision-making processes more accessible to those who are directly affected by them? Although organizational researchers have suggested numerous decentralization strategies in recent years, these ideas have not been integrated with the theory of participatory democracy.

6. What is the most appropriate organizational unit within which to practice participatory democracy? "Participatory-democracy units could be overburdened with problems and decisions that they could not handle by themselves or with functions that could be performed far more effectively or efficiently elsewhere. A major criticism of participatory democracy that any systematic theory must confront is that the primary problems of our world and its national communities are not amenable to solutions by small-scale democracy.... Participatory democracy would proliferate decision-making units with essentially parochial concerns, absorbing all attention in the trival at the expense of what is significant" (Cook and Morgan, 1971:28–29).

7. Finally, will participatory democracy result in collective decisions that adequately serve the public interest? This process could seriously impede the process of negotiation and bargaining through which many public issues are resolved, producing only incessant strife among a multiplicity of individuals and organizational units. In addition, "decision-making may be not only inefficient but also incompetent. Since participatory democracy would place the power to make decisions in the hands of ordinary citizens to a far greater extent, a question inevitably arises as to the likelihood that these citizens will make 'good' decisions" (Cook and Morgan, 1971:34).

It is quite obvious that we still have much to learn about designing and operating adequate systems of participatory democracy. Nevertheless, this theory does provide a set of goals toward which we can strive as we seek to extend the basic principles of democracy to all spheres of social life.

Sociopolitical Pluralism

A basic tenet of classical political liberalism, we noted earlier, is that the individual rather than the organized group or community is the fundamental political actor. Participatory democracy accepts this premise and urges all individuals to become highly involved in political affairs. Both classical liberalism and participatory democracy therefore discount the political role of organizations, often viewing them as potentially dangerous "factions" whose special interests will often conflict with the general welfare (Ricci, 1971:11).

As a consequence of this distrust of organizations, traditional democratic theory rests on what Robert Nisbet (1962:253) calls a "unitary conception" of society, in which the only two viable political units are the individual and the national government. Influence is seen as flowing directly from the people to the government through elections, without any intermediate stages of aggregation in interest organizations. This conception of the political state was largely developed in France during the eighteenth century, as an outgrowth of prevailing rationalistic conceptions of man and society, and as an attack on the crumbling feudal social structure. As described by Nisbet:

> State and individual were the two elements of the unitary theory of democracy. The abstract individual was conceived as the sole bearer of rights and responsibilities. The State, conceived in the image of people who lay incorruptible beneath the super-structure of society, would be the area of fraternity and secular rehabilitation. All that lay between these two elements — gilds, churches, professions, classes, unions of all kinds — were suspect for their fettering influence upon the individual and their divisive consequences to the people's State. [1962:253]

Potential consequences of this unitary conception of society — as observers from Tocqueville onward have often charged — are that individuals are left powerless in the face of government, elections become largely a public popularity contest or the means through which the established regime reaffirms its legitimacy, the people become available for manipulation by elites through mass movements, and the nation drifts toward the model of a "mass society." In Nisbet's (1962:250) words: "By focusing on the abstract political mass, this view of the people becomes administratively committed at the outset to a potentially totalitarian view of the State."

As a response to this unitary conception of the state, the theory of sociopolitical pluralism offers a model of society that emphasizes the crucial political role of private-interest associations. It argues that political democracy in modern nations requires a foundation of strong interest organizations throughout the society that can continually exert influence on the government. "If democracy involves participation and influence in decision-making processes, then the extent to which a society is democratic depends on the degree of citizen participation in associations which are not overtly political as well as in explicitly political associations" (Berry, 1970:16).

The Pluralist Model

Although the idea of sociopolitical pluralism can be traced back to Plato's *Republic,* it was Alexis de Tocqueville's *Democracy in America* that first presented this model as a necessary social basis for democracy. Tocqueville argued that the breakdown or absence of traditional hierarchies of feudal authority in contemporary societies would lead to conditions of mass equality, which in turn provided fertile ground for a "tyranny of the majority" that would destroy individual freedom in the name of "popular democracy." To replace traditional aristocracies in modern societies, Tocqueville (1961:128–33) called for the creation of multitudes of voluntary associations. "Amongst the laws which rule human societies there is one which seems to be more precise and clear than all others. If men are to remain civilized, or to become so, the art of associating together must grow and improve, in the same ratio in which the equality of conditions is increased."

As elaborated by numerous contemporary writers, the theory of sociopolitical pluralism calls for a complex network of interest organizations throughout society, each of which possesses its own power base and hence can function relatively independently of the government. Sometimes called "intermediate organizations" because of their structural location between the people and the national government, these associations must rest on voluntary membership derived from shared interests and concerns. They must be entirely private, or outside the formal government, to ensure that they remain autonomous sources of power. Each association should be limited in its sphere of activities, so that it cannot become too inclusive of its members' lives. Either separately or in links with one another, these organizations must extend from the grass-roots level of individual participation up to the national level, where they interact with the government. And most important, if they are to affect political decision making, these intermediate organizations must possess sufficient resources of one kind or another to effectively exert influence on governmental bodies and leaders.

Some of these organizations, such as political parties, nonpartisan citizens' associations, political action groups, and lobbies, may participate regularly in the political system. But most of them will normally be nonpolitical, entering the political arena as "parapolitical actors" only when their particular organizational interests are involved. Such parapolitical organizations might include labor unions, business and professional associations, civic organizations, recreational associations, ethnic groups, fraternal associations, "cultural" associations, or churches. Regardless of how frequently or extensively these organizations become politically active, however, the crucial feature of the pluralistic model is that all of them remain voluntary and autonomous, so as to provide citizens with independent power bases outside the formal government.

To prevent a highly pluralistic society from being torn apart by intense conflicts arising among its component organizations as each one seeks to attain its own particular goals, the model also specifies several necessary integrative conditions: (a) crosscutting rather than cumulative interests on various issues, to prevent cleavages among organizations from becoming too deep or irreconcilable; (b) overlapping memberships, with individuals (especially leaders) belonging to several different organizations; (c) interdependent activities, to keep organizations functionally interrelated; and (d) consensus on a set of procedural rules for resolving conflicts and reaching collective decisions. In David Berry's (1970:112) words, "It is the strength of the multiple memberships of associations and the extent to which these are overlapping rather than superimposed upon conflicting interests in society that is significant in maintaining social integration and democracy." None of the major writers on pluralism have specified in any detail how these integrative conditions are to be attained, however, so that the model is more of an ideal than a blueprint for a democratic society.

Although the distinction is not commonly made, there are actually two different versions of pluralist theory. The mobilization version of pluralism focuses on the role of nonpolitical voluntary associations in mobilizing individuals to become active in political affairs. The mediation version of pluralism is concerned, not with individuals' actions, but with the role of intermediate organizations as mediators of political influence between the citizens and the government. Let us examine both versions in greater detail.

The Mobilization Process

Numerous studies have discovered that people who belong to voluntary associations of all kinds are more likely than others to participate in many forms of political activity (Milbrath, 1965; Verba and Nie, 1972). To explain this widespread relationship, the argument is made that membership and involvement in nonpolitical interest organizations activates people for political participation. The concept of social mobilization is derived from Karl Deutsch (1961), who describes it as "the process in which major clusters of old social, economic, and psychological commitments are eroded or broken and people become available for new patterns of socialization and behavior." He uses this concept in the context of modernizing societies, referring to activities that move people from traditional to "modern" ways of life. However, the idea is equally applicable to modernized societies if we assume that many traditional patterns of social activities in these societies are inimical to involvement in political affairs. People caught in these traditional patterns must be mobilized through involvement in new social contexts such as voluntary associations if they are to become politically active.

Several reasons can be given to explain the dynamic process through which nonpolitical organizational involvement leads to political participation: (1) Association membership broadens one's sphere of interests and concerns, so that public affairs and political issues become more salient to the individual. (2) It brings one into contact with many diverse people, and the resulting social relationships draw the individual into a wide range of new activities, including politics. (3) It gives one training and experience in social interaction and leadership skills that are valuable in the political sphere. (4) It provides one with multiple channels through which he or she can act to exert influence on politicians and the political system.

The importance of this political mobilization process for political democracy has been expressed by Gabriel Almond and Sidney Verba in these words:

> The organization member, compared with the nonmember, is likely to consider himself more competent as a citizen, to be a more active participant in politics, and to know and care about politics. He is, therefore, more likely to be close to the model of the democratic citizen . . . Membership in some association, even if the individual does not consider the membership politically relevant, and even if it does not

involve his active participation, does lead to a more competent citizenry. Pluralism, even if not explicitly political pluralism, may indeed be one of the most important foundations of political democracy. [1963:321–22]

The Mediation Process

In addition to mobilizing their members for political activity, the special-interest voluntary associations that pervade a pluralist society enact an influence-mediating process between individual citizens and the government. Each intermediate organization brings together a number of people with similar concerns and goals, provides means through which these members can acquire information about relevant public issues, enables them to pool their resources to generate greater collective influence than could be exercised by an single individual, and provides an established channel through which they can exert this influence "upward" on political decisions and policies. To some extent, they also protect individuals from direct manipulation by elites through the mass media or state-controlled programs (Kornhauser, 1959).

At the same time, intermediate organizations serve governmental leaders by providing necessary information about public interests and needs, as well as an established means through which these leaders can reach "downward" to large numbers of constituents in order to deal effectively with their problems and concerns. Governmental leaders are simultaneously insulated from immediate dependence on mass public opinion and fear of overthrow by mass movements or revolution, which enables them to take socially necessary but unpopular actions (Kornhauser, 1959).

The mediation process thus bridges the influence gap between citizens and the government that is ignored by traditional democratic theory, making it possible for individuals to exercise far more extensive and meaningful influence on political decisions and policies than would ever be possible through occasional mass voting or sporadic mass movements. Robert Presthus expresses the process as follows:

According to pluralist theory, voluntary groups play a critical role in a democratic system. Linchpins between government and the individual in a complex society, they become the most important means of direct access to those with political power. In the sense that they help shape public policy they are parapolitical. By hammering out a consensus among their members, which then becomes part of the raw material from which political parties manufacture their policies, they become part of the political system.... In sum, voluntary organizations are essential instruments of pluralism because they make possible citizen influence on government. [1964:241]

Problems of Sociopolitical Pluralism

Although pluralism is sometimes described as the unofficial political philosophy of the United States, a number of theoretical criticisms are frequently levied against it. Several of these are briefly mentioned in the following paragraphs.

1. The viability of a pluralist society is questionable when large proportions of the population do not belong to any special-interest voluntary associations, and when a majority of those who do belong to such organizations are only nominal members who take little or no part in the affairs of their organizations. To the extent that this situation prevails—as is presently the case in the United States and most other modern societies—neither the mobilization nor the mediation process can occur. Individuals will not acquire the experiences and skills necessary for political participation, and the organizations will not function as influence channels between citizens and government.

2. The theory implicitly assumes a "natural harmony of interests" among all parts of the society, or consensus on basic values, lack of deep social cleavages, and absence of strong ideologies and extremist politics. Only under such conditions will diverse actions by competing, self-oriented, special-interest organizations result in social unity and promotion of the general welfare. Lacking these conditions, pluralism can either paralyze or destroy a society, since attachment to intermediate associations does not by itself ensure commitment to the total society. As society changes, some organizations are bound to feel adversely affected and deprived, while others will develop new aspirations and goals. In both cases, these organizations may decide that the existing social and political orders are not adequate and reject them in favor of extremist ideologies or bitter intergroup conflict.

3. As new interests arise in a society, new organizations are often formed to promote these interests. But it is often difficult for such organizations to gain legitimacy as accepted players in the political system. This is particularly likely to happen if they advocate radically new ideas or extensive social change. And if such organizations are not recognized by others as representing legitimate collective interests, they cannot enact an influence-mediating role.

4. There is a pervasive tendency in all organizations to drift toward centralized, oligarchic control, as noted over sixty years ago by Robert Michels (1966) in his famous "iron law of oligarchy." To the extent that this process occurs, an organization can neither effectively teach its members political participation skills nor provide an effective influence channel for exerting influence on the government. Some theorists (Lipset, et al., 1956) have argued that internal oligarchy may be necessary if special-interest associations are to speak with a strong voice in political affairs, but this negates the fundamental principal of open participation in decision making and reduces the system to a set of pluralistic elites. Each of these "strategic elites" (Keller, 1963) tends to dominate its own sphere of activity and to encounter little interference from other elites. "A pluralism of elites does not necessarily produce a competitive situation among elites" (Bachrach, 1967:37).

5. In modern nations in which the state tends to predominate over all other sectors of society, private, limited-action associations may have little influence on the government, no matter how well organized they may be. Can such organizations ever exercise any positive influence on public decision making to promote their interests, or are they forever doomed to enacting the role of "veto groups" (Riesman et al., 1954) that can only act negatively to block decisions they oppose? And if most, if not all, of these intermediate organizations lack effective autonomous power resources, they can easily be coopted by the government to become nothing more than agents for carrying out governmental policies.

6. Even if organizations do possess sufficient power resources with which to effectively exert influence on public decision making, they frequently lack viable channels for carrying out this process. The theory of sociopolitical pluralism, as presently envisioned, does not identify any practical influence mechanisms. The theory specifies the role that intermediate organizations should enact in political affairs, but says nothing about how this role is to be carried out. We shall return to this question in greater detail in chapter 8.

These various criticisms of the pluralist model indicate that it is not an ideal blueprint for promoting political democracy in modern societies. Indeed, if political elites were capable of infiltrating and gaining control of the major interest organizations in a society, they could conceivably convert a pluralist society into a totalitarian state under their complete direction. Nevertheless, the pluralist model does suggest that a viable network of autonomous intermediate organizations throughout a society might provide a means of diffusing the exercise of social power among many different parts of society, thereby giving individual citizens numerous opportunities to participate in the governmental process. If this model were effectively implemented, it could provide an organizational foundation for both political democracy and meaningful involvement by all citizens in the operation and continual transformation of their society.

3. Individual
Political Participation

For the past two hundred years, Western nations have been struggling with the questions of what roles citizens should play in political processes and who should be entitled to enact these roles. As T.H. Marshall (1965) has shown, this pervasive movement to extend and expand the rights of citizenship has been fraught with conflict and is presently nowhere near resolution. The central tenet of political democracy is that all qualified citizens should enjoy full rights and opportunities for meaningful political participation. Widespread citizen involvement in politics does not necessarily result in political democracy; but if citizens fail to participate actively in political affairs, they will certainly remain politically powerless. Yet what constitutes meaningful and effective participation in politics?

Beginning with Charles Merriam and Harold Gosnell's (1924) pioneering study of voting turnout in the 1923 Chicago Mayoral election, literally hundreds of empirical studies have examined the extent to which different kinds of people engage in various kinds of political actions. Much of this literature is summarized by Lester Milbrath (1965), while Sidney Verba and Norman Nie's (1972) extensive analysis of data from a national sample survey provides numerous insights into American political participation. Nevertheless, two fundamental questions are inadequately answered by these previous studies.

First, in what ways do individuals become involved in politics? This chapter approaches that topic from two different perspectives: the political roles that people enact, and the dimensions into which political actions can be grouped. The chapter closes with a discussion of the factors that induce people to become politically active.

Second, to what extent do various social settings or contexts promote the process of social mobilization emphasized by participatory democracy and sociopolitical pluralism? In the following chapter we shall examine mobilization linkages between seven different social contexts and six dimensions of political participation. Subsequent chapters will then explore three aspects of this mobilization process in greater detail.

Implicit throughout this research is the assumption that citizen participation in politics is a desirable activity. That supposition is limited in two crucial respects, however. First, democratic theory says only that citizens should have the opportunity to participation in politics, not that everyone must participate equally. As Morris Jones (1954) has pointed out, the right to freedom of action is hypocritical unless it includes the right to be politically apathetic and uninvolved if one chooses. Other writers have gone even further, arguing that nonparticipation by some portions of the population may reflect general satisfaction with the political system (Lipset, 1960:32) or even contribute to the functional effectiveness of the system by excluding uninformed individuals (Berelson et al., 1954). As David Berry (1970:122–28) has demonstrated, however, all such arguments explicitly or implicitly assume that democracy depends ultimately on basic value consensus. If democracy is instead viewed as a set of political procedures for promoting conflict and change, then mass participation is to be welcomed and encouraged — though still never mandated.

Second, there is no guarantee in democratic theory that political participation will lead to the exercise of meaningful influence in the political system. We commonly assume that the reason for voting or otherwise taking part in politics is to exert some influence, no matter how small, on political decisions and policies. But whether or not this actually occurs depends on many features of the political system other than the extent of citizen participation. As critics of contemporary societies — from Mosca (1939) to Mills (1956) — have repeatedly asserted, even with full enfranchisement of the entire adult population, most of the major political decisions are normally made by small sets of dominant elites. Hence, we are never justified in assuming that participation automatically ensures the exercise of political influence.

Research Data

The data on individual political participation reported in this and the following four chapters are taken from the 1968 Indianapolis Area Project of the Institute of Social Research at Indiana University. The population for this survey research project was the urbanized area of Indianapolis as defined by the 1960 census, including the central city and its immediate suburbs. A sample of 750 persons was randomly selected to represent the entire adult population.[1] These respondents were personally interviewed in their homes by trained interviewers.

Because the data are drawn entirely from one community, the findings cannot be generalized statistically beyond the population of Indianapolis. However, there is no reason to believe that Indianapolis is not relatively typical of most medium-sized cities in the United States, so that we might expect many of these findings to be at least roughly duplicated in other communities. Moreover, Robert Alford's study of political participation in four Wisconsin communities revealed that, despite wide variations among the political and economic systems of these cities, such systemic differences had few effects on rates of individual political participation. "While varying from city to city, local involvement is almost entirely due to characteristics of the individual, and not to the political context in which he is located . . ." (Alford, 1969:160). The present analysis therefore focuses entirely on characteristics of individuals, and does not include any structural or cultural features of the Indianapolis community.

Political Participation Roles[2]

Several previous writers have described sets of roles that individuals can enact within the political system, although these schemes tend to be rather imprecise in both their theoretical justifications and operational definitions of those roles. W.S. Robinson (1952) divided participants into the three categories of "spectators" (who regard elections as mass spectacles), "citizens" (whose primary concern is how to vote), and "partisans" (who

---

1. The sampling procedure used in the study was "probability sampling with quotas." This procedure, developed by the National Opinion Research Center, uses random probability sampling to first select census tracts from the total urbanized area, and then blocks (or in this case, pairs of adjacent blocks) within these selected tracts. Within each block (or pair of blocks) it uses quota sampling, in which the interviewer is instructed to begin at one corner of the block and go around it in a clockwise direction, stopping at every dwelling to see if it contains an available respondent who fits one of five categories: male under 30, male between 30 and 65, male over 65, employed female, and unemployed female. (These factors of age for men and employment for women are the variables that most directly affect availability for interviewing.) The interviewer is given a quota for the number of people in each category who must be interviewed in that block — determined by the composition of its population — and continues around the block until completing the assigned number of interviews. This procedure increases the sampling error somewhat (usually less than 10 percent), but it provides considerable savings in time and costs. For additional details of this sampling process, see Sudman (1966).

2. The following discussion of political participation roles is taken by permission from Marvin E. Olsen, "A Model of Political Participation Stratification," Journal of Political and Military Sociology, Vol. 1, Fall 1973, pp. 183-200.

seek to ensure the election of their candidates and party). Somewhat more elaborate is Robert Agger and Vincent Ostrom's (1956) scheme of "non-participants," "workers" (people who take an active part in public issues, but do not participate in any political discussions or meetings), "listeners" (people who attend meetings at which community policy questions are discussed), "talkers" (people who talk frequently with others about community policy issues), and "advisors" (people to whom others come for advice on these issues). However, these roles are geared more to involvement in informal community issues than to participation in the formal political system. Robert Dahl (1961:99–103) argued that political activists could be classified as either leaders or subleaders, and that both groups were typically split into numerous segments with conflicting interests and values. Lester Milbrath (1965:17–22) placed participants into the three categories of "spectators," "transactionals," and "gladiators" on the basis of their involvement in political affairs.

A more elaborate typology of political roles was developed by Sidney Verba and Norman Nie (1972:73–81). It consists of "the totally inactive," "the voting specialists" (who vote regularly but engage in no other political activities), "the parochial activists" (who contact governmental officials on minor local or personal issues), "the communalists" (who participate actively in nonpartisan voluntary community associations and programs), "the campaigners" (who are active in party and campaign affairs), and "the totally active" (who do all of these things). Their scheme was derived from a national survey of the United States and is more empirically grounded than the earlier efforts. Nevertheless, they did not relate their role typology to the existing theoretical literature on political participation. Nor did they empirically test the thesis (suggested by Robert Lane, 1959, and Lester Milbrath, 1965) that political participation tends to form a cumulative ladder, so that persons enacting any given role also perform — or have performed in the past — all roles lying below it on the participation ladder.

The typology of political participation roles outlined here rests on the assumption that political activity can be conceptualized as one aspect of the broader process of social stratification. Each role thus constitutes a level or stratum in a hierarchy of political participation. The six roles or strata comprising this model are given both conceptual and operational definitions, and they are justified on theoretical grounds drawn from existing sociological and political science literature. From top to bottom, these participation roles/strata are Leaders, Activists, Communicators,

Citizens, Marginals, and Isolates.[3] Conceptual definitions and relevant operational variables for each role are given in Table 3.1, while the following paragraphs sketch each role in more detail and refer to the literature sources from which each was derived.

Role Descriptions

Political *Leaders*.   By virtue of their elected or appointed positions in the formal governmental structure, Leaders normally exercise dominant power in the political system. There is wide variation among them in the amount of authority and influence they exercise, however, depending on their positions and actions. Leaders tend to share and defend a common political subculture that defines the rules and norms according to which the game of politics is to be played, and which legitimizes their authority. Nevertheless they are frequently divided into several competing subgroups according to political philosophies and partisan policies, with resulting conflicts and cleavages that prevent them from becoming a monolithic set of elites.[4]

Political *Activists*.   These active members of political parties, other political organizations, and parapolitical voluntary associations operate outside the formal governmental structure, yet exercise considerable influence on the political system through their collective efforts. Except for those involved in the political parties, however, Activists commonly become politically active only when issues or programs impinge directly upon their organizations' particular spheres of interest and concern, so that their political involvement is relatively specialized. They typically express considerable concensus in support of democratic political procedures and

---

3. These six strata differ from those of Verba and Nie (1972:77) in four main ways: (1) Verba and Nie did not include a category of Leaders operating within the formal political system. (2) My Activist stratum roughly (though not entirely) corresponds to their two categories of communalists and campaigners. Their distinction may be of considerable value, and might have been incorporated into this model if it had been available when the model was formulated, but it is relevant to note that they found these two categories to be more highly correlated ($r = .52$) than any of the others. (3) Because they defined political participation only in terms of overt activity, they included nothing corresponding to my Marginal stratum (4) Their category of parochial activists is largely included within my stratum of Communicators.

4. In his study of New Haven politics, Dahl (1961) used the concept of political leaders essentially as it is defined here. Milbrath (1965:22) also places officeholding at the top of his hierarchy of political involvement.

Table 3.1
Political Participation Strata: Conceptual Definitions and Operational Variables

Stratum	Conceptual Definition	Operational Variables
Leaders	Persons who are directly involved in government	At some time have either (a) served as a member of a public board, committee, or other body of some kind, or (b) been elected to public office
Activists	Persons who engage in organized political action within private organizations	At some time have either (a) done volunteer work or held office in a political party, or (b) participated directly in some kind of political activity conducted by a voluntary interest association (regardless of whether or not the organization's stated purposes are political in nature)
Communicators	Persons who receive and communicate political information, interests, beliefs, or values	At some time have both (a) received a political message by attending some kind of political meeting or speech, and (b) communicated a political message by writing to or otherwise contacting a public official, writing a letter to the editor of a newspaper, or displaying a political button, sticker, or other sign
Citizens	Persons who perform the expected responsibilities of citizens, but take no other part in politics	At the present time (a) have knowledge of the political system and recent political events, (b) hold opinions of some kind on several current political issues, (c) have a political party preference (including Independent), and (d) are registered to vote and have voted in at least half of all recent elections
Marginals	Persons who have only minimal and transitory contacts with the political system	Within the past few months have both (a) had some minimal exposure to political news via the mass media or reading partisan literature, and (b) felt some interest in a political issue or at least once discussed a political topic with another person
Isolates	Persons who rarely or never participate in politics in any way	Do not qualify for any of the above strata

42

norms, but they often conflict sharply with one another concerning substantive issues of all kinds.[5]

Political *Communicators*.   As individuals, they can have some impact on the political system through their communicative actions, but this influence is severaly limited because their communications are not usually reinforced by organized political forces. Hence the extent of Communicators' political influence depends largely on the receptiveness of Citizens to their messages and the willingness of Activists and Leaders to listen to and act on their views. Communicators tend to be fairly knowledgeable and concerned about political affairs; they constitute the "politically attentive public" called for by democratic political theory. They can, therefore, perform a vital linking function between Leaders and Activists and the masses of Citizens and Marginals.[6]

Political *Citizens*.   Individually, Citizens have little impact on the political system, but collectively they constitute the power foundation of a democratic political system. Political parties are the principal vehicles through which the collective influence of Citizens is organized and exercised, but with the exception of primary elections, Citizens have little impact on party decisions and policies. Moreover, many Citizens only minimally fulfill the requirements of a "politically attentive public," and party identifications and voting choices of most Citizens are affected much more by socioeconomic class, ethnicity, and childhood political socialization than by rational considerations of political issues.[7]

Political *Marginals*.   Their minimal contacts with the political system are almost entirely private actions, so that they have virtually no actual impact on the system. Marginals are potentially available for political mobilization by office seekers, party workers, and opinion molders, however, if the issues involved touch directly on their own lives or personal

---

5. Involvement of individuals in politics through participation in nongovernmental organizations has been central to the theory of sociopolitical pluralism, from Tocquerville (1961) to Berry (1970:13-30). The term *activist*, in its present meaning, was introduced by Freeman et al. (1963). Some writers have included the upper portion of the Activist stratum (i.e., leaders of private organizations) in the "political class," but this obscures the critical distinction between Leaders, who act within the formal government, and Activists, who operate in private organizations.

6. The idea of political communicators is taken from Katz and Lazarsfeld's (1955) concept of "opinion leaders" in the "two-step flow of information," although it here includes upward as well as downward communications.

7. The concept of the citizen role pervades the writings on democratic political theory and is particularly crucial for Nisbet's (1962) conception of "unitary democracy" and the notion of "sense of citizen duty" developed by Campbell et al. (1954).

concerns. But any such political activity will usually be sporadic and will rarely lead to sustained involvement.[8]

Political *Isolates*.   As a result of their being almost entirely cut off from the political system, Isolates rarely have any impact or influence on political affairs. Despite their deprived political status, they are not likely to protest or rebel against their status; their political ignorance and apathy normally result in either passive acquiescence toward, or withdrawal from, all political matters. Hence they are highly impervious to political mobilization for almost any cause. They are outside the political system and are quite likely to remain there.[9]

Role Characteristics

The validity of a conceptual model such as this cannot be directly tested, but we can use empirical data to describe several characteristics of these roles and the people who enact them.

An initial matter to investigate is the proportion of the population occupying each role. Previous studies of political participation suggest that very few people enact a leadership role, that relatively small minorities of people are activists or communicators, that the bulk of the population falls into the citizen category, and that substantial minorities are either marginals or isolates. Hence the overall distribution of people within the political participation hierarchy should be approximately diamond shaped.

Respondents in the Indianapolis survey were assigned to the six political strata from the top downward. All persons who qualified as Leaders were first placed in that stratum. Among the people remaining, all individuals meeting the criteria for Activists were then assigned to that stratum, and so on down the participation ladder. The Isolates are thus a residual group of those persons who did not qualify for any of the higher strata. The percentages of people falling into each stratum were as follows: Leaders, 3 percent; Activists, 14 percent; Communicators, 13 percent; Citizens, 30 percent; Marginals, 18 percent; and Isolates, 22 percent. The overall distribution only roughly resembles a diamond, but it generally

8. Although the term *Marginals* is taken from the early literature on assimilation of immigrants, an equivalent concept was introduced into the realm of political participation by Katz and Piret (1964) in their discussion of "circuitous participation" as "a silent form of participation in political affairs."

9. Perhaps the best-known discussion of political isolation in the sociological literature is Kornhauser's (1959:74–93) analysis of mass society. See also Milbrath's (1965:21–22) discussion of political "apathetics."

substantiates our theoretical expectations. Probably the most notable departure is the relatively large size of the Isolate stratum, although Verba and Nie's (1972:79) "inactive" category also comprised 22 percent of the American population.

Do these roles form a cumulative participation ladder or hierarchy, so that persons in any given stratum also qualify for all lower levels (except for the Isolate level)? This can be determined with Guttman scaling analysis, which indicates whether or not a set of categories is cumulative in a single dimension. The resulting Coefficient of Reproducibility is .96 and the Minimum Marginal Reproducibility is .76, which tells us that the top five political strata are almost wholly cumulative for this sample. Since these data were all gathered at one point in time, they do not reveal whether or not people actually "climb the ladder" of political participation one rung at a time, passing upward through the various strata in a stepwise fashion. Only a longitudinal study could investigate that possibility. But we can infer from our data that the members of any given political participation stratum have had at least some prior or current experience with all the lower-ranking roles (except the Isolate role).

We can also examine the social and economic characteristics of the people occupying each political stratum and describe their most significant characteristics. The following paragraphs note the features on which the members of each stratum differ by 10 percent or more from the figures for the total sample.[10]

Political *Leaders* are disproportionately males, over age sixty, whites, liberal Protestants, college graduates with high nonmanual occupations and considerable wealth, and long-time residents of Indianapolis (forty years or more). They are also frequent participants in community service projects and belong to many voluntary associations which they attend regularly and to which they often give leadership. More than one-fourth of them identify themselves as "community leaders." They indeed comprise social and economic as well as political elites, and their influence is clearly felt throughout many realms of social life.

The political *Activists* are especially likely to be college graduates and to have high incomes ($12,000 or more in 1968) and considerable wealth. They are also participators in community service projects and active members of several voluntary associations which they attend fairly regularly and in which they often hold responsible positions. In addition, they

---

10. See Olsen (1973) for the data on which the descriptions are based.

are fairly likely to perceive themselves as "community activists." With quite high socioeconomic status (though no higher occupational status than Communicators) and extensive involvement in all kinds of social activities, these are the people who "make things go" in the community.

Political *Communicators* are disproportionately marked by being middle aged (forty to forty-nine), having one to three years of college education, and earning comfortable incomes ($8,000–$12,000 in 1968). They are also more likely than average to be familiar with many of their neighbors, to have taken part in several community service projects, and to belong to three or more voluntary associations (although they are not so likely to participate actively in these organizations). We thus have a picture of middle-aged, middle-class people who are at least minimally involved in many social activities but who lack the socioeconomic or organizational status to become community and political leaders, and who therefore largely confine their "extracitizenship" political activities to communicating with others.

Members of the *Citizen* stratum do not differ significantly from the total sample on any of the characteristics investigated here. They are modal socially and economically as well as politically.

Political *Marginals* are especially characterized by being under age thirty, high school graduates, recent migrants to the community (less than four years' residency), nonparticipants in community service projects, and not members of (or participants in) any voluntary associations. Thus, although Marginals are not much more active politically than Isolates, they are quite different kinds of people. They are not disadvantaged in terms of socioeconomic status, nor are they isolated from their neighbors or the mass media. Rather, they are moderately well educated, most hold skilled blue-collar jobs, and they receive medium-range incomes. Their political marginality appears to be largely a result of their being young newcomers to the community who have not yet become involved in community events and voluntary associations.

Political *Isolates* are distinguished by being disproportionately females, under age thrity, conservative Protestants, poorly educated (eight years or less), in low-status manual occupations, and financially poor (incomes under $4,000, and total wealth less than $5,000 in 1968). They are also more likely than other people to know none of their neighbors, to have virtually no exposure to serious television programs, to take no part in community service projects, to describe themselves as isolated from the community, and not to belong to any voluntary associations. In short, these people with no links to the political system also tend to occupy the most disadvantaged statuses on a number of other stratification dimensions and to be relatively isolated from almost every other realm of social life.

In sum, this model of political participation roles suggests that individuals can be classified into one of six rather distinct types of political actors. The most common of these is the Citizen role, while relatively small numbers of people are more deeply involved in politics as Leaders, Activists, or Communicators. At the other end of the scale, considerable numbers of people are only minimally involved in politics as Marginals or remain outside the political arena as Isolates. These six political roles form a cumulative hierarchy, so that we may conceive of them as a ladder of increasing political involvement.

An alternative way of approaching the question of how people become involved in politics is to examine the kinds of actions they take, which is the concern of the following section.

Dimensions of Political Actions

Much of the existing literature on political participation deals primarily or exculsively with rates of voting. On the occasions when the focus has been broadened to include other kinds of political activities, the usual procedure has been to measure several diverse forms of participation and then combine them into a single index.[11] The assumption underlying the construction of all such unidimensional indexes is that political participation is essentially a unitary type of activity despite its many situational manifestations. As Robert Alford and Eugene Lee (1968) noted, however: "We know from many studies of communities that this may not be a valid assumption. People are involved in a variety of groups, with a variety of demands upon local government, and these demands are not necessarily all aggregated in one place by one body of decision-makers. . . ." Let us therefore conceive of political participation as a multidimensional process,

---

11. This procedure was employed by Woodward and Roper (1950), Campbell et al. (1954), Dahl (1961), Erbe (1964), Alford (1968), Nie et al. (1969), and Palma (1970).

consisting of several distinct (though interrelated) dimensions, each of which can be separately investigated.[12]

To encompass as many different kinds of political actions as possible, six dimensions of political participation were identified for this study. These are termed the Cognitive, Expressive, Electoral, Organizational, Partisan, and Governmental participation dimensions. In contrast to the four "modes of participation" derived by Verba and Nie (1972) in a "brutally empirical manner," these six dimensions of political involvement were all constructed on theoretical grounds from the current literature on political activity. Each dimension can be measured with two different but related empirical indexes. These dimensions and their indexes are described in the following paragraphs.

Cognitive Participation

As an individual comes into contact with the political system, whether through interpersonal contacts, the mass media, associational activities, or party campaigning, one's first response is likely to be some kind of cognitive activity. That is, one may acquire new information, question or reject previously held knowledge, formulate new opinions on current issues, change present opinions, or reject the message being received. Such cognitive activities can vary along several axes, but all involve some degree of reorientation in the individual's "cognitive mapping" of the political system.[13] Cognitive political participation can be measured with indexes of a person's (a) knowledge of the political system and political problems, and (b) extent of opinion formation on current political issues.

---

12. The only full-scale multidimensional model of political participation thus far utilized in empirical research is Sidney Verba and Norman Nie's (1972:56–73) four "modes of participation." Applying factor analysis to data from a national sample survey, they extracted four separately identifiable factors: (1) campaign activity, consisting of persuading others how to vote, working for a party or candidate, attending a political meeting, contributing money to a party, and belonging to a political club; (2) voting, based on the last two presidential and several local elections; (3) communal activity, consisting of forming a group and working with others on local problems, active membership in a community problem-solving organization, and contacting local or national leaders concerning public issues; and (4) particularized contacting, or contacting leaders concerning personal problems. The first three of these modes were moderately interrelated, with campaign activity and communal activity correlated at .52, and voting correlated with both of them at .31 and .28, respectively. Particularized contacting, on the other hand, was unrelated to any of the other modes. Despite the attention given by Verba and Nie to identifying these four dimensions of participation, however, in their subsequent data analysis they frequently revert to the procedure of combining all the dimensions into a single political participation index.

Expressive Participation

Like the previous dimension, expressive participation is a personal activity, but in this case the individual makes at least a minimal commitment to the political system in some way. Beyond merely acquiring and processing information or opinions, one responds in some manner to political events. Such responses might be either intrapersonal or interpersonal in nature. On the intrapersonal level, expressive participation can be measured with an index of a person's degree of interest in political matters. On the interpersonal level, it can be measured with an index of the extent to which one discusses politics with others.

Electoral Participation

In this society, the minimum demand on citizens for overt participation in the political system is to vote in elections. To do this, however, they must first be officially registered as voters. In addition, considering the great importance of political parties in the U.S. political system, holding some kind of party preference is quite crucial for both registration and voting. Hence having a party preference, being registered, and voting fairly regularly together comprise this electoral participation dimension. More specifically, it can be measured with indexes of (a) holding a party preference and understanding some of the basic differences between the major parties, and (b) being registered and actually voting in local and national elections.

Organizational Participation

One way of becoming more involved in politics beyond voting is to participate in political activities within voluntary associations. An individual can either join an organization (other than a political party) that is specifically political in nature (such as the League of Women Voters) or take part in politically oriented actions within normally nonpolitical associations. In either way, one is entering the political arena through a voluntary interest association that is attempting to exert influence on the political system. Consequently, organizational political participation can be measured with indexes of an individual's membership and activity

---

13. This dimension of cognitive participation is fairly similar to the concept of "circuitous participation" suggested by Fred Katz and Fern Piret (1964), which they described as "a silent form of participation in political affairs."

within (a) political but nonpartisan organizations, and (b) nonpolitical special-interest associations.

Partisan Participation

The individual who takes part in political party activities of one kind or another becomes directly involved in the political system. He or she takes a position toward candidates or issues and publicly identifies himself or herself as a political partisan. One's degree of commitment to a party and partisan positions can vary from marginal to total, however. Some people merely put a bumper sticker on their automobile, while others give long hours of voluntary service to their party or candidate. To take account of this variation in depth of partisan commitment, partisan political participation can be measured with indexes of (a) casual partisan activities such as wearing a campaign button or contributing money to a party or candidate, and (b) intense partisan involvement as evidenced by doing volunteer work for a political party or serving on a party committee.

Government Participation

This dimension of political activity involves interacting with or taking part in formal government at the local, state, or national levels. Most individuals' contacts with government are undoubtedly sporadic and transient, such as occasionally talking with a local official or writing to a congressman about an issue of concern to them. A few individuals do become involved participants in governmental affairs, however, by sitting on public boards and committees or holding public office. Consequently, governmental political participation can be measured with indexes of (a) minor government-related activities such as writing a letter to a public official or attending a meeting of a governmental board or council, and (b) major governmental involvement such as serving as a citizen member of a governmental committee or commission or holding elective office.

General Features

Three general features of these six political participation dimensions may be noted. First, the dimensions are arranged in rough order of increasing "depth" or "intensity" of political participation. The amount of participation within each dimension can vary from none to continual, but the dimensions do seem to follow a natural progression in terms of the nature or quality of participation. This does not imply that individuals necessarily tend to progress through the dimensions in order as they become increasingly involved in political affairs, or that the average rate of participation necessarily declines steadily from the first to the last dimension. Nevertheless, this rough "intensity" ordering is useful in conceptualizing the general nature of political participation.

Second, the six dimensions can be divided into two broad categories that we might term "passive" activities — cognitive, expressive, and electoral participation — and "active" ones — organizational, partisan, and governmental participation. In other words, the first three dimensions are composed of actions that do not demand much motivational strength or expenditure of energy by the individual, while the latter three dimensions do involve some degree of active commitment and involvement. Although this distinction is obviously quite crude, it suggests that the reader oriented toward social-psychological characteristics might want to give particular attention to the first three dimensions, while the reader who is more interested in overt political action will want to concentrate on the last three participation dimensions.

Third, all six dimensions are moderately interrelated, indicating that these various forms of political participation do not occur in isolation from one another. Table 3.2 gives the matrix of correlation coefficients between each pair of dimensions in the Indianapolis study, as well as the range of scores, the mean score, and the standard deviation for each index.[14] At the same time, none of these correlations is high enough to suggest serious overlaps between any of the dimensions. Each dimension can therefore be conceptualized as a separate form of the overall process of political participation. All six dimensions will be utilized in the analyses of the social contexts of political participation reported in the following chapter.

---

14. In the Indianapolis study, each political participation dimension was measured with two separate indexes, as suggested in the descriptions of the dimensions. More specifically, these were as follows. (1) Cognitive participation: (a) political knowledge, based on questions about the names of the mayor of Indianapolis and the two U.S. senators from Indiana, the final outcomes of bills considered by the Indiana State Legislature on abolishing the death penalty and legalizing abortion, and the percentage rate of the federal income tax surcharge at that time; and (b) political opinions, based on whether or not the individual held an opinion of any kind (regardless of its nature or strength) on each of sixteen issues concerning foreign relations, domestic governmental programs, civil rights activities, and civil liberties problems. (2) Expressive participation: (a) political interest, based on questions about the respondent's amount of interest in political issues and activities at the community, state, national, and international levels; and (b) political discussion, based on frequency of discussion of political topics with neighbors, relatives, personal friends, and coworkers. (3) Electoral par-

Political Inducements

The preceding sections of this chapter described the roles that individuals enact within the political system and several dimensions of political activity, but they said nothing about the process through which people are induced to become politically active. Traditional political theory has commonly assumed that this mobilization process occurs through political communications (often via the mass media) and party contacts (such as door-to-door canvassing). In contrast, both participatory democracy and sociopolitical pluralism look outside the realm of politics for inducements to political participation.

The Social Mobilization Thesis

Participatory democratic theory argues that participatory experiences in the work place and other social settings will teach people political skills and increase their interest in political processes. The theory of sociopolitical pluralism, meanwhile, asserts that the political mobilization

---

ticipation: (a) party preference, based on whether or not the respondent had a party preference (including being an independent) on both the local and national levels, and whether one perceived any differences between the two major parties; and (b) registration and voting, based on whether or not the person was currently registered, and whether he or she voted in the last local election, the 1966 congressional election, and the 1964 and 1960 presidential elections. (4) Organizational participation: (a) political organizations, based on membership and participation in one or more organizations directly concerned with political affairs; and (b) voluntary association political activities, based on the number of times the respondent had taken part in political activities conducted by nonpolitical interest associations to which he or she belonged. (5) Partisan participation: (a) partisan activities, based on questions about displaying a campaign button, bumper sticker, or poster, contributing money to a party or candidate, and attending a party rally, meeting, or other gathering; and (b) partisan involvement, based on frequency of doing volunteer work for a political party, plus serving on a committee or holding office in a party. (6) Governmental participation: (a) governmental activities, based on questions about writing letters to state or federal legislators, interacting with local officials concerning a public issue or problem, and attending a formal meeting of a public committee, board, commission, or council; and (b) governmental involvement, based on whether the respondent had ever served as a member of any public committee, board, commission, or council, and whether he or she had ever been a candidate for elective public office (regardless of the outcome of the election).

Each of these twelve indexes was constructed by assigning points to a respondent's answers to its component items, summing the person's total points for that set of questions, and then collapsing the overall distribution of these scores for all respondents into a series of categories ranging from None to High. The rule followed when collapsing total scores into the index categories was to have each category contain approximately the same number of respondents, insofar as possible. Nine of the twelve indexes consist of six categories, but participation rates were too low to allow for more than three categories for the indexes of political organizations, voluntary association political activities, and governmental involvement. Finally, a single combined index score was assigned to each respondent for each participation dimension by summing that person's scores on the two indexes comprising that dimension.

Table 3.2

Ranges, Means, Standard Deviations, and Intercorrelations of the Six Political Participation Dimensions

Participation Dimensions	Range	Mean	S. D.	Intercorrelations (Pearsonian r 's)				
				Expressive	Electoral	Organizational	Partisan	Governmental
Cognitive	0–10	5.74	2.48	.57	.41	.15	.30	.37
Expressive	0–10	3.87	2.66	—	.42	.30	.44	.42
Electoral	0–10	6.70	2.85		—	.19	.37	.28
Organizational	0–5	0.18	0.72			—	.42	.37
Partisan	0–10	1.88	2.66				—	.41
Governmental	0–7	0.99	1.61					—

process occurs largely within special-interest voluntary associations. These two perspectives can easily be combined into a more inclusive social mobilization thesis. This thesis holds that the more extensively and intensively a person becomes involved in all aspects of his or her social environment — including one's voluntary associations, work place, community, social class, and family — the more likely one is to participate in political affairs. Political participation is seen as an integral part of the total web of social conditions in which one lives, so that one will become politically active to the extent that one's total social environment encourages and supports involvement in politics. Expressed in action terms: activate people in one or more realms of their social existence and they will tend to participate actively in politics.

Stated in these broad terms, the social mobilization thesis does not specify (a) which social settings or contexts have the strongest and most direct effects on political involvement, or (b) which dimensions of political participation are most affected by the social mobilization process. Both of those questions will be addressed in the research reported in the following chapter, which employs the social mobilization thesis as a general theoretical framework for investigating the effects of seven different social contexts on six dimensions of political participation.

Political Orientations

To provide a theoretical linkage between social involvement and political participation, many writers have included in their models one or more political orientations as intervening variables. In essence, they suggest that social mobilization generates knowledge and attitudes necessary for political activity, which in turn motivate people to act politically. For example, Nie, Powell, and Prewitt (1969) examined the factors of political efficacy (a feeling that one is capable of influencing political events), citizen duty (the feeling that one has an obligation to take part in political affairs), level of political information, perceived stake in the society, and attentiveness to politics. Other writers have examined such orientations as political trust (a feeling of confidence that public officials are adequately performing their functions), faith in democracy as a legitimate and viable political process, identification with the political system, and satisfaction with it (Palma, 1970).

In addition to the basic question of how these orientations become instilled in individuals, however, is the vexing issue of whether they are actually necessary or whether social involvement can lead directly to political participation regardless of one's political orientations. Nie, Powell, and Prewitt (1969), for instance, discovered that almost two-thirds of the observed relationships between voluntary association involvement and a general index of political participation formed a direct linkage that did not pass through any of the orientations included in their study. Moreover, since these kinds of political orientations tend to be relatively stable and enduring through time, is it possible to alter them sufficiently to bring previously apolitical people into the political arena?

Another way of viewing these political orientations, consequently, is to see them as outcomes of political activity rather than as necessary preconditions. From this perspective, the social mobilization process would not depend on any cognitive or attitudinal changes, although any such changes that did result from political participation would serve to reinforce and perpetuate those activities.

Alternative Theses

As a final note to this discussion of inducements to political participation, let us briefly examine two alternative explanations of this process.

The party contacts thesis focuses on the time-honored practice by political parties of attempting to interact personally with as many individuals as possible. The assumption underlying this approach is that such direct contacts give people the feeling that the parties are personally interested in them, that the issues at stake are of immediate relevance to them, and that they can influence party and public affairs by taking part in politics. Party contacts can take numerous forms, including door-to-door canvassing, personal visits by a party worker to one's home or work place, distributing party literature through the mail, or just casual conversations with party supporters. Judging by the amount of campaign efforts and funds expended on these kinds of activities, it would appear that political parties generally place great reliance on them as inducements to political participation.

What are the dynamics underlying this mobilization process? Do personal contacts by political parties actually induce people to become more active politically? Or might it be that people who respond to such contacts are already predisposed to political activity as a result of extensive social involvement in various realms of their lives? From a practical perspective, this form of political inducement is easily implemented, but does it actually have any effects on political participation? We shall address that question with empirical data in chapter 7.

The personal benefits thesis stresses the ancient practice of providing direct payoffs to individuals for political activity. Based on a conception of human beings as calculating actors who continually seek to derive benefits from their actions, this inducement process operates by offering individuals something they desire in return for their participation in politics. The proffered payoff may be as tangible as money or a job or a business contract. It may also be more intangible — for example, creation of economic conditions that enhance one's financial affairs, enactment of a new public program that directly or indirectly benefits the individual, or even vague promises of "protecting the environment" or "upholding traditional moral virtues." The logic underlying this inducement process can be justified by several lines of psychological and economic reasoning, and political parties and machines have frequently used it to their great advantage.

Nevertheless, an inescapable practical problem haunts the personal benefits approach as an inducement to political participation. Continually providing benefits to individuals in exchange for their political activities sooner or later drains a party and the entire political system of its available resources. Moreover, since different people frequently seek different payoffs from the political system, it is frequently impossible to satisfy more than a small number of people at any one time. A political system that relies primarily or solely on providing personal benefits as a means of inducing political activity will therefore undoubtedly prove either moribund or unstable over time.

Because these two alternative processes of party contacts and personal benefits occur within the realm of politics, they have been the main foci of attention in the political science literature on political participation. In contrast, the social mobilization process incorporates a much broader perspective, with the result that there has been relatively little theorizing or research on this topic. To compensate for that deficiency, the research project reported in the next chapter was designed primarily to investigate the social mobilization thesis as an explanation of political participation.

4. Social Contexts
of Political Participation

Despite the importance of citizen participation for democratic political systems, in practice large numbers of Americans have little or nothing to do with politics. In Indianapolis, these people constituted 40 percent of the population, with 18 percent classified as marginal to the political system and 22 percent isolated from it. And only 30 percent of the people in that study engaged in any political activities beyond the routine citizen duty of voting, with 13 percent in the role of political communicators, 14 percent being political activists, and 3 percent political leaders. How might the democratic goal of widespread and meaningful citizen participation in politics be more fully realized?

Goals of the Study

The social mobilization thesis sketched in chapter 3 argues that individuals can be mobilized for political participation through involvement in all kinds of nonpolitical social activities. But what kinds of social conditions or activities are the most relevant and effective for this mobilization process? The research reported in this chapter addresses that question by examining seven different social contexts in which the political mobilization process can occur. Three of these contexts — one's sociodemographic location, parents' activities, and social and economic statuses — are essentially fixed, at least in the short run. To the extent that they affect political participation, therefore, relatively few possibilities exist for altering current participation rates. In contrast, the other four

contexts — one's job influence, mass media exposure, community attachment, and association involvement — are quite variable and hence provide
considerable flexibility for mobilizing political participation.

Each of these social contexts is examined in relation to each of the six
dimensions of political actions discussed in the previous chapter. In addition, the most relevant factors from all seven social contexts are brought
together in a combined analysis that explores the total mobilization process
in a more integrated manner.

The data for these analyses are all taken from the Indianapolis study of
political participation described in chapter 3. When examining the data for
descriptive purposes, separate percentages are given for the two indexes
comprising each participation dimension, since the narrower scope of
these indexes makes them more intuitively meaningful. When performing
correlation and regression analyses, however, only a single coefficient for
the combined index for each dimension is reported, so as to be as parsi-
monious as possible in identifying significant relationships. The three
most commonly reported statistics in these latter analyses are (a) the
zero-order correlation coefficient r, which indicates the basic relationship
between two variables; (b) multiple R coefficients, which when squared
indicate the total amount of variation in the dependent variable explained
by all the predictor variables in combination; and (c) partial beta coefficients, which indicate how much the dependent variable is affected by a
standardized change in a designated predictor variable while holding
constant the effects of all the other predictor variables in that analysis.[1]
All relationships reported here are statistically significant using the F-test
and the .05 probability level, so that presumably they represent real
relationships in the total population rather than just artifacts of the sampling procedures.

Most of the relationships examined in this chapter have been investigated by many previous studies. For example, we already know with
considerable certainty that "income is positively correlated with political
participation" (Milbrath, 1965:120). Most of this previous research has

---

1. Correlation and regression analyses assume that all relationships are linear (rather than curvilinear in some manner) and additive (rather than interactive). To test for linearity, all relationships
were also examined using multiple classification analysis (Andrews et al., 1967), which does not
assume linearity, and large discrepancies between the two sets of corresponding coefficients were
given special attention. Tests for interaction were beyond the statistical scope of this study, but
assuming additivity when interaction may in fact be occurring is a conservative strategy, since
it results in less explained variation than might be obtained if one did take interaction effects
into account.

suffered from three serious limitations, however, all of which are evident in that generalization.

First, and perhaps most serious, almost all of these studies have conceptualized the process of political participation as a single dimension of behavior, ignoring the possibility that it may actually consist of several distinct dimensions. Rather than treating political participation as a general phenomenon, we should be able to explain why people do or do not discuss politics with friends, vote in elections, belong to political clubs, or work for political parties.

The second limitation is that most previous research has been content to examine one explanatory variable (such as income) at a time, and has not attempted to carry out more complex multivariate analyses in which several interrelated predictor variables are examined simultaneously. Perhaps, for instance, the observed relationship between income and voting turnout is only a spurious consequence of the fact that both variables are directly related to level of education. A few recent studies (e.g., Palma, 1970; Verba and Nie, 1972) have performed some multivariate analyses, but only with small numbers of predictor variables.

The third limitation results from failure to measure the strengths of the relationships between predictor and participation variables. Knowing that participation increases with income tells us nothing about how strong, and hence important, this relationship actually is. Consequently, there is no way of deciding whether income is a stronger or weaker predictor of participation than some other variable such as media exposure.

The research reported here attempts to surmount all three of these limitations by (a) conceptualizing and measuring political participation as a multidimensional process, (b) examining a large set of predictor variables using multivariate statistical analysis techniques, and (c) focusing on strengths of observed and controlled relationships, as measured by zero-order, partial, and multiple regression coefficients.[2]

Sociodemographic Location

The sociodemographic factors of sex, age, race, and religion are vital determinants of a person's location in social space and therefore indirectly

2. The only previous study of political participation that has attempted to surmount all three of the above methodological limitations is Sidney Verba and Norman Nie's (1972) research based on a 1967 national sample survey. Their findings are discussed in subsequent chapters whenever relevant, but it should be noted at the outset that their study did not include many of the social variables investigated here. Although this Indianapolis study is based on a single metropolitan area, its analysis is broader in scope and depth than Verba and Nie's work.

affect most forms of social involvement and political participation. Most previous research has discovered correlations between each of these socio-demographic variables and political participation, although many of the relationships were rather weak.[3] In general:

1. Men are more likely than women to participate in many aspects of politics, although these differences appear to be slowly disappearing.

2. In general, political participation rates are very low among people in their twenties, increase steadily from about age thirty until the fifties, and then decline again, although this decline is caused largely by lower levels of education and income among elderly persons rather than by old age.

3. Blacks tend to participate less often than whites in most kinds of political activities, but when socioeconomic status is held constant, political participation rates among blacks are as high as or even higher than rates among whites at the same status level.

4. Jews generally participate much more extensively in political affairs than do persons of other religions, while those with no religious preferences are the least active politically. Most studies have found somewhat higher rates of political participation among Roman Catholics than Protestants, but there are wide variations among Protestant denominations.

Theoretical Rationale

Despite the heterogeneity of these sociodemographic factors, their effects on political participation are compatible with our overall social mobilization thesis. Women, young people, blacks, and nonreligious people — all of whom have lower-than-average rates of political activity — occupy social statuses in this society that undoubtedly hinder or restrict their involvement in many types of social activities. This constriction in turn prevents them from being mobilized into political participation. In contrast, men, middle-aged people, whites, and those with commonly accepted religious beliefs are not socially limited by their sociodemographic characteristics and may even benefit from them.

More specifically, the observed relationships between each of these sociodemographic factors and political participation might be explained in the following ways. The greater participation of men, in contrast to women, is undoubtedly due to traditional cultural norms that have discour-

---

3. A complete listing of all studies prior to 1965 that dealt with these sociodemographic variables is given in Milbrath (1965:134–41). Five relevant studies worthy of note that have been published since 1965 are by Orum (1966), Glenn and Grimes (1968), Alford and Scoble (1968), Palma (1970), and Verba and Nie (1972:138–73).

aged women from becoming politically active. The relationship between age and political participation is probably a result of the increasing social ties, commitments, and responsibilities that usually come with middle age. Low rates of political participation by blacks in the United States are clearly caused by racial discrimination and low socioeconomic status. The most likely explanation for the unusually high rates of political activity among Jews lies in their unique cultural heritage stressing active manipulation of the social environment. The above-average political participation rates found among Roman Catholics can perhaps be explained in terms of a sense of community that to some degree unites all Catholics. And finally, persons with no religious preference may also be socially isolated in other ways.

Basic Findings

Relationships occurring between sex, age, and race and each of the political participation indexes are reported in Table 4.1.[4] In this and all subsequent tables reporting basic relationships, two kinds of information are given for each participation dimension: (a) the percentage of respondents with "high" (i.e., top third) scores on each of the component indexes comprising that dimension, and (b) the product-moment correlation coefficient r (which is numerically equivalent to beta in these cases) for the combined dimensional index. In addition, at the bottom of the table are given mean percentages and r's across all six dimensional indexes, plus N's.

As expected, men score higher than women on all of the participation indexes except political organizations and partisan involvement, but most of these differences are rather slight. Only on the Cognitive participation dimension is there a sharp sex difference, with men knowing more about politics and holding more political opinions than women. The overall mean coefficient for all six participation dimensions is just .11.

As also anticipated, most forms of political involvement increase with age until the forties or fifties and then decline somewhat. The two exceptions to this generalization are Partisan and Governmental participation, both of which are most frequent among people in their sixties. Because of these curvilinear tendencies, all of the regression coefficients (except for

---

4. For presentation in these tables, the political participation indexes have all been dichotomized as close to the sixty-seventh percentile ("high") as possible. However, on some of the indexes — such as political organizations — the "high" category consists of considerably fewer than one-third of the respondents, since few people had ever done those activities.

Table 4.1

Sex, Age, and Race Related to the Political Participation Indexes

Political Dimensions and Indexes	Sex		Age					Race	
	M	F	21–29	30–39	40–49	50–59	60+	W	B
Cognitive participation									
Percent high knowledge	48%	27%	29%	37%	45%	42%	42%	41%	20%
Percent high opinions	58%	36%	50%	51%	57%	41%	30%	47%	43%
Combined index r		.27		NS[a] (eta = .17)[b]					.17
Expressive participation									
Percent high interest	37%	28%	24%	31%	41%	38%	30%	33%	26%
Percent high discussion	27%	16%	25%	19%	25%	24%	10%	21%	17%
Combined index r		.15		NS (eta = .17)					NS
Electoral participation									
Percent high party pref.	36%	33%	25%	28%	39%	44%	42%	32%	44%
Percent high registration & voting	39%	37%	8%	35%	50%	58%	50%	38%	39%
Combined index r		NS		.31 (eta = .33)					NS
Organizational participation									
Percent high VA activities	7%	6%	4%	6%	6%	15%	4%	7%	5%
Percent high political organization	2%	4%	3%	5%	2%	4%	2%	3%	3%
Combined index r		NS		NS (eta = .13)					NS
Partisan participation									
Percent high activities	33%	25%	15%	23%	36%	41%	35%	28%	31%
Percent high involvement	20%	20%	11%	16%	23%	26%	27%	20%	20%
Combined index r		NS		.18 (eta = .20)					NS
Governmental participation									
Percent high activities	29%	22%	12%	29%	37%	29%	23%	26%	20%
Percent high involvement	6%	2%	0%	3%	3%	5%	8%	4%	2%
Combined index r		.10		.11 (eta = .16)					NS
Mean percent high	29%	21%	17%	24%	30%	31%	25%	25%	23%
Mean r		.11		.15 (eta = .19)					NS
N	356	394	182	164	146	117	139	595	154

[a]NS = not significant.
[b]Eta is a correlation coefficient obtained with multiple classification analysis, which does not assume linearity.

62

Electoral participation) are nonsignificant or very low. Multiple classification analysis, which does not assume linearity, was therefore used to obtain an eta coefficient for each dimension. These etas are all significant and higher than the corresponding r's. The mean eta for age is .19.

In regard to race, the only index on which whites score significantly higher than blacks is political knowledge, so that the correlation for the Cognitive dimension is .17. The coefficients for all the other dimensions are nonsignificant, as is the overall mean coefficient.

The sample was not large enough to permit analysis of each Protestant denomination separately, so Protestants were divided into the two categories of "conservatives" (including all Pentecostal churches, Church of Christ, Disciples of Christ, Nazarene Church, and all Baptists), and "liberals" (including Methodists, Presbyterians, Lutherans, Episcopalians, Congregationalists, community churches, and Unitarians). Two other religion categories are Roman Catholics and those with no preference. Only six Jews fell into the sample, which is too small a number for generalizations, but data on these people are reported for comparison purposes. Because these five religious categories are not ordered in any manner, multiple classification etas rather than r's are given in Table 4.2.

The main discovery of this analysis is that religious preference forms a rough dichotomy in respect to political participation. Liberal Protestants and Roman Catholics tend to be more active politically than conservative Protestants and those with no preference. In general, religious preference is a relevant but not particularly strong predictor of political participation, with a mean eta of .16.

Multivariate Analyses

The first question to be investigated here is whether the observed correlations between the sociodemographic characteristics and the political participation dimensions represent real relationships, or whether they are simply spurious consequences of underlying correlations between these characteristics and one's social and economic statuses. To test this possibility, each of the political participation indexes was regressed on each of the four sociodemographic variables while holding constant the effects of education, occupation, and income. The resulting partial beta coefficients for sex are virtually identical to the zero-order coefficients in Table 4.1, indicating that these control variables have no effects on the observed participation differences between men and women. The effect of these controls on age, however, is to raise the participation scores of

Table 4.2

Religious Preference Related to the Political Participation Indexes

Political Dimensions and Indexes	Conservative Protestants	Liberal Protestants	Religious Preference — Roman Catholics	No preference	Jews	eta
Cognitive participation						
Percent high knowledge	20%	49%	47%	47%	100%	
Percent high opinions	42%	52%	57%	40%	17%	
Combined index eta						.22
Expressive participation						
Percent high interest	24%	40%	41%	31%	33%	
Percent high discussion	16%	28%	25%	19%	0%	
Combined index eta						.20
Electoral participation						
Percent high party pref.	31%	39%	36%	33%	33%	
Percent high registration & voting	31%	49%	42%	29%	50%	
Combined index eta						.15
Organizational participation						
Percent high VA activities	5%	9%	9%	3%	50%	
Percent high political organization	2%	6%	3%	2%	0%	
Combined index eta						.10
Partisan participation						
Percent high activities	35%	36%	30%	24%	83%	
Percent high involvement	8%	14%	7%	10%	0%	
Combined index eta						.13
Governmental participation						
Percent high activities	17%	34%	36%	19%	50%	
Percent high involvement	1%	6%	5%	5%	17%	
Combined index eta						.16
Mean percent high	19%	30%	28%	22%	36%	
Mean eta						.16
N	309	222	106	106	6	

people over age fifty on all the political dimensions, so that all the relationships for age become linear or nearly so and the partial betas are all slightly larger than the corresponding etas in Table 4.1.[5]

With race, these controls totally erase the observed tendency for blacks to score lower than whites on political knowledge, indicating that the lower scores of blacks in this area are due entirely to their socioeconomic (particularly educational) disadvantages. In addition, the relationship between race and Electoral participation now becomes significant in a reversed direction — with blacks scoring higher than whites. In short — as explored more fully elsewhere (Olsen, 1972) — race is apparently no longer a barrier to full participation in this community. When these controls are applied to religious preference, finally, its relationships with all the political participation dimensions become very low or nonsignificant. Thus, most of the observed differences among religions in political participation rates are due to their varying socioeconomic statuses.

Age and sex are clearly the most important sociodemographic characteristics affecting political participation. Moreover, because they are unrelated to one another, none of their relationships with any of the political participation dimensions is significantly altered when the other variable is held constant. The multiple R coefficients produced by age and sex in combination can therefore be taken as summary indicators of the effects of sociodemographic location on each of the political participation dimensions. These figures are as follows: Cognitive participation, .29; Expressive participation, .21; Electoral participation, .33; Organizational participation, .13; Partisan participation, .20; Governmental participation, .17; mean R, .22.

Conclusions

To briefly summarize this section, we have found the following relationships. (a) The expected tendency for men to be more politically active than women occurs only on the Cognitive, Expressive, and Governmental dimensions, and only in the Cognitive area is the difference between men and women at all noticeable. Controlling for socioeconomic status does not appreciably alter these patterns. (b) The predicted curvilinear relationship between age and political participation was found to exist in all areas

---

5. When only education is held constant, the coefficients for age with Cognitive, Electoral, and Partisan participation increase in magnitude over the zero-order coefficients. In other words, if it were not for their relatively greater education, younger people would be even less politically active than they are.

except intense involvement in partisan and governmental affairs, where older people predominate. All of these relationships become more nearly linear in form when socioeconomic status is controlled, however. (c) Only in the area of political knowledge do whites score significantly higher than blacks, and this difference disappears entirely when education is held constant. Consequently, race can be discarded as a useful predictor of political participation. (d) Roman Catholics tend to be relatively active in most areas of politics, and persons with no religious preference are relatively inactive. Liberal Protestants are slightly more active than Catholics, while conservative Protestants score even lower than those with no preference. This pattern is consistent across all dimensions of political participation, but the relationships become extremely weak when socioeconomic status is held constant.

From the perspective of policy formation, the sociodemographic context does not appear to impose major barriers to active participation in politics. On the whole, blacks and women are no longer handicapped in the political arena, although youth does seem to restrict political participation. Perhaps, however, the dramatic political events of the past two decades are slowly making politics more salient to young people.

Parents' Activities

Almost all previous research on long-term effects of the political socialization process has dealt with the transmission from parents to children of political attitudes, values, and preferences.[6] Very little attention has been given to the effects of parental political activities on a person's participation in politics as an adult. Our present knowledge about this aspect of political socialization is summarized by Lester Milbrath (1965:43) in the statement that "family experience has a profound impact on a person's exposure to political stimuli and on his activity level in politics." This generalization obviously does not say a great deal, and neither Milbrath nor later studies (David, 1965; Greenstein, 1965) attempt to specify what kinds of family experiences have how much influence on what kinds of political participation. In this section we shall address these more detailed questions.

Theoretical Rationale

A theoretical explanation of why the children of politically active parents also tend to participate extensively in politics is found in the idea of

---

6. This literature has been summarized by Hyman (1959) and more recently by Langton (1969).

the "politicized family." Dwaine Marvick and Charles Nixon (1961:209) describe this as "a family in which political matters receive both substantial and sustained attention, and in which skills in the analysis of public issues are supplemented by examples of adult political participation . . ." In such a family, the adults stimulate each other to become more aware of and informed about political issues, they discuss politics together and raise each other's level of interest in politics, they motivate each other to register and vote and to support candidates in elections, and they willingly make adjustments in family routines necessitated by active involvement in political affairs. At the same time, the children in a politicized family learn to be interested in and concerned about political affairs, they acquire extensive political knowledge and participation skills that facilitate involvement in politics, and they internalize the norm that political activity is important.

This line of reasoning is fully compatible with the social mobilization thesis, although that perspective suggests that other forms of parental involvement — such as membership in interest associations — should also politicize a child and prepare him or her for active political participation as an adult. Most of the effects of parental activities are undoubtedly modified by one's adult circumstances such as statuses and roles, but this does not negate the relevance of the political socialization process to later political participation.

Basic Findings

The indicators of parents' political activities included in this analysis are whether they held party preferences, how frequently they discussed politics and voted, and whether they participated actively in political organizations, partisan affairs, or governmental activities. An index of parents' political actions was constructed from these items. As an indicator of parents' social involvement, respondents were asked the number of voluntary associations to which the parent of the same sex belonged when the respondent was a youth. Observed relationships between these two parental variables of voluntary association membership and political actions and each of the political participation indexes are given in Table 4.3.

The number of voluntary associations to which one's parent belonged is related to all forms of political participation except involvement in governmental affairs. The coefficients for the Cognitive, Expressive, and Partisan participation dimensions are moderately strong, while the figures for the other three dimensions are somewhat weaker. Overall, the mean *r* for this variable is .21. Quite clearly, having a parent who belongs to

Table 4.3

Parents' Memberships in Voluntary Associations and the Index of Parents' Political Actions Related to the Political Participation Indexes

Political Dimensions and Indexes	Parents' VA Memberships				Index of Parents' Political Actions			
	0	1	2	3+	Low	Occasional	Moderate	High
Cognitive participation								
Percent high knowledge	31%	41%	42%	58%	24%	37%	47%	48%
Percent high opinions	40%	54%	50%	60%	30%	43%	60%	65%
Combined index r			.26				.33	
Expressive participation								
Percent high interest	24%	38%	40%	52%	18%	29%	39%	58%
Percent high discussion	17%	27%	16%	38%	9%	17%	30%	37%
Combined index r			.28				.40	
Electoral participation								
Percent high party pref.	31%	37%	42%	49%	30%	37%	32%	48%
Percent high registration & voting	33%	42%	42%	54%	32%	41%	37%	50%
Combined index r			.17				.20	
Organizational participation								
Percent high VA activities	7%	5%	4%	10%	6%	5%	9%	6%
Percent high political organizations	3%	3%	4%	10%	2%	3%	5%	6%
Combined index r			.12				.11	
Partisan participation								
Percent high activities	23%	33%	27%	54%	18%	26%	34%	49%
Percent high involvement	14%	27%	20%	49%	12%	19%	22%	38%
Combined index r			.24				.24	
Governmental participation								
Percent high activities	20%	28%	29%	40%	20%	25%	21%	48%
Percent high involvement	3%	8%	3%	3%	4%	4%	4%	4%
Combined index r			.19				.15	
Mean percent high	21%	36%	30%	46%	26%	29%	31%	39%
Mean r			.21				.24	
N	228	132	91	65	246	194	213	94

several voluntary associations does affect a child's political socialization and can influence him or her to become actively involved in politics as an adult.

The index of parents' political actions displays roughly similar patterns, although the coefficients for the Cognitive and Expressive dimensions are somewhat stronger than with association memberships. The mean *r* in this case is .24, which suggests that the extent to which one's parents took part in political affairs definitely influences all aspects of one's adult political participation.[7]

Multivariate Analyses

The first question to be investigated here is whether the variable of parents' association memberships directly affects one's political participation, or whether this linkage occurs indirectly through the intervening variable of one's own voluntary association involvement. To resolve this issue, we must reexamine the relationships for parents' association memberships while holding constant the number of voluntary associations to which the respondent presently belongs. The resulting partial beta coefficients are virtually unchanged from the original zero-order coefficients reported for this variable in Table 4.3, which indicates that parental membership in voluntary associations directly affects one's adult political activities regardless of whether one joins any organizations.

The next step is to examine the effects of each of these parental variables — association memberships and political actions — while holding constant the effects of the other. This analysis also yields multiple regression coefficients for the two measures in combination. The results of this analysis are reported in the first three columns of Table 4.4, where we see that both variables do have effects on all forms of political activity that are independent of the other factor. In fact, most of the partial betas for both variables are only slightly lower than the corresponding zero-order coefficients. In addition, all of the multiple *R*'s for the two variables in combination are noticeably higher than either of their component coefficients, so that we can considerably increase our explanatory power by

---

7. The variables of mother's and father's levels of education and father's occupational status were also investigated. Both parental education measures correlated moderately with the Cognitive and Expressive participation dimensions, were unrelated to Electoral participation, and were only weakly correlated with the remaining three political dimensions. The mean *r* in both cases was .15. Father's occupation was only weakly related to all six political participation dimensions. When extent of parent's political action was held constant, however, all of these correlations became nonsignificant or nearly so.

Table 4.4

Partial and Multiple Relationships of Parents' Voluntary Association Memberships and Political Actions with the Combined Political Participation Indexes, Plus Zero-Order and Partial Relationships for the Combined Parents' Activities Index

Political Dimensions	Partial Betas Simultaneous Controls		Multiple R's	Combined Parents' Activities Index	
	Parents' VA Memberships	Parents' Political Actions		Zero-Order r's	Partial Betas Controlling Sex, Age, Education, and Socio-economic Status
Cognitive participation	.21	.27	.36	.37	.23
Expressive participation	.22	.34	.44	.44	.32
Electoral participation	.14	.17	.24	.25	.19
Organizational participation	.10	.10	.15	.15	.10
Partisan participation	.20	.18	.29	.30	.26
Governmental participation	.16	.11	.21	.21	.10
Mean coefficients	.17	.20	.28	.28	.20

utilizing both parental variables. Consequently, these two variables were combined into a single index of parents' activities. The zero-order correlations between this combined parental index and each of the political participation indexes are reported in the fourth column of Table 4.4. These coefficients, which are almost identical to their corresponding R's, can be taken as summary indicators of the effects of parental social and political involvement on one's own political participation.

The final step in this analysis is to determine whether the combined index of parents' activities is directly related to political participation, or whether its effects are mediated through such intervening variables as sex, age, education, occupation, and income. The last column in Table 4.4 gives the partial betas for the parents' activities index with each of the political participation dimensions while holding constant the effects of those other factors. Although all of these coefficients are somewhat lower than the corresponding zero-order coefficients in the previous column, all remain significant. We are therefore justified in retaining the index of parents' activities as an independent predictor of political participation.

Conclusions

Theoretically, these findings suggest that one's parents play an important role in initiating the social mobilization and political socialization processes that lead to later political participation. Parental involvement in voluntary associations and political actions tends to expand and intensify the social and political environment in which the child lives and to create a politicized family. Regardless of the individual's sex, age, education, occupational status, or income, these parental influences tend to carry over into his or her adult life and stimulate participation in all realms of politics.[8]

Pragmatically, this factor of parents' activities cannot be manipulated as a means of mobilizing adults to become more involved in politics. Consequently, as we examine the effects of other social factors on political participation, we must continually ask whether these effects occur independently of the social and political activities of one's parents. Only those social conditions that lead to political participation regardless of the extent of parental activities can be utilized as political mobilization procedures.

---

8. These data do not permit a test of the "politicized family" idea in regard to one's present marriage, since the study did not include any measures of the political actions of the respondents' spouses. Additional analyses not reported here did reveal, however, that political participation is generally unrelated to such family characteristics as marital status, number of children, time spent together, and patterns of decision making.

Social and Economic Statuses

Without exception, every previous study of political participation has discovered moderate to strong correlations between various social and economic status measures and all types of political activity.[9] The generalization that "the higher one's socioeconomic status, the more extensively one will participate in political activities" has come to be regarded as almost a universal social law. Verba and Nie (1972:129–33) attached so much importance to the relationship between socioeconomic status and political participation that they constructed a "standard SES model" as an analytical baseline and argued that all other social factors "can be thought of as modifying the working of the standard socioeconomic model."

Despite the apparent validity of this generalization, however, many questions derived from it still remain unanswered. Is it equally applicable to all forms of political participation, or does socioeconomic status correlate more highly with some kinds of political activities than with others? Do the usual empirical indicators of socioeconomic status — education, occupation, income — have separate effects on political participation (in all its various forms), or are all three variables measuring essentially the same underlying phenomenon? Do the various socioeconomic status indicators remain related to all forms of political participation after the effects of sociodemographic and parental factors are held constant? We shall attempt to answer these questions in this section.

Closely related to this variable of one's current social status is the process of status mobility, both upward and downward. A few previous studies have found a slight tendency for upwardly mobile people to be more active politically than those who are not mobile, and for those who are downwardly mobile to be less active than others. These findings are not consistent, however, and some of the studies contradict each other (Milbrath, 1965:117–19). We shall therefore also examine the effects of both generational and career occupational mobility, as well as generational educational mobility, on all forms of political participation.

Theoretical Rationale

A variety of arguments have been proposed to explain the observed relationships between social and economic statuses and political participa-

---

9. A long list of these studies is given in Milbrath (1965:220–34), and these relationships are discussed in more detail by Lane (1959:220–34). More recently research by Alford and Scoble (1968), Nie et al. (1969), Berry (1970:70–73), and Palma (1970:143–44) also confirmed these relationships.

tion. We shall examine two of them — the intellectual sophistication and socioeconomic power arguments — that are compatible with the general thesis of social mobilization. Both argue that the higher one's statuses, the more likely one is to be mobilized into social activity and hence into political participation. They differ sharply, however, in their explanations of this process and the types of status they emphasize.

The intellectual sophistication thesis places primary emphasis on education as the main factor influencing participation in politics. The argument is that the greater one's cognitive capabilities and sophistication — as indicated primarily by amount of education completed — the more one will know about the political system, the more attention and interest one will give to politics, the more complete will be one's understanding of political issues, the more seriously one will take his or her citizen responsibilities, and the better prepared one will be to take part in political activities. From this perspective, the variables of occupation and income appear to be correlated with political participation only because they are strongly influenced by one's educational level.

The socioeconomic power thesis, in contrast, focuses primarily on occupational status and to a lesser extent on amount of income. The argument here is that one's capability of exerting influence or power in various realms of social life determines one's social privileges and prestige and hence the amount of resources (e.g., time, energy, possessions) one can commit to political activities. The more resources one possesses, the more extensively one will employ them in an effort to obtain favorable outcomes from the political system. This thesis therefore predicts that holding constant occupational status and income should eliminate the observed correlations between education and political participation.

In addition to addressing these two theoretical arguments focusing on one's statuses, we must also ask why upwardly mobile people may be more politically active than those who are downwardly mobile. Perhaps the simplest explanation would be that individuals attempting to raise their socioeconomic statuses sometimes use political activity as a mobility route, while those who are falling in status may blame the political system for their plight. Beyond this, we quickly become enmeshed in complex arguments involving psychological factors such as class identification, feelings of relative deprivation, and reference-group orientations. Before proceeding further in that direction, however, we must ask if the process of mobility by itself — apart from the status levels of origin or destination — is in fact related to different forms of political participation.

Perhaps upwardly mobile people are politically active simply because they now occupy high-status positions, and vice versa. To check that possibility, our analyses of social mobility will include controls for one's current statuses.

Basic Findings

Three measures of education were originally devised to test the intellectual sophistication thesis: (a) total amount of education, (b) type of education (e.g., academic, professional, general, vocational), and (c) educational mobility in relation to the parent of the same sex. Relationships between amount of education and each of the political participation indexes are given in Table 4.5. No data are included for type of education or educational mobility because both these variables were found to be completely unrelated to all forms of political participation. (Educational mobility by itself displays small, U-shaped curvilinear relationships with three of the participation dimensions, but these all disappear when amount of education is held constant.)

Amount of education is significantly related to all the political indexes, and some of its coefficients are rather strong. In particular, education has dramatic consequences for Cognitive and Expressive participation. The coefficient for the Governmental dimension is also moderately high, although almost all of this relationship occurs on the index of governmental activity (e.g., writing letters to congressmen) rather than on the index of direct governmental involvement. In contrast, the correlations between education and the Electoral, Organizational, and Partisan dimensions are much weaker. Nevertheless, college graduates score noticeably higher than all other persons on most of the political indexes — but especially on the Partisan and Governmental dimensions. The mean r for education is .29.

The most commonly used indicator of socioeconomic power is the occupational status of the head of the household, since this factor will affect a family's income and other resources, its prestige in the community, and many of the activities and social relationships of the family members.[10] A four-category occupational scheme was devised for this study: (a) low manual, including all unskilled laborers, private household

10. A more basic but very crude measure of occupational power is the distinction between heads of households who are presently employed (either full-time or part-time) and those who are not (including those who are retired, disabled, laid off, unemployed, students, or homemakers). The 147 respondents in this sample who fell into the latter category did score lower than the others on the Cognitive and Expressive dimensions, but the remaining relationships were nonsignificant.

Table 4.5
Amount of Education Related to the Political Participation Indexes

Political Dimensions and Indexes	Amount of Education				
	0–8 Years	9–11 Years	12 Years	13–15 Years	16+ Years
Cognitive participation					
Percent high knowledge	14%	23%	36%	57%	66%
Percent high opinions	29%	34%	51%	61%	58%
Combined index *r*			.46		
Expressive participation					
Percent high interest	16%	19%	35%	46%	52%
Percent high discussion	7%	17%	22%	26%	40%
Combined index *r*			.44		
Electoral participation					
Percent high party pref.	28%	33%	29%	39%	51%
Percent high registration & voting	32%	35%	36%	37%	56%
Combined index *r*			.21		
Organizational participation					
Percent high VA activities	2%	4%	7%	10%	15%
Percent high political organizations	1%	1%	3%	6%	8%
Combined index *r*			.14		
Partisan participation					
Percent high activities	23%	22%	24%	33%	52%
Percent high involvement	17%	16%	18%	22%	34%
Combined index *r*			.16		
Governmental participation					
Percent high activities	10%	13%	27%	34%	53%
Percent high involvement	3%	2%	3%	2%	10%
Combined index *r*			.30		
Mean percent high	15%	18%	23%	31%	42%
Mean *r*			.29		
N	146	159	198	157	89

workers, and semiskilled operatives; (b) high manual, composed of all skilled craftsmen, public service workers, and foremen; (c) low non-manual, including all clerical workers, salespersons, proprietors of small businesses (less than five employees), and farm owners; and (d) high nonmanual, composed of executives, managers, owners of large businesses, technicians, public officials, and professionals.[11] Relationships

11. In this scheme, retired, disabled, laid off, and unemployed persons were classified according to their last regular job, and full-time college students were coded as high nonmanual. Hence the only persons excluded from the classification scheme were female heads of households who were not employed.

between this occupational status scheme and the political participation indexes are given in the left-hand side of Table 4.6.

In general, most of these coefficients for occupation are slightly smaller than the corresponding ones for education, but they follow the same pattern. That is, the strongest relationships occur on the Cognitive and Expressive dimensions, the Governmental participation dimension ranks third (again because of governmental activities rather than involvement), and the remaining dimensions of Electoral, Organizational, and Partisan participation have much lower coefficients. Another interesting feature of these scores is the sharp break on most of the indexes between manual and nonmanual occupations, which suggests that the traditional distinction between the "working" and "middle" classes in American society is still a meaningful class division in regard to political participation. The average r for occupational status is .24.[12]

It might be argued that both career (movement during one's lifetime) and generational (movement in relation to one's father) occupational mobility should be relevant to the socioeconomic power argument, since those who have moved upward in occupational status have increased their opportunities for exerting social influence. These analyses revealed, however, that career mobility is unrelated to any of the political participation measures, that generational mobility is significantly related only to the Cognitive dimension, and that controlling for present occupational status reduces this latter relationship to nonsignificance. Hence no data are given for either of these variables.

Another commonly employed indicator of socioeconomic power is annual income, defined for this study as the total gross (pretax) income of all family members from all sources in 1967. As seen in the right-hand side of Table 4.6, amount of annual family income is related to all the political indexes, although only the coefficients for the Cognitive and Expressive dimensions are at all high. Following the previously observed patterns for both education and occupation, the Governmental participation dimension ranks third, while the remaining relationships are quite weak. In terms of income categories, people falling in the $0–$3,999 and $4,000–$7,999 groups (in 1968) tend to have relatively similar scores on most of the political indexes, which is to say that apparently income must rise above

---

12. Very similar results were obtained using Duncan occupational scores (Duncan, 1961:109–38), except that several of the coefficients were slightly lower (so that the average r was .22). These two measures of occupational status are themselves correlated at .84.

Table 4.6
Occupational Status and Annual Family Income Related to the Political Participation Indexes

Political Dimensions and Indexes	Occupational Status				Annual Income			
	Low Manual	High Manual	Low Non-manual	High Non-manual	$0–3,999	$4,000–7,999	$8,000–11,999	$12,000–or More
Cognitive participation								
Percent high knowledge	19%	30%	55%	51%	4%	27%	42%	58%
Percent high opinions	29%	46%	55%	57%	26%	45%	55%	62%
Combined index r			.34				.36	
Expressive participation								
Percent high interest	16%	25%	44%	49%	27%	29%	38%	36%
Percent high discussion	15%	18%	23%	30%	12%	18%	22%	24%
Combined index r			.33				.27	
Electoral participation								
Percent high party pref.	27%	35%	35%	41%	33%	35%	31%	41%
Percent high registration & voting	39%	33%	47%	47%	37%	34%	38%	49%
Combined index r			.19				.16	
Organizational participation								
Percent high VA activities	3%	4%	10%	11%	3%	5%	8%	11%
Percent high political organizations	1%	4%	7%	13%	3%	3%	4%	5%
Combined index r			.13				.10	
Partisan participation								
Percent high activities	24%	22%	37%	37%	28%	22%	31%	37%
Percent high involvement	15%	14%	31%	25%	18%	17%	22%	25%
Combined index r			.15				.12	
Governmental participation								
Percent high activities	13%	19%	32%	42%	18%	16%	28%	44%
Percent high involvement	4%	4%	5%	14%	5%	2%	3%	5%
Combined index r			.28				.22	
Mean percent high	17%	21%	32%	35%	19%	21%	27%	33%
Mean r			.24				.21	
N	164	253	248	167	131	241	201	144

the national median (about \$8,000 in 1968) before it begins to effect political participation. The mean r for income is .21.

Multivariate Analyses

The question of which variable or variables provide the best indicator(s) of socioeconomic power can be answered by simultaneously relating occupational status and annual income to the political participation dimensions. The resulting partial betas for each factor (controlling the other) and multiple R's are given in Table 4.7. Both sets of partial coefficients are considerably reduced from their original zero-order values, and those for income with Organizational and Partisan participation become nonsignificant. The rest of the coefficients do remain significant, however, with the figures for occupation being somewhat higher than those for income on all dimensions except Cognitive participation. The mean partial coefficient for occupation is .19, compared to only .11 for income, which means that occupational status is generally a more powerful predictor of political participation than is annual family income. All of the multiple R's obtained with both variables in combination are stronger than the corresponding zero-order coefficients for either variable, nevertheless, so that we gain some additional predictive power by using both variables rather than just one. Consequently, a combined index of socioeconomic status was constructed by summing respondents' scores for occupational status and annual income. Relationships between this SES index and the six political participation dimensions are given in the right-hand column of Table 4.7. In general, these figures are quite similar to the corresponding multiple R's.

Our next concern is to test the competing arguments of the intellectual sophistication and socioeconomic power theses concerning political participation. The first perspective says that amount of education is the crucial determining factor, so that controlling it should eliminate the relationships for occupational status and income. The second perspective asserts that occupational status and income are the crucial variables, so that controlling them (or the combined SES index) should destroy the relationships for education.[13] We can simultaneously evaluate both of these predictions by examining the data in Table 4.8.

The first two columns in this table give partial beta coefficients for education and the SES index, holding constant the effects of the other

---

13. Education and the SES index are correlated at $r = .60$.

Table 4.7
Partial and Multiple Relationships of Occupational Status and Annual
Income, as Well as the Socioeconomic Status Index, with the Combined
Political Participation Indexes

Political Dimensions	Partial Betas Simultaneous Controls		Multiple *R*'s	SES Index *r*'s
	Occupa- tional Status	Annual Income		
Cognitive participation	.23	.16	.41	.40
Expressive participation	.28	.14	.36	.35
Electoral participation	.16	.10	.22	.21
Organizational participation	.10	NS	.13	.13
Partisan participation	.11	NS	.15	.15
Governmental participation	.23	.14	.32	.30
Mean coefficients	.19	.11	.27	.26

factor. Since both variables remain significantly related to four of the participation dimensions, we conclude that each has independent effects on political activity and that both theoretical arguments are valid. The mean net effects of education (.16) are somewhat greater than those of SES (.12), however. These data also tell us that the intellectual sophistication thesis is more useful than the socioeconomic power thesis for predicting Cognitive and Expressive political participation, neither thesis is particularly useful in respect to Organizational and Partisan participation, the socioeconomic argument is somewhat more applicable to Electoral participation, and both have equal effects on Governmental participation.[14] Finally, the multiple *R*'s based on both variables provide summary indicators of the effects of one's social and economic statuses on political participation.

Our final concern here is to make sure that both education and socioeconomic status have effects on political participation that are independent of sociodemographic and parental factors. The fourth and fifth columns in Table 4.8 show the partial beta coefficients for education and the SES index while simultaneously controlling for age, sex, and parents' activities. Most of these figures are somewhat but not greatly lower than their

14. Further detailed analyses revealed that the partial coefficients for occupation are higher than the corresponding ones for education only on the two indexes of registration and voting and partisan involvement. Insofar as previous research has found occupation to be a better predictor of political participation than education (e.g., Palma, 1970:148–49), that finding has probably resulted because these studies used a single compound index of political participation that relied heavily on the two activities of voting turnout and volunteer party work.

Table 4.8

Partial and Multiple Relationships of Education and the Socioeconomic Status Index with the Combined Political Participation Indexes, Both with and without Additional Controls

Political Dimensions	Partial Betas Simultaneous Controls		Multiple R	Partial Betas Controlling Sex, Age, and Parents' Activities	
	Education	SES Index		Education	SES Index
Cognitive participation	.30	.23	.47	.37	.32
Expressive participation	.33	.16	.44	.32	.27
Electoral participation	.10	.16	.23	.22	.19
Organizational participation	.10	NS	.14	.11	.13
Partisan participation	NS	NS	.16	.11	.13
Governmental participation	.20	.19	.35	.32	.28
Mean coefficients	.17	.12	.30	.24	.22

corresponding zero-order coefficients, while those for education with Electoral and Governmental participation are somewhat higher. In short, both education and socioeconomic status affect all dimensions of political participation regardless of one's sex, age, or extent of parents' activities.

Conclusions

Although we began this section already knowing — on the basis of previous research — that socioeconomic status is related to political participation, we have discovered several new features of this relationship. We have found that (a) educational attainment generally explains more variation in political participation rates than does occupational status, while annual family income is a relatively weak predictor of most forms of political activity; (b) neither educational nor occupational status mobility affect participation in politics, once one's present status levels are taken into account; (c) none of the observed relationships between either education or socioeconomic status and the political participation indexes are seriously affected by one's age, sex, or parents' activities; and (d) both the intellectual sophistication and socioeconomic power theses are valid explanations of political participation.

In addition, these analyses also reveal that education, occupation, and income all exert considerably more influence on passive than on active forms of political participation. All three status measures are useful primarily as predictors of one's political knowledge, political opinion holding, political discussion, and political interest, plus the single active index of contacts with governmental officials. In contrast, they are considerably less relevant for holding a party preference, registering and voting, partisan activities and involvement, and direct governmental involvement. We cannot, therefore, speak of any general effects of socioeconomic status on political participation. Here is striking evidence for the importance of treating political participation as a multidimensional phenomenon.

From an applied policy perspective, finally, these findings suggest that, as the overall educational, occupational, and income levels of the population slowly rise through time, more and more people will become informed and concerned about politics, if not actively involved in political affairs. This expectation is not particularly encouraging for anyone attempting to stimulate rapid increases in voting, political organizational involvement, or partisan political activity, however. To mobilize greater participation in these political activities, we must clearly look for approaches that have more immediate and broader consequences.

Job Influence

Although the participatory democracy model places considerable emphasis on the work place as a training ground for political participation, no previous research has systematically investigated the nature and characteristics of one's job in relation to political activity. The only generalization that can be gleaned from the existing literature is that — as we have already seen — the higher one's occupational status, the more likely one is to participate in politics. But even that generalization is clouded by the fact that occupational status has usually been measured for the head of the household, not the individual respondent, so that married women have been assigned their husband's rather than their own job statuses.

Theoretical Rationale

The participatory democracy thesis maintains that experience with exercising influence and authority on the job will carry over into the political realm, causing individuals to become more politically active (Pateman, 1970). Hence we would expect to find direct relationships between job influence or authority and most forms of political participation.

Another relevant theoretical argument comes from studies of community power systems. From Hunter (1953) and Dahl (1961) onward, these writings have stressed the importance of occupationally based influence in determining which individuals wield political power in the community. Most of this work has focused on differences in power between such occupational categories as businessmen and politicians. Underlying such categorizations, however, are more basic factors, including the amount of formal authority and informal influence associated with various occupations. Hence this perspective also argues that the more influence one exercises at work, the higher will be one's levels of political activity.

In a broader sense, our general social mobilization perspective also suggests that amount of influence on the job should be a relevant determinant of political participation. Responsibility, authority, and influence relationships constitute social bonds that link the individual into his or her job context, and the greater this job involvement, the stronger the mobilizing process leading to political activity.

Basic Findings

This analysis is limited, by necessity, to the 592 respondents (79 percent of the sample) who were employed either part- or full-time in the labor force. The 158 respondents not in the labor force did not differ significantly from the employed persons in their levels of political participation, however. Respondent's occupation was measured with the same four-category scale used for heads of households. We would not expect these two measures — occupation of respondent and of household head — to differ greatly in their correlations with the political participation indexes, since they are identical measures except in the case of employed married women. In fact, the coefficients for respondent's occupation are so similar to those for heads of households reported in Table 4.6 that they need not be repeated here. The only noteworthy difference between these two sets of figures is that the coefficients for respondent's occupation are consistently lower (by .02 to .04) than those for head's occupation.

Three other indicators of job influence were also investigated in this study: (a) self-employment versus working for others, on the assumption that self-employed persons exercise considerably more influence over their work than do employees; (b) number of people (if any) that one supervises at work; and (c) a subjective evaluation by the respondent of the amount of influence exercised on the job. The results of these analyses can be very briefly summarized without data. Self-other employment is unrelated to all the political participation indexes. Number of subordinates and perceived amount of influence evidence weak zero-order relationships with some of the political participation indexes, but these cannot be considered meaningful until we hold constant the factor of occupational status, which heavily affects both of these job influence measures. Adding this control variable to the regression equations severely reduces most of the coefficients for both measures, and when age and amount of education (which similarly affect job influence) are also held constant, all of these coefficients become nonsignificant.[15]

Conclusions

All of these findings suggest that the social mobilization process does not occur at work, and that the influence or other features of one's job are essentially irrelevant for one's political participation. This generalization does not necessarily negate the emphasis of participatory democracy theory on the work place as a training ground for political democracy, but it does indicate that, if this process occurs at work, it is much more complex

---

15. Investigations of such other job characteristics as size of work place, years on the job, hours worked per week, and general job satisfaction all failed to disclose any significant relationships with any forms of political participation.

and subtle than indicated by amount of job influence or status. Consequently, the entire job context was discarded from further analysis in this study.

Mass Media Exposure

The mass media provide channels of communication reaching far beyond the small circles of individuals with whom we personally interact. Television, radio, newspapers, and magazines constantly bombard us with all varieties of messages — including many that are explicitly or implicitly political in nature. But how effective are the mass media in mobilizing individuals for political participation?

Numerous empirical studies have discovered relationships between various kinds of media exposure and political activity. As expressed by Robert Lane (1959:288), "Those who are more exposed to the media . . . are more likely to be interested in politics, vote, discuss politics, . . . have more opinions and more political information, have a firm party preference." At least three important questions remain unanswered by this previous research, however. First, do the various media all have approximately equal effects on political participation, or are some media more influential than others? Second, is media exposure equally related to all forms of political participation? Third, are all of these correlations between mass media exposure and political activity merely a spurious consequence of one's level of education, or do they persist after education and other background factors are held constant? In this section we will attempt to answer these questions.

Theoretical Rationale

Despite extensive documentation of the relationship between mass media exposure and at least some forms of political participation, little attention has thus far been given to explaining why this relationship occurs. Our general social mobilization thesis appears to be quite relevant in this context, however. Presumably a person who gives considerable attention to the mass media will become aware of current events and problems in the community and society, acquire some knowledge of public issues, and in general broaden the scope of his or her relevant social environment. All of these consequences of media exposure should have mobilizing effects on individuals, and hence eventually stimulate them to become more actively involved in political activities. In the words of

David Berry (1970:93–94), "A high level of exposure to the mass media may be regarded as an indicator of social integration in that people who are more exposed to the media are more likely to have more information about and to be more interested in social and political affairs."

Like all applications of the social mobilization thesis, this is a two-step process, with media exposure mobilizing the individual to become more involved in his or her social world, which in turn leads to increased political participation. Thus it is not just exposure to political news that stimulates a person to become politically active, but rather exposure to all media messages of an informational nature.

Basic Findings

Three different types of mass media exposure were measured for this analysis: (1) number of hours per week spent listening to informational or public affairs programs on television or radio; (2) number of daily newspapers read regularly; and (3) number of magazines containing serious information read regularly. Data for these three measures are not given here but can be summarized briefly. Number of magazines read proved to be the best predictor of most types of political participation. It was significantly and moderately strongly related to all of the political indexes except party preference, with a mean r of .25. The next best predictor of political activity was number of newspapers read regularly, which correlated significantly with all twelve political indexes, although its mean r was only .21. Exposure to television and radio, in contrast, was significantly related to only eight of the twelve political indexes, its mean r was just .12, and almost all of the variation of this measure occurred between those people with virtually no exposure and all other respondents. Because all three of these media exposure measures remain significantly related to political participation when the other two measures are held constant, they were combined into an index of mass media exposure. The coefficients for this index, reported in Table 4.9, provide summary indicators of the effects of mass media exposure on political participation.

All of the coefficients for this media exposure index are moderately to relatively high. Its relationships with Cognitive and Expressive participation are particularly strong, and the coefficient for Governmental participation is almost as high. Overall, the mean r for media exposure is .30. Thus exposure to the mass media is quite crucial for almost all types of political participation, but especially for the more passive forms.

Table 4.9
Mass Media Exposure Index Related to the Political Participation Indexes

Political Dimensions and Indexes	Mass Media Exposure Index			
	Low	Below Average	Above Average	High
Cognitive participation				
Percent high knowledge	13%	22%	42%	56%
Percent high opinions	20%	41%	50%	50%
Combined index r			.37	
Expressive participation				
Percent interest	5%	23%	32%	57%
Percent high discussion	1%	14%	21%	37%
Combined index r			.39	
Electoral participation				
Percent high party pref.	15%	31%	39%	39%
Percent high registration & voting	28%	28%	37%	54%
Combined index r			.24	
Organizational participation				
Percent high VA activities	1%	3%	6%	9%
Percent high political organization	0%	2%	3%	8%
Combined index r			.17	
Partisan participation				
Percent high activities	11%	19%	31%	43%
Percent high involvement	6%	12%	20%	32%
Combined index r			.28	
Governmental participation				
Percent high activities	2%	15%	28%	45%
Percent high involvement	0%	2%	5%	9%
Combined index r			.32	
Mean percent high	8%	18%	26%	37%
Mean r			.30	
N	68	223	303	156

Multivariate Analyses

We must now consider the possibility that many or all of these relationships for mass media exposure are merely spurious consequences of the fact that better-educated people are quite likely to be exposed to the media and to participate in politics. To test this hypothesis, we reexamine the correlations for the mass media index while holding constant the effects of education. The resulting partial beta coefficients are shown in the left-hand column of Table 4.10. The figures for the Cognitive and Expressive political dimensions are noticeably reduced from the corresponding zero-order coefficients because of the strong correlation between education and these two political dimensions. Nevertheless, both these partial betas, as well as those for the other four political dimensions, remain significant and moderately strong, with mean beta = .22. Hence exposure to the mass media can mobilize people to become politically active regardless of their educational attainment.

Finally, to make sure that mass media exposure affects political participation independently of all other background factors, we control simultaneously for education, socioeconomic status, sex, age, and parents' activities. The resulting partial beta coefficients are given in the right-hand column of Table 4.10. These additional controls further reduce the coefficients for mass media exposure with each of the political dimensions, but all the relationships remain significant.

Conclusions

In answer to the questions raised at the beginning of this section, we have discovered that (a) the extent of one's magazine and newspaper reading has much greater influence on political participation than does television and radio exposure; (b) mass media exposure in general is related most strongly to Cognitive and Expressive political participation, and least strongly to Electoral participation; and (c) mass media exposure exerts at least some effects on all types of political participation regardless of one's level of education or other background characteristics.

Theoretically, these relationships can be explained in terms of the social mobilization thesis. Reading magazines and newspapers, watching television, and listening to the radio bring one into closer contact with the community and society and heighten one's sense of involvement in his or her social environment. This mobilization process, in turn, encourages the person to take part in political activities.

Table 4.10
Partial Relationships of the Mass Media Exposure Index and the Combined
Political Participation Indexes, Controlling Education and Other Variables

Political Dimensions	Partial Betas	
	Controlling Education	Controlling Sex, Age, Education, Socioeconomic Status, and Parents' Activities
Cognitive participation	.23	.18
Expressive participation	.26	.22
Electoral participation	.20	.10
Organizational participation	.15	.11
Partisan participation	.25	.20
Governmental participation	.24	.18
Mean coefficients	.22	.17

Pragmatically, we conclude that, despite their impersonal nature, mass communications do indeed mobilize political participation across all sectors of society. Although the mass society image of millions of people being blindly manipulated by political elites via the mass media is undoubtedly grossly exaggerated, exposure to the mass media — especially the printed word — clearly does stimulate people to think about and be interested in politics.

Community Attachment

The local community is the arena in which most of our daily social interactions transpire and that encompasses many of the associations in which we work, study, worship, and recreate. It is also the arena for many forms of political activity. We would therefore expect the extent and strength of a person's ties with his or her community to affect political participation to a considerable extent. Community attachment can be measured in at least three different ways: (a) residency measures, such as length of residency in the community or in one's present home, or home ownership; (b) activity measures, concerning participation in various kinds of community events, projects, and other public functions; and (c) interpersonal measures, pertaining to frequency of informal interaction with neighbors, friends, and relatives in the community. All three of these measurement approaches are utilized in this section.

The most firmly established empirical generalization in this area is that "the longer a person resides in a given community, the greater the likelihood of this participation in politics" (Milbrath, 1965:133). Since most of the studies from which this generalization is derived focused solely on voting, however, it would be more accurate to say only that length of residency is related to voting turnout, leaving problematic the question of whether or not length of residency correlates significantly with other forms of political action. An alternative measure is home ownership, which Alford and Scoble (1968) found to be the only community attachment variable with any noteworthy effects on overall political involvement. Another residency measure used occasionally in previous research has been length of residency at the same address (Berry, 1970:80), but its correlations with political participation are generally weak.

Concerning community activities, a number of previous studies have found that "persons who are active in community affairs are much more likely than those not active to participate in politics" (Milbrath, 1965:17). This generalization has been found to hold true in several different Western nations, and with socioeconomic status controlled. Finally, since a considerable portion of most people's daily lives is spent in informal social interaction with relatives, friends, and neighbors, the extent of one's interpersonal relationships would appear to be another vital aspect of community attachment that could affect political activity. There has been no previous research on this topic, however.

In short, beyond the substantiated correlation between length of community residency and voting turnout, we have relatively little firm evidence at the present time concerning the relevance of community attachment for political participation.[16] In this section we shall explore and compare the effects of the three types of community attachment measures on each of the political participation indexes.

Theoretical Rationale

The social mobilization thesis is fully applicable to this community context. As an individual's community involvement increases, he or she should become mobilized for active participation in political affairs. As expressed by Lester Milbrath (1965:133), "persons who are well inte-

---

16. Verba and Nie (1972:229–47) gave considerable attention to the effects of "the community context" — e.g., community size and type — on political participation rates. They found interesting variations across six types of communities, leading them to conclude that "the nature of the community does make a difference in participation over and above the effects of the characteristics of the individual citizens who live there." Their research did not investigate individual's rates of involvement in the community, however.

grated into their community tend to feel close to the center of community decisions and are more likely to participate in politics." The causal link between community involvement and political participation is readily apparent, since politics is so closely tied in with community decisions, programs, and activities. Hence a person who has lived in a community for some period of time, who takes part in community affairs, and who interacts frequently with others, is quite likely to be "pushed" or "pulled" into political activities.

Basic Findings

The observed relationships between length of community residence and the political participation indexes are reported in the left-hand side of Table 4.11. The most striking finding here is that community residency is rather strongly correlated with the registration and voting index, which is in accord with all previous research on voting turnout. (This relationship is not merely a result of residency requirements for voter registration, since voting turnout rises constantly through forty or more years of residency.) Otherwise, length of residence in the community is only weakly related to Partisan participation, and it is completely unrelated to all other forms of political participation except the political knowledge index.

The principal findings concerning the two other residency measures can be summarized without data. Length of residency at one's present address is an even poorer predictor of participation in politics than is community residency. It is significantly but rather weakly related only to the Electoral (.20) and Governmental (.11) participation dimensions. Home ownership — dichotomized as "owning" (outright or mortgaged) or "not owning" (renting or living in free housing) — is significantly related to all the political dimensions except Organizational participation, but these relationships are quite weak and the mean r is just .12. This measure thus has broad but fairly inconsequential predictive power across the various dimensions of political activity.

In contrast to the straightforward residency approach to measuring community attachment, the activity approach argues that meaningful attachment to one's community develops only as one actively participates in various kinds of community affairs. In this study, respondents were asked how frequently they attended public community events (e.g., fairs, parades, outdoor concerts) and took part in public service projects (e.g., fund drive, school canvass, cleanup campaign). Scores on these two items were combined into an index of community activities, data for which are

Table 4.11

Community Residency and Community Activities Index Related to the Political Participation Indexes

Political Dimensions and Indexes	Length of Community Residency				Community Activities Index			
	0–4 Years	5–19 Years	20–39 Years	40+ Years	None	Below Average	Above Average	High
Cognitive participation								
Percent high knowledge	22%	33%	42%	42%	30%	27%	43%	52%
Percent high opinions	53%	41%	49%	44%	37%	50%	50%	47%
Combined index r		NS					.22	
Expressive participation								
Percent high interest	31%	30%	35%	30%	20%	25%	42%	43%
Percent high discussion	16%	20%	26%	16%	14%	16%	27%	29%
Combined index r		NS					.31	
Electoral participation								
Percent high party pref.	19%	33%	36%	42%	27%	33%	36%	43%
Percent high registration & voting	11%	36%	36%	58%	38%	50%	62%	76%
Combined index r			.31				.27	
Organizational participation								
Percent high VA activities	3%	7%	9%	6%	4%	6%	11%	12%
Percent high political organization	1%	4%	5%	2%	1%	5%	2%	11%
Combined index r		NS					.14	
Partisan participation								
Percent high activities	19%	22%	32%	36%	23%	19%	34%	43%
Percent high involvement	12%	17%	20%	26%	11%	15%	22%	36%
Combined index r			.15				.23	
Governmental participation								
Percent high activities	21%	26%	25%	28%	14%	13%	27%	52%
Percent high involvement	1%	4%	3%	5%	3%	3%	3%	6%
Combined index r		NS					.34	
Mean percent high	17%	23%	26%	28%	18%	22%	30%	38%
Mean r		NS					.25	
N	102	181	275	190	180	219	196	154

given in the right-hand side of Table 4.11. All six coefficients for this index are statistically significant, and those for Expressive and Governmental participation are relatively high, while the figures for the Cognitive, Electoral, and Partisan dimensions are lower but still noteworthy. The mean r is .25. This community activities index is thus a moderately strong predictor of most forms of political participation.

The third approach to measuring community attachment is to determine the extent of one's informal interaction with relatives, neighbors, and friends. Respondents were asked the number of each kind of relationship they presently had and how frequently they interacted with these people. From these items were constructed indexes of relatives interaction, neighbors interaction, and friends interaction. None of the relationships for the relatives interaction index is statistically significant, however, indicating that this kind of interpersonal relationship has no effects on political participation. Data for the neighbors and friends indexes are reported in Table 4.12.

Although all six of the coefficients for the neighbors interaction index are significant, none of them is particularly high. The strongest relationships occur on the Cognitive, Expressive, and Governmental dimensions, and the mean r for this index is .21. Interaction with neighbors is therefore a relevant but not particularly strong predictor of all types of political participation. The figures for the friends interaction index are fairly similar to, though generally lower than, the corresponding ones for neighbors, so that the mean r is only .19. Thus interaction with friends is a slightly weaker predictor of political participation than is interaction with neighbors.

At this point in the analysis of community attachment, we have three residency measures, one activity measure, and two interaction measures that relate at least moderately to political participation. But which of these variables provide the best predictors of participation in politics, independent of other factors?

Multivariate Analyses

We begin by examining the three residency variables while holding constant certain background variables. Length of community residency, we saw, is significantly correlated with just Electoral and Partisan participation. But if we control for age, on the grounds that persons with longer community residency will on average be older, the beta for Electoral participation drops to .16, while Partisan participation becomes nonsignif-

Neighbors Interaction and Friends Interaction Indexes Related to the Political Participation Indexes

Political Dimensions and Indexes	Neighbors Interaction Index				Friends Interaction Index			
	Low	Below Average	Above Average	High	Low	Below Average	Above Average	High
Cognitive participation								
Percent high knowledge	23%	31%	43%	45%	24%	38%	38%	43%
Percent high opinions	36%	41%	49%	55%	28%	43%	52%	54%
Combined index r			.25				.19	
Expressive participation								
Percent high interest	17%	28%	37%	42%	17%	31%	38%	36%
Percent high discussion	3%	18%	22%	38%	4%	13%	25%	37%
Combined index r			.29				.31	
Electoral participation								
Percent high party pref.	27%	34%	36%	39%	21%	30%	38%	45%
Percent high registration & voting	27%	39%	39%	42%	26%	42%	37%	40%
Combined index r			.16				.19	
Organizational participation								
Percent high VA activities	4%	6%	7%	11%	3%	5%	7%	8%
Percent high political organization	0%	3%	3%	8%	0%	2%	3%	7%
Combined index r			.15				.14	
Partisan participation								
Percent high activities	18%	24%	31%	40%	16%	29%	29%	35%
Percent high involvement	5%	19%	34%	27%	12%	18%	20%	27%
Combined index r			.17				.14	
Governmental participation								
Percent high activities	8%	20%	29%	37%	13%	23%	24%	36%
Percent high involvement	1%	2%	4%	7%	3%	4%	3%	4%
Combined index r			.22				.18	
Mean percent high	14%	22%	28%	33%	14%	23%	26%	31%
Mean r			.21				.19	
N	124	197	290	139	104	236	240	169

icant. Adding sex, education, and socioeconomic status as additional controls does not alter this situation. Hence community residence is apparently relevant only to Electoral participation — or more precisely, to voting turnout — and does not appear to affect any other form of political activity once a person's age is taken into account.

Similar results occur with address residency when age is controlled. The beta for Electoral participation drops to .12, and the relationship with Governmental participation becomes nonsignificant. Adding sex, education, and socioeconomic status as additional controls again produces no further changes. Consequently, community residency remains a somewhat better predictor of Electoral participation than is address residency, and we can discard the latter variable in favor of the former.

With the home ownership measure, we must control both age and socioeconomic status, since older and higher-status people are more likely to be homeowners. When these controls are applied, all the partial beta coefficients for home ownership become nonsignificant, showing that this factor has no independent effects on political participation.

Our next consideration is whether the indexes of interaction with neighbors and friends are measuring essentially the same thing, since as the questions were framed, the friends with whom respondents interacted could also be neighbors. Examination of the partial betas for each index, holding constant the effects of the other, reveal that interaction with neighbors has more independent effects on political participation than does interaction with friends. Specifically, the betas for neighbors are higher than the corresponding figures for friends on the Cognitive, Organizational, Partisan, and Governmental dimensions, and only slightly lower on the Expressive and Electoral dimensions. The mean beta for neighbors interaction is .15, compared to .10 for friends interaction. Moreover, three of the six multiple R's produced by the two measures in combination are actually lower than the corresponding zero-order coefficients for neighbors interaction alone. On the basis of these findings, only the neighbors interaction index was retained as an indicator of interpersonal attachment to the community.

Thus far we have discovered that within the community attachment context the two strongest predictors of political participation are the community activities and neighbors interaction indexes. The next step is to simultaneously relate both of these measures to the political participation indexes, to make sure that each has some independent effects on political activity. The resulting partial beta coefficients are shown in the two left-hand columns of Table 4.13. All of the figures for community activities are significant, and most of them are moderately strong. The coefficients for neighbors interaction are somewhat lower than the corresponding figures for community activities in all areas except Cognitive participation, but all of them also remain significant.

Since both variables have independent effects on all types of political participation, their multiple R's — also given in Table 4.13 — are all somewhat higher than the corresponding zero-order coefficients for either one alone, with mean $R = .29$. Consequently, a single community attachment index was constructed by summing respondents' scores on the community activities and neighbors interaction indexes. The zero-order coefficients for this combined index on each of the political participation dimensions, given in the fourth column of Table 4.13, are almost identical to the corresponding multiple R's, so that use of this single combined index entails virtually no loss of predictive power.

Finally, this community attachment index is related to the six political participation dimensions while controlling for the effects of sex, age, parents' activities, education, and socioeconomic status. As seen in the right-hand column of Table 4.13, all of these betas remain significant, and those for Expressive, Electoral, Partisan, and Governmental participation are still moderately strong. Attachment to one's community through participation in community activities and interaction with one's neighbors definitely affects one's participation in all realms of politics, regardless of other background factors.

Conclusions

The three approaches to measuring community attachment used in this section — residency, activity, and interaction — were all found to be relevant for explaining at least some forms of political participation. After considering a number of alternative variables, we selected the community activities index and the neighbors interaction index as the most useful empirical indicators of community attachment. The combined community attachment index constructed from both these measures relates moderately strongly to all political participation dimensions, even with other background variables controlled.

From a theoretical perspective, the results of this analysis provide considerable substantiation for the social mobilization thesis. None of the measures of community attachment used here refer specifically to politics, yet they all influence various forms of political participation.

Table 4.13

Partial and Multiple Relationships of the Community Activities and Neighbors Interaction Indexes with the Combined Political Participation Indexes, Plus Zero-Order and Partial Relationships for the Combined Community Attachment Index

Political Dimensions	Partial Betas		Multiple R's	Combined Community Attachment Index	
	Community Activities Index	Neighbors Interaction Index		Zero-order r's	Partial Betas Controlling Sex, Age, Parents' Activities, Education, and SES
Cognitive participation	.17	.20	.30	.29	.18
Expressive participation	.27	.20	.38	.36	.26
Electoral participation	.24	.10	.28	.28	.19
Organizational participation	.11	.11	.18	.17	.12
Partisan participation	.19	.12	.25	.24	.20
Governmental participation	.29	.15	.37	.35	.26
Mean coefficients	.21	.15	.29	.28	.20

Once again we find evidence of a two-stage process, in which various kinds of social involvement in turn mobilize individuals to become politically active.

From an applied point of view, the length of time a person has lived in a community cannot be manipulated — but except for voting turnout this factor is not important. Much more important is the extent to which the individual participates in all kinds of community events and projects. Although people cannot be coerced into taking part in these kinds of community activities, they can certainly be encouraged to do so by developing events and projects that will attract interest, publicizing them extensively, organizing them effectively, and providing some form of direct benefits to those who attend. Informal interaction among neighbors is more difficult to encourage on a broad scale, but techniques such as organizing block or neighborhood groups to deal with local problems should certainly stimulate greater interaction among neighbors. By thus involving individuals in their communities through formal activities and informal interaction, it is possible to promote more extensive participation across all dimensions of politics.

Association Involvement

Although Alexis de Tocqueville's (1961:141) observation that "Americans of all ages, all conditions, and all dispositions, constantly form associations" has never been fully realized, voluntary associations of many diverse types pervade American society. One of the six dimensions of political activity utilized throughout this study has been organizational participation, involving both political activities undertaken within non-political associations (measured with the voluntary association political activities index) and membership in explicitly political organizations (measured with the political organizations index). In this section, however, we shall examine the full range of our respondents' memberships and activities within all types of voluntary associations.

As with socioeconomic status, in a broad sense we already know the answer to the question, How does involvement in voluntary associations relate to participation in politics? Every previous study of political participation that has included any measure of associational involvement has found these two factors to be positively correlated. Moreover, these relationships are often of fairly strong magnitude, they remain significant after socioeconomic status has been controlled, and they are remarkably consistent across many Western societies (Alford and Scoble, 1968; Berry, 1970:358; Erbe, 1964; Palma, 1970:194; Verba and Nie, 1972:172–208). In fact, Nie, Powell, and Prewitt (1969) state definitively that "Organizational involvement is the predictor variable with the most strength . . . . The citizen who is an active member of social groups is more likely to be a political participant than the citizen with few or no organizational involvements . . . . In addition . . . , the relationship between social status and political activity is weaker and less consistent crossnationally than the relationship between organizational involvement and political activity." What more is there to learn about this topic?

Much more. For example, which is more important in stimulating political participation, the number of associations to which one belongs or the degree of one's involvement in these organizations? Several studies (Alford and Scoble, 1968; Berry, 1970:54–57; Lane, 1959:196; Verba and Nie, 1972:184–86) have indicated that members who regularly attend organizational meetings are more politically active than nonattenders, and that persons who hold offices or are otherwise deeply involved in their associations are the most politically active of all. In this study, consequently, we shall examine several different levels of associational involvement.

Another topic that has not been explored is whether involvement in different kinds of associations has differential consequences for political participation. Labor unions have been singled out for special attention in several studies, but the resulting evidence as to whether or not union membership leads to increased political activities is presently inconclusive (Milbrath, 1965:131–32). And what about all other kinds of voluntary associations? We shall separately examine several different types of organizations in this section.

Voluntary associations can also be classified according to whether or not they ever enter the political arena as parapolitical actors by taking organizational stands on public issues or engaging in other partisan actions. Can membership in completely nonpolitical organizations stimulate individuals to become more politically active, or does this mobilization process occur only in parapolitical associations?

Finally, at the present time we also lack adequate data concerning the impact of associational involvement on the different dimensions of political participation. Does the basic relationship between associational and political participation occur with all forms of political activity, or just some of them?

Theoretical Rationale

The social mobilization thesis was originally derived from studies of the political effects of voluntary association involvement, and it is perhaps most directly relevant to this social context. According to the socio-political pluralism model, to the extent that people become involved in interest associations of all kinds — regardless of whether or not these organizations ever have anything to do with politics — they will become available for mobilization into active political participation. Gabriel Almond and Sidney Verba have summarized the argument thusly:

> The organization member, compared with the nonmember, is likely to consider himself more competent as a citizen, to be a more active participant in politics, and to know and care about politics. He is, therefore, more likely to be close to the model of the democratic citizen.... Membership in some association, even if the individual does not consider the membership politically relevant, and even if it does not involve his active participation, does lead to a more competent citizenry. Pluralism, even if not explicitly political pluralism, may indeed be one of the most important foundations of political democracy. [1963:321–22]

Moreover, this mobilization process within voluntary associations appears to operate among people of all socioeconomic statuses. It thus provides a means of politicizing lower-status people who would otherwise likely remain outside of the political arena (Ambrecht, 1975). Consequently, voluntary interest associations might well be viewed as the primary social settings for the social mobilization process.

Basic Findings

To measure voluntary association membership, each respondent was asked how many (if any) organizations he or she belonged to within each of thirteen categories: unions, fraternal, veterans and patriotic, civic, educational, youth serving, cultural, nationality and civil rights, sports and hobby, professional and scientific, social and recreational, charitable and welfare, and church sponsored.[17] The respondent was then asked a series of questions about each organization to which he or she belonged.

---

17. Churches were not considered to be voluntary associations in this research, but church-sponsored and church-related groups were. Political organizations were also included on the list read to respondents but are excluded from this analysis of voluntary association participation since they are counted in the political organizations index.

Whereas most previous studies have ascertained only the number of organizations to which respondents belonged, three alternative "counting measures" are employed here: (a) the total number of voluntary associations to which the person belonged (henceforth abbreviated as "VA's a member"); (b) the number of associations whose meetings he or she attended at least half the time (abbreviated "VA's attend"); and (c) the number of associations in which he or she had ever held an official position (abbreviated "VA's held a position"). Relationships between each of these measures and the political participation indexes are given in Table 4.14.

The most striking feature of these data is the strength of all the relationships, with mean r's of .27 for VA's a member, .24 for VA's attend,[18] and .27 for VA's held a position. Moreover, the relationships for each measure tend to be remarkably uniform across all the political indexes, and all three measures display relatively similar patterns of relationships across the various participation dimensions. Thus, neither of the more restrictive measures — number of VA's attended regularly or number of VA's in which the respondent ever held a position — provide any more explanation of political participation than does a simple count of the number of organizations to which a person belongs.

All three of these measures overlap, however, so we must ask if organizational membership per se has any political consequences, apart from the compounding effects of attendance and involvement. Sidney Verba and Norman Nie (1972:184–86) have argued that active participation in organizations is much more important than passive membership in stimulating people to participate in politics, although mere membership does raise participation scores slightly. To investigate this possibility, let us examine the partial relationships for VA's a member while controlling for both VA's attend and VA's held a position, thus removing all the effects of attendance and involvement from the membership count. The resulting partial betas are as follows: Cognitive participation, .23; Expressive participation, .20; Electoral participation, .11; Organizational participation, NS; Partisan participation, .14; and Governmental participation, .14. These findings indicate that membership by itself does increase par-

---

18. To make sure that the somewhat lower correlations for the "VA's attend" measure were caused by the fact that it does not take into account either the frequency with which meetings are held or exactly how many of these meetings the person actually attends, a more complex VA attendance index was also constructed, based on the total number of meetings a respondent had attended during the past year. The resulting relationships with the political participation indexes were only about .01 higher than the corresponding figures for "VA's attend," however, so that the average coefficient for the index was just .25.

Table 4.14

Three Alternative Counting Measures of Voluntary Association Participation Related to the Political Participation Indexes

Political Dimensions and Indexes	Number of VA's a Member				Number of VA's Attend Regularly			Number of VA's Ever Held a Position		
	0	1	2	3+	0	1	2+	0	1	2+
Cognitive participation										
Percent high knowledge	25%	39%	36%	63%	32%	37%	55%	31%	46%	59%
Percent high opinions	40%	47%	50%	57%	42%	52%	53%	44%	52%	50%
Combined index r			.26			.20			.20	
Expressive participation										
Percent high interest	22%	35%	37%	46%	25%	24%	42%	27%	43%	46%
Percent high discussion	11%	22%	31%	33%	15%	26%	35%	17%	24%	38%
Combined index r			.30			.27			.27	
Electoral participation										
Percent party pref.	25%	42%	37%	42%	28%	43%	44%	29%	48%	45%
Percent high registration & voting	27%	38%	42%	58%	29%	48%	55%	30%	52%	65%
Combined index r			.25			.25			.26	
Organizational participation										
Percent high VA activities	0%	6%	11%	21%	1%	12%	23%	2%	13%	26%
Percent high political organization	0%	2%	6%	11%	1%	3%	13%	1%	7%	15%
Combined index r			.25			.27			.30	
Partisan participation										
Percent high activities	17%	31%	28%	53%	22%	32%	50%	21%	44%	53%
Percent high involvement	10%	19%	23%	43%	12%	29%	36%	11%	35%	47%
Combined index r			.29			.23			.31	
Governmental participation										
Percent high activities	12%	24%	26%	57%	14%	38%	48%	15%	40%	64%
Percent high involvement	2%	3%	4%	10%	2%	4%	11%	2%	6%	9%
Combined index r			.27			.24			.27	
Mean percent high	16%	26%	28%	41%	19%	29%	39%	19%	34%	43%
Mean r			.27			.24			.27	
N	298	217	105	129	455	175	118	530	124	94

101

ticipation in five of the six political dimensions, and particularly in the areas of Cognitive and Expressive participation. Since Verba and Nie were examining political activities that correspond roughly to our Electoral, Organizational, and Governmental dimensions, it is not surprising that they emphasized active over passive organizational involvement. The results of this study, in contrast, indicate that passive membership does have important consequences for most forms of political participation.

To take account of the fact that membership, attendance, and position holding in voluntary associations all affect participation in politics, these three counting measures were combined into an index of voluntary association involvement. For each organization to which an individual belonged, he or she received one point for passive membership, two points for attending at least half the meetings, or three points if he or she had ever held an official position in the organization. The coefficients for this index — reported in Table 4.15 — provide summary indicators of the effects of association involvement on political participation.

All of the relationships for this VA involvement index are noticeably stronger than the corresponding figures for the three separate counting measures, and the mean r of .36 is the highest average coefficient among all the predictor variables in this study. As with the earlier measures, the relationships for this index are also remarkably uniform across all dimensions of political participation. Because this index is clearly a better predictor of political participation than are any of the separate measures, it will be utilized throughout the rest of the study.[19]

Thus far we have been considering only aggregate measures of membership or activity in all kinds of voluntary associations, without taking into consideration the nature or purpose of these organizations. We must now ask whether some types of associations are more relevant than others for the political mobilization process. Respondents were classified as either belonging or not belonging to at least one organization within each of the thirteen categories of associations listed above. This

---

19. A fourth counting measure of associational involvement investigated in this analysis was the number of associations to which a respondent belonged that had ever been politically active in any way (within the memories of the respondents). Its coefficients with the political participation dimensions are lower than the corresponding figures for the other three measures: Cognitive, .20; Expressive, .25; Electoral, .19; Organizational, .25; Partisan, .27; Governmental, .18; and mean, .22. This finding is of direct relevance to the social mobilization argument that participation in voluntary associations of all kinds mobilizes people for politics, regardless of whether or not these organizations are themselves politically active. Because of its low coefficients, this measure was omitted from further consideration.

Table 4.15
Voluntary Association Involvement Index Related to the Political Participation Indexes

Political Dimensions and Indexes	Voluntary Association Involvement Index			
	Low	Below Average	Above Average	High
Cognitive participation				
Percent high knowledge	25%	40%	37%	64%
Percent high opinions	40%	49%	49%	55%
Combined index r		.32		
Expressive participation				
Percent high interest	22%	31%	44%	44%
Percent high discussion	11%	21%	30%	34%
Combined index r		.37		
Electoral participation				
Percent high party pref.	25%	36%	46%	42%
Percent high registration & voting	27%	33%	48%	61%
Combined index r		.33		
Organizational participation				
Percent high VA activities	0%	3%	13%	23%
Percent high political organization	0%	1%	5%	15%
Combined index r		.34		
Partisan participation				
Percent high activities	17%	26%	35%	56%
Percent high involvement	10%	13%	32%	44%
Combined index r		.35		
Governmental participation				
Percent high activities	12%	18%	33%	57%
Percent high involvement	2%	2%	5%	9%
Combined index r		.42		
Mean percent high	16%	23%	31%	42%
Mean r		.36		
N	298	190	144	117

member/nonmember dichotomy, while an extremely crude measure, nevertheless produces some interesting results that can be summarized without
reporting the detailed data. Membership in labor unions, first of all, is
not significantly related to any of the policial participation indexes. This
is due to at least two factors: (a) Union members generally have lower
educational and socioeconomic statuses than do nonmembers, which reduces their likelihood of being politically active. When these two status
variables are held constant, all of the coefficients for union membership
increase in magnitude and some become significant. (b) For many workers, union membership is merely a requirement for obtaining a job, and
the union has very little impact on them personally. If we examine only
those union members who at least occasionally attend meetings, however,
we find that these people are considerably more active politically than are
passive members and nonmembers. If we also control for education and
socioeconomic status in this analysis, active union membership relates
significantly to all six dimensions of political participation.

With all other types of associations, meanwhile, members score higher
than nonmembers on all six political participation indexes. A few of these
relationships are too weak to be significant, but every kind of associational
membership is significantly related to most forms of political participation. Looking at the mean correlation coefficients, the strongest overall
relationships occur with nationality and civil rights groups (.20), youth-
service (e.g., Scouts) organizations (.17), and business and civic (.15) and
professional and scientific (.15) associations. These types of organizations
might all be described as instrumental or community-action oriented in
their concerns and programs. The remaining mean coefficients range from
.14 down to .10 (for sports and hobby groups), but all are significant.[20]

The obvious conclusion to be drawn from this analysis of types of
voluntary associations is that, with the exception of labor unions, the
nature of one's organizations makes relatively little difference in regard to
political participation. Put differently, membership in almost any kind of
voluntary association will tend to mobilize people for increased political

20. Although churches were not considered to be voluntary associations in this analysis, the social
mobilization thesis would assert that church membership and attendance should also mobilize individuals to become more active in politics. Previous research has found that regular church attenders
are somewhat more likely than other people to participate actively in some kinds of political affairs,
but these relationships have been rather weak (Milbrath, 1965:137). In this study, both church
membership and frequency of attendance at religious services were found to relate significantly but
very weakly to all the political participation dimensions except Organizational participation. The mean
coefficients for these two variables were .12 and .11, respectively. These relationships are not affected
when religious preference is held constant.

activity. Consequently, for the remainder of this study we shall use only the combined voluntary association involvement index and not differentiate among types of organizations.

Multivariate Analyses

One of the most frequently debated questions in the literature on political participation is whether socioeconomic status (education, occupation, and income) or organizational participation has greater independent effects on a person's political activities. Since these two variables are always found to be interrelated (in this study, the VA participation index is correlated with education at .40 and with the SES index at .46), it is possible that the observed correlations between either of them and political participation are spurious results of the underlying relationship between the two predictor variables. Most previous research on this topic (Erbe, 1964; Alford and Scoble, 1968; Nie et al., 1969; Verba and Nie, 1972:200–205) has favored organizational participation as having more independent effects on political participation than do any status measures, although none of this earlier work has involved multiple regression analysis with several different political dimensions.

To resolve this debate, in Table 4.16 the three predictor variables of education, socioeconomic status (based on occupational status and family income), and the index of association involvement are simultaneously related to the six political participation dimensions. The partial beta coefficients in the three left-hand columns of this table indicate that voluntary association involvement has much greater effects on political activity than does either education or socioeconomic status. On the Electoral, Organizational, Partisan, and Governmental dimensions, association involvement is clearly the dominant factor, since most of these partial betas for education and socioeconomic status are not even significant. Education is more important on the Cognitive and Expressive dimensions, but in both cases associational participation also has some independent effects. The results of this analysis thus unequivocally favor association participation as a determinant of political activity.

In addition to controlling for education and socioeconomic status, let us also hold constant the effects of the other background variables of sex, age, and parents' activities. Partial beta coefficients for the VA involvement index under these extensively controlled conditions are given in the fourth column of Table 4.16. The beta for Cognitive participation has now become very small, indicating that almost all of the zero-order correlation

Table 4.16
Partial Relationships of the Voluntary Association Involvement Index with the Political Participation Indexes, Controlling Various Other Variables

Political Dimensions	Partial Betas				
	Simultaneous Controls			VA Involvement Index	
	Education	Socio-economic Status	VA Involvement Index	Controlling Sex, Age, Parents' Activities, Education, and SES	Controlling VA Political Activities Index
Cognitive participation	.27	.19	.13	.11	.23
Expressive participation	.29	NS	.21	.19	.25
Electoral participation	NS	NS	.27	.23	.24
Organizational participation	NS	NS	.35	.35	.17
Partisan participation	NS	NS	.32	.30	.26
Governmental participation	.14	NS	.33	.31	.25
Mean coefficients	.12	NS	.27	.25	.23

with this dimension is due to other factors. The relationships between voluntary association involvement and the other five political dimensions all remain significant and moderately strong, however.

Our final analysis is to calculate partial beta coefficients for the VA involvement index while holding constant the extent to which a respondent's associations have taken any kind of political action such as supporting a candidate or taking a public stand on a political issue. This will enable us to make one further test of the argument that organizational participation can mobilize individuals into political activity even if their organizations have nothing to do with politics. A voluntary association political actions index was constructed for this analysis and related to the political participation dimensions, along with the VA involvement index. The partial betas for the latter measure, given in the right-hand column of Table 4.16, are all significant and moderately strong under these controlled conditions. The social mobilization thesis is thus once again supported, for association involvement can mobilize people for political participation regardless of whether or not these organizations ever enter the political scene.

Conclusions

In answer to the questions raised at the beginning of this section concerning the apparently universal relationship between associational and political participation, we can now offer the following generalizations:

1. The three counting measures of associational memberships, associations attended regularly, and associations in which one has held an official position are all related fairly strongly to political participation.

2. Both passive membership and active involvement in an organization can mobilize people for political participation.

3. Association membership, attendance, and position holding have additive effects on political participation, so that the combined voluntary association involvement index provides the best predictor of political participation of all the variables examined in this study.

4. With the exception of membership in labor unions (because of their semi-involuntary and "working-class" nature), members of all types of voluntary associations tend to be more politically active than nonmembers, although this tendency is most evident with action-oriented instrumental organizations.

5. Voluntary association involvement is more effective than education or socioeconomic status in mobilizing individuals for Electoral,

Organizational, Partisan, and Governmental political participation, and it also has some independent effects on Cognitive and Expressive participation.

6. Involvement in voluntary associations is related to all forms of political activity regardless of the extent to which these organizations have engaged in political actions.

These empirical generalizations provide strong support for the social mobilization version of pluralistic theory. Membership, attendance, and position holding in almost all kinds of associations — regardless of whether or not they have any connections with the political system — tend to draw individuals out of their purely private lives and expand their social environments. As they come into contact with a broader range of new people, ideas, activities, and social roles, participants in organizations become mobilized for increased political activity.

These findings also point to an extremely effective and practicable procedure for stimulating more widespread political participation. If we can actively involve people in voluntary associations, regardless of their specific nature, these people are then more likely to become active in a variety of political affairs. This mobilization process appears to operate regardless of one's educational or socioeconomic level and hence provides a viable means of bringing lower-status people into the political arena. Although it is true, as Verba and Nie (1972:205) argue, that association participation mobilizes more high-status than low-status people because of the greater propensity of high-status people to join organizations, organizational involvement can overcome the handicaps to political participation imposed on people by low statuses.

The Total Social Mobilization Process

We have now examined in considerable detail seven different social contexts — sociodemographic, parental, socioeconomic status, job, mass media, community, and associational — that may affect the ways and extent to which people participate in politics. These various contexts do not exist in isolation, however, but rather interpenetrate and influence one another in countless ways. Hence, to understand the full impact of the total social environment on political participation, we must bring together and analyze jointly these various contexts.

Only four previous studies of political participation have used multivariate analysis to explore the relative mobilization effects of two or more different social contexts. William Erbe (1964) used survey data from three small Iowa towns to compare the effects of socioeconomic status (measured with education, occupation, and income) versus voluntary association participation (measured with the Chapin Social Participation Scale) on political participation (measured with Woodward and Roper's Political Participation Scale). He found zero-order correlations (Somer's "d") of .33 for SES and .37 for VA participation, and partial correlations (holding constant the effects of the other variable) of .20 for SES and .26 for VA participation.

Robert Alford and Harry Scoble (1968) examined the effects of several different "classes of factors" on political participation, including social status, organizational participation, community attachment, and religion and ethnicity. Their measure of political participation was a composite index of items covering political information, political interest, political meeting attendance, and voting turnout. Using survey data from four medium-sized Wisconsin cities, they found that socioeconomic status (education, occupation, and income) and organizational participation (membership and attendance) had approximately equal effects on political activity, both independently and with the other variable controlled. Home ownership also remained correlated with political participation when the other two variables were controlled.

Norman Nie, G. Bingham Powell, Jr., and Kenneth Prewitt (1969) confined their analysis of social variables to socioeconomic status (measured with education, occupation, income, and an interviewer's rating), organizational involvement (organizational membership and attendance, participation in an economic marketplace, and involvement in group leisure activities), and urban residence. Their research had the advantage, however, of using data drawn from national samples in five different societies. Their dependent variable was a single index of political participation, composed of measures of discussing politics, contacting local and national authorities, involvement in political campaigns, and membership in political organizations and parties. They found that organizational involvement related quite strongly to political participation in all five nations (United States, .52; United Kingdom, .48; Germany, .48; Italy, .49; Mexico, .52), while socioeconomic status produced a high correlation only in the United States (United States, .43; United Kingdom, .30; Germany, .18; Italy, .28; Mexico, .24). Urban residence was not significantly related to political participation in any of these cases. They concluded that: "The two variables [of social class and organizational involvement] alone account for all the difference between the participation levels of citizens in the more and less developed societies."

Sidney Verba and Norman H. Nie (1972), finally, considered socio-economic status to be the principal social factor affecting political participation ($r = .37$). Consequently, when they examined the effects of age, race, and organizational participation on political activities they consistently controlled for the effects of SES, showing that each of these other variables had independent effects on political participation. Unfortunately, they did not report the partial coefficients necessary to compare the relative net effects of these various predictor variables.

In short, previous multivariate analyses of political participation have been severely limited in (a) the range of predictor variables included, (b) the measurement of political participation (usually a single composite scale), and (c) the extensiveness of the data analysis. In this final section we shall attempt to move considerably beyond previous studies in all three directions, in order to gain a more comprehensive understanding of the total social mobilization process.

Mobilization Factors

From the preceding analyses of the various social contexts, eight factors have emerged as particularly important in mobilizing individuals to participate in politics. These are the sociodemographic variables of sex and age, the index of parents' activities (both political and associational), education, socioeconomic status (based on occupation and income), the index of mass media exposure, the community attachment index (combining community activities and neighbors' interaction), and the combined voluntary association involvement index. Our concern here is to ask how these eight social variables are interrelated, in terms of both correlations and causal paths.

The matrix of zero-order correlations among these eight variables is given in Table 4.17. Except for sex (which is unrelated to all the other factors except community attachment) and age (which is unrelated to parents' activities and SES), these variables are all interrelated to some degree. But in what ways are they influencing one another? What kind of causal model can we construct with these variables?

Let us begin by designating the factors of parents' activities, sex, age, and education as exogenous variables, since for any particular adult they were all determined at some time in the past (ignoring those who are continuing their education). None of these factors except education can possibly be manipulated as a means of increasing present levels of political participation, and obtaining a higher education is a long-term process. The

Table 4.17
Social Variables Correlation Matrix

	Age	Parents' Activities	Education	SES	Mass Media Exposure	Community Attachment	VA Involvement
Sex	NS	NS	NS	NS	NS	$-.12^a$	NS
Age	—	NS	-.17	NS	.11	.23	.12
Parents' activities		—	.34	.34	.25	.18	.27
Education			—	.61	.34	.19	.40
Socioeconomic status				—	.39	.29	.46
Mass media exposure					—	.38	.36
Community attachment						—	.41
Voluntary association involvement							—

[a]Females are slightly more likely than males to be involved in their communities.

inverse relationship between age and education is important here, since it will result in these two factors having opposite effects on other variables (such as media exposure) to which they are both related. We shall omit from our model the correlations between parents' activities and both education and SES, since they do not represent direct causal links. They are, rather, spurious consequences of the fact that one's parents' social statuses (educational, occupational, and income levels) are related to both the parents' activities and their children's current educational and SES levels.

Because socioeconomic status is highly influenced by one's earlier education, it becomes the first endogenous predictor variable in the causal model. The remaining three predictor variables — media exposure, community attachment, and voluntary association involvement — can then be located subsequent to SES since they are all strongly influenced by it. But in what order shall we place them, since each one undoubtedly affects the other two? On theoretical grounds, we might argue that some amount of media exposure is necessary to learn about community events and voluntary associations before one can become active in those latter areas, which would give it causal priority. It might also be argued that some amount of community attachment probably precedes association involvement for most people. A stronger argument for this particular ordering can be made on empirical grounds, however. When each bivariate relationship is examined while controlling for the third variable, the partial coefficients between media exposure and community attachment and between community attachment and association involvement both remain moderately strong, but the relationship between media exposure and association involvement becomes nonsignificant. This suggests that community attachment is in fact an intermediate phenomenon lying between the other two in a causal sequence.

With these considerations in mind, we can construct the causal path model shown in Figure 4.1. The purpose of this model is to suggest a likely pattern of causal effects among the various social factors that mobilize individuals for political participation. The coefficients on the paths in this model are partial betas, indicating the effects of a prior variable on a later one, net of the effects of all other prior variables. Of the four exogenous variables, education is clearly the most important, since it has very strong effects on socioeconomic status, and also affects mass media exposure and association involvement. Of the endogenous predictor variables, socioeconomic status is the most crucial, since it has direct effects on mass media exposure, community attachment, and association involvement.

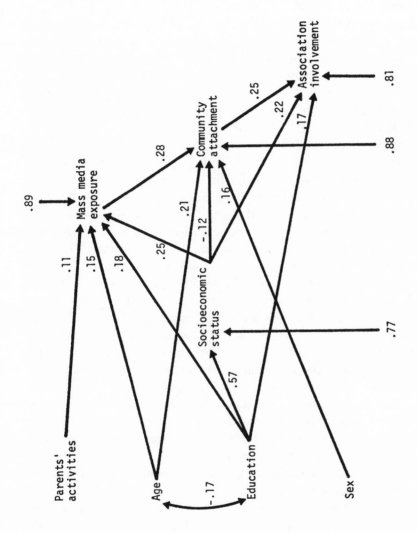

Figure 4.1 Causal Model of Relevant Social Variables

113

Political Participation

As a convenient means of summarizing the main findings from the preceding sections of this chapter, coefficients for the zero-order relationships between each of the eight predictor variables and the six political participation dimensions are shown in Table 4.18. Looking across the mean coefficients for the eight social variables at the bottom of the table, we see that the overall effects of sex (.11) and age (.19) are rather weak; the next five factors — parents' activities (.28), education (.29), socioeconomic status (.26), mass media exposure (.30), and community attachment (.28) — all have approximately similar overall effects on political participation; and association involvement (.36) is clearly the most powerful predictor variable.

Another way of examining this table is to go through the six political participation dimensions, identifying the two predictor variables with the highest correlations on each dimension. For Cognitive participation these are the two status variables of education (.46) and socioeconomic status (.40). Education (.44) is also important in relation to Expressive participation, together with parents' activities (.44). Apparently, therefore, involvement in these first two, rather passive, dimensions of political participation is largely the result of a learning process that can occur in childhood, in school, at work, or via the mass media (since that index is also rather highly correlated with both these dimensions). Electoral participation, as we have already noted, is uniquely related to age (.33), but also to association involvement (.33). On all three of the remaining active political dimensions, voluntary association involvement is the dominant social variable, with r's of .34, .35, and .42, respectively. No other social factors correlate at all strongly with Organization participation; parents' activities (.30) is the second-most-powerful predictor of Partisan participation, and community attachment (.28) ranks second on Governmental participation. Thus the most effective way of involving people in the latter four dimensions of politics is to encourage them to join voluntary associations.

The next step is to include all eight predictor variables in a single multiple regression equation with each dimension of political participation. The resulting partial betas and multiple R's are reported in Table 4.19.

Since sex is uncorrelated with most of the other social variables, its net relationships with the various political dimensions are almost the same as its zero-order relationships. Men continue to score substantially higher than women on Cognitive participation (.25), and slightly higher on the

Table 4.18
Zero-Order Relationships between Eight Social Variables and the Six Political Participation Dimensions

Political Dimensions	Sex	Age[a]	Parents' Activities	Education	Socio-economic Status	Mass Media Exposure	Community Attachment	VA Involvement
Cognitive participation	.27	.17	.37	.46	.40	.37	.29	.32
Expressive participation	.15	.17	.44	.44	.35	.39	.36	.37
Electoral participation	NS	.33	.25	.21	.21	.24	.28	.33
Organizational participation	NS	.13	.15	.14	.13	.17	.17	.34
Partisan participation	NS	.20	.30	.16	.15	.28	.24	.35
Governmental participation	.10	.16	.21	.30	.30	.32	.35	.42
Mean	.11	.19	.28	.29	.26	.30	.28	.36

[a]Coefficients for age are etas from Multiple Classification Analysis.

Table 4.19

Partial and Multiple Relationships between Eight Social Variables and the Six Political Participation Dimensions

Political Dimensions	Partial Betas								Multiple R's	
	Sex	Age[a]	Parents' Activities	Education	Socio-economic Status	Mass Media Exposure	Community Attachment	VA Involvement	R	R^2
Cognitive participation	.25	.07	.17	.23	.11	.14	.12	NS	.60	.35
Expressive participation	.12	NS	.26	.21	NS	.16	.17	.09	.60	.35
Electoral participation	NS	.34	.14	.11	NS	NS	.14	.14	.51	.26
Organizational participation	NS	NS	NS	NS	-.09	NS	NS	NS	.32	.12
Partisan participation	.07	.20	.22	NS	-.10	.13	.10	.21	.47	.22
Governmental participation	.11	.14	NS	.15	NS	.10	.18	.22	.52	.27
Means										
Direct effects	.09	.12	.13	.12	—	.09	.12	.16		
Indirect effects	.01	.06	.01	.15	.09	.06	.04	—		
Total effects	.10	.18	.14	.27	.09	.15	.16	.16	.51	.26

[a]To make the relationships for age approximately linear, the top three categories of 50–59, 60–69, and 70+ were collapsed in this analysis.

Expressive (.12), Partisan (.08), and Governmental (.11) dimensions. (Further analyses of the twelve separate political indexes revealed that the partial coefficients for sex are higher than the corresponding zero-order figures on the political opinions, political interest, and governmental activities and involvement indexes.) In other words, when everything else is equal, the tendency for men to be more politically active than women is slightly greater than first appeared. Sex has no direct effects on Electoral or Organizational participation, however. Overall, the mean direct effects of this variable on all forms of political activity — shown in the third line from the bottom in Table 4.19 — are .09. Its average indirect effects transmitted through community attachment to the six political dimensions — shown in the second line from the bottom in the table — are a negligible .01. Hence the mean total effects of this variable — given in the bottom line of the table — are just .10.

Age continues to evidence a fairly strong relationship with Electoral participation (.34) under these controlled conditions (especially with the registration and voting index, for which the partial beta is .42). Partisan (.20) and Governmental (.14) participation also still increase with age to a notable extent. In contrast, the beta for Cognitive participation is just barely significant, and the figures for Expressive and Organizational participation are nonsignificant. The mean partial beta for the direct effects of age across all areas of politics is .12. In addition, age is important in the total social mobilization process because of its influences on socioeconomic status, mass media exposure, and community attachment. For the six political dimensions taken together, its average indirect effects through these variables are .06, which gives age a mean total effects coefficient of .18.

Parents' activities are now seen to be particularly important as a determinant of Expressive and Partisan (.22) political participation, while the partial coefficient for the Cognitive dimension (.17) is somewhat lower. This predictor variable also exerts some independent effects on Electoral participation, (.14) but none on Organizational or Governmental participation, with a resulting mean direct effects coefficient of .13. The only indirect effects of this variable operate through mass media exposure (.01). The mean total effects of parents' activities are therefore .14.

Education is important primarily as a determinant of the first two dimensions of Cognitive (.23) and Expressive (.21) participation. Its direct effects on Electoral (.11) and Governmental (.15) participation are weaker but still significant. Education is not significantly related to Organizational or Partisan participation in this multivariate analysis, however, so that its mean direct effects beta is merely .12. We must not overlook the fact, however, that in the total social mobilization process education plays a crucial role in determining one's socioeconomic status, mass media exposure, and voluntary association involvement. Consequently it exerts considerable indirect effects on political participation through these other variables, for an average indirect effects coefficient of .15. The mean total effects figure for education across all dimensions of political participation is therefore a noteworthy .27.

Perhaps the most interesting finding in this analysis is that socioeconomic status (occupation and income) retains only one significant and very weak positive relationship — with Cognitive participation (.11) — under these extensively controlled conditions. However, its net relationships with Organizational ($-.09$) and Partisan ($-.10$) participation become significant in an inverse direction. In other words, with everything else equal, lower-status people are slightly more likely than higher-status people to become involved in politics through organizations and political parties. Not only does the total social mobilization process overcome the disadvantages of low status in these two areas of politics, but it actually gives low-status individuals a slight advantage. The nonsignificant betas for the Expressive, Electoral, and Governmental dimensions, meanwhile, indicate that in these areas low status is neither an advantage nor a disadvantage. Because of these opposing positive and negative direct effects, the overall mean for socioeconomic status across all dimensions of political participation is nearly zero. This variable does influence media exposure, community attachment, and association involvement, however, and hence through them has an indirect effect of .09 on politics — which is therefore also its total effects coefficient.

Rather surprisingly, mass media exposure becomes a rather weak predictor of all forms of political activity in this multivariate analysis. Its highest relationship is with Expressive participation (.16), while its betas for the Cognitive (.14), Partisan (.13), and Governmental (.10) dimensions are quite low, and those for Electoral and Organizational participation are nonsignificant. The overall mean beta for media exposure is only .09, which indicates that in general it has relatively few direct effects on political activity. In our causal path model, however, media exposure does affect community attachment to a considerable extent, so that its average indirect effects are .06, giving it a mean total effects figure of .15.

Community attachment is now found to exert moderate net influence on Governmental (.18) and Expressive (.17) participation, and some influence on Electoral (.14), Cognitive (.12), and Partisan (.10) participation, while the beta for Organizational participation is nonsignificant. The mean direct effects figure for this variable is .12, while the average figure for indirect effects through associations involvement is .04, which gives community attachment a total effects coefficient of .16.

Finally, voluntary association involvement is no longer significantly related to Cognitive participation; its effects on Expressive participation are quite small (.09); and its effects on Electoral participation (.14) are not much greater. At the same time, however, association involvement continues to exert moderately strong independent effects on Organizational (.32), Partisan (.21), and Governmental (.22) participation, which gives it a mean beta for direct effects across all six political dimensions of .16 — which is the highest such figure in the table. In our path model this variable is at the end of the causal chain, and so it cannot have any indirect effects through other causal variables, which leaves its total effects at .16.

To summarize, let us review the row of mean direct effects for the eight predictor variables. We see that voluntary association involvement (mean $r = .16$) has the most influence across all dimensions of politics, followed by parents' activities (mean $r = .13$). The three factors of age, education, and community attachment then rank third in terms of overall influence (all with mean r's = .12). Next come sex and mass media exposure (both with mean $r = .09$), with even less effects. Finally, socioeconomic status has no significant direct effects across all political participation dimensions.

A somewhat different picture emerges when we also take indirect effects into consideration. From this perspective, education is unquestionably the most important determinant of overall political participation (mean total effects = .27). Age is then the second most influential factor (mean total effects = .18), although we must remember that much of this influence is concentrated in Electoral participation. The three "current activity" variables of association involvement (mean = .16), community attachment (mean = .16), and media exposure (mean = .15) appear to all have approximately equal total effects across all the political dimensions. This pattern is due to the nature of our causal model, however, which allows media exposure to exercise indirect effects through both the other two variables and community attachment to have indirect effects through association involvement, but does not allow the latter variable any indirect effects at all. This unidirectionality (or recursiveness) was imposed on the causal model to keep it relatively manageable, although in reality all three of these variables undoubtedly influence each other in reciprocal processes. Consequently, association involvement must in fact exercise some indirect effects on political participation through the other two variables, and similarly with community attachment.[21]

Thus far we have been looking at the data in Table 4.19 in terms of the relative effects of the various predictor variables, but alternatively we can also examine these data in terms of each of the six political dimensions. Beginning with Cognitive participation, sex (.25) and education (.23) have the greatest net effects in this area, and the multiple R for all predictor variables in combination is .60 ($R^2 = .35$). On the Expressive dimension, education (.21) remains relatively important, but the most influential factor is parents' activities (.26), while the multiple R in this case is also .60 ($R^2 = .35$).

The factor of age (.34) totally dominates the Electoral participation dimension, with all the other social variables having only small net effects or being irrelevant (sex, socioeconomic status, and media exposure). The multiple R is .51 ($R^2 = .26$). Similarly, Organizational participation is totally dominated by association involvement (.32), and the only other

---

21. Verba and Nie (1972:133–36) argued that most of the effects of socioeconomic status and other social variables on political participation were mediated through the intervening psychological variable of "civic orientations," as measured by a composite index of interest in and attention given to politics, political efficacy, political knowledge, and perceived role in the community. They did not, however, look at the effects of civic orientations on political participation while holding constant their predictor social variables, so that their analysis does not indicate whether or not civic orientations have any independent effects on political participation. In this study, political interest, attention, and knowledge were conceptualized as forms of political participation, but the two variables of political efficacy (Campbell et al., 1954) and political trust (Olsen, 1969) were investigated as intervening psychological factors. Efficacy was found to relate significantly and moderately strongly to all six participation dimensions, with mean $r = .29$, but trust relates significantly only to Expressive, Organizational, and Governmental participation, and its mean coefficient is not significant. When efficacy is added to the general regression equations with the eight social variables, only the betas for Cognitive (.10), Expressive (.11), and Governmental (.11) participation remain significant, and these effects are so weak that they are of little substantive importance. When trust is included in these equations, all of its betas become nonsignificant. Conversely, holding constant the effects of efficacy and/or trust does not significantly reduce the betas for any of the eight predictor social variables. From this analysis we conclude that neither political efficacy nor political trust (a) has any important direct effects on any forms of political participation, or (b) acts as an intervening factor between the social variables investigated in this study and any forms of political participation. This finding corroborates the conclusion of Nie, Powell, and Prewitt (1969) that the link between voluntary association involvement and political participation does not pass through any intervening psychological variables such as efficacy or trust. If Verba and Nie's (1972) concept of "civil orientations" does act as an intervening variable, therefore, it is only because their index also includes political interest, which is highly related to all other forms of political activity.

significant factor is socioeconomic status in an inverse direction. Consequently, the multiple R for this dimension is only .35 ($R^2 = .12$).

On the dimension of Partisan participation, the three factors of age (.20), parents' activities (.22), and association involvement (.21) are all about equally effective as predictor variables. The resulting multiple R is .47 ($R^2 = .22$). On the last dimension of Governmental participation, voluntary association involvement (.22) exerts the most net effects, followed by community involvement (.18), and the multiple R is .52 ($R^2 = .26$).

As a final summary figure, we note that the mean multiple R across all six political dimensions is .51 ($R^2 = .26$), which indicates that in this overall sense we can predict just over one-fourth of the total variance in political participation with these eight predictor variables.

In Figure 4.2, the mean direct effects coefficients for each predictor variable across all six political participation dimensions have been added to the causal path model given in Figure 4.1. This completed path model thus diagrams the total network of presumed causal net effects from all relevant predictor variables to overall political participation.

Conclusions

A considerable amount of analytical ground has been covered in this section, but the main findings that emerge from these multivariate analyses can be summarized in a set of six propositions.

1. In terms of average direct and indirect effects, education provides the most effective means of mobilizing people for political activity. These effects of education are focused primarily on the two passive dimensions of Cognitive and Expressive participation, however, and they have considerably less relevance for the other four dimensions.

2. Similarly, the average total effects of age on political participation are notable, but this influence is exerted principally on the Electoral and Partisan participation dimensions.

3. The three current activities — association involvement, community attachment, and media exposure — are themselves moderately interrelated, but each exercises independent effects on political participation. The total effects of association involvement are somewhat (but not excessively) greater than those of the other two variables, with community attachment ranking second. Association involvement is particularly important as a means of mobilizing individuals in the more active dimensions of Organizational, Partisan, and Governmental participation; media ex-

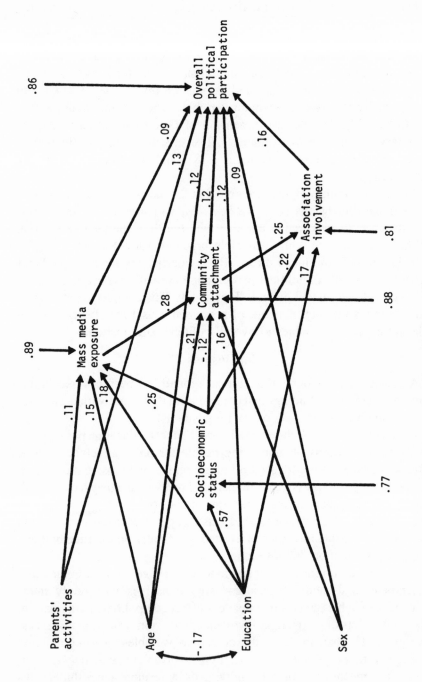

Figure 4.2 Causal Model of Overall Political Participation

posure is most important in the passive Cognitive and Expressive dimensions; and the effects of Community attachment are spread relatively evenly across all the political dimensions.

4. Parents' activities, as an indicator of the strength of one's childhood political socialization, have considerable direct effects on Expressive and Partisan participation and lesser direct effects on Cognitive and Electoral participation but virtually no indirect effects through the other predictor variables.

5. Socioeconomic status (based on occupation and income) has no overall direct effects across all forms of political participation, and on the Electoral and Partisan dimensions its small direct effects operate inversely, with lower-status people being slightly more active. This variable does have some indirect positive effects on political participation through association involvement, community attachment, and media exposure.

6. Men tend to be much more knowledgeable and opinionated than women about politics, regardless of all other factors, and also to be slightly more active on several other political dimensions. On the average, however, these direct effects are relatively small, and sex has virtually no indirect political effects through other variables.

From a methodological perspective, this analysis has repeatedly demonstrated the necessity of (a) treating political participation as a multidimensional phenomenon, with each dimension being influenced by a unique set of causal factors; and (b) using a multivariate analytical approach that determines the amount of direct and indirect effects each predictor variable exerts on each political dimension, net of all other causal factors.

Theoretically, this analysis has produced considerable empirical evidence in support of the social mobilization thesis. Although social mobilization is undoubtedly only one of several processes through which individuals can become involved in politics, it does appear to operate in all dimensions of political participation with noticeable impact.

Pragmatically, this analysis suggests both long-term and short-term answers to the question of how to get people involved in politics. The long-term approach looks first to education, taking the hopeful stance that, as the general level of education continues to rise in the population, more and more people will become oriented toward and concerned about politics. This approach also looks to the current aging trend in American society with the hope that, as the population becomes older and more mature, its level of political participation will consequently rise. The short-term approach to stimulating political participation, meanwhile, looks first to membership and involvement in voluntary associations of all kinds as a means of mobilizing individuals for political activity. Supplementing this process — or substituting for it if association involvement is unavailable — are the companion social mobilization processes of becoming attached to one's community and being exposed to information via the mass media. These processes apparently lead to greater participation in politics at all occupational and income levels. And finally, since education, aging, and these three types of social activities (as well as the mediating factor of socioeconomic status) are themselves all interrelated and rising, we are led to predict that, for the foreseeable future, all forms of political participation are likely to increase steadily in the United States and other modern societies.

5. *Voluntary Association Participation and Political Activity*

We discovered in the preceding chapter that membership and involvement in voluntary interest associations was the single best predictor of most forms of political activity, which provided convincing support for the social mobilization theory of political participation. This chapter expands that analysis in four directions: (1) examining rates of participation in several different kinds of voluntary associations; (2) evaluating the relative effects of passive membership versus active involvement on four selected forms of political activity; (3) exploring the specific effects of involvement in different kinds of associations on political participation; and (4) comparing these data from the Indianapolis study with the results of a similar survey conducted in Sweden. These comparative analyses will indicate whether the relationships between voluntary association participation and political activity in the United States are peculiar to this society or also occur in other industrial societies.

Involvement in interest associations of all kinds is often held to be a vital requisite for the maintenance of political democracy; "If democracy involves participation and influence in decision-making processes, then the extent to which a society is democratic depends on the degree of citizen participation in associations which are not overtly political as well as in explicitly political associations" (Berry, 1970:16). Interest associations are often said to play an especially vital role in the Swedish political

Adapted by permission from Marvin E. Olsen, "Interest Association Participation and Political Activity," *Journal of Voluntary Action Research*, vol. 3, Fall 1974, pp. 17–33.

system, providing a second means, in addition to voting, through which citizens can exert political influence. David Jenkins (1968:86) writes: "The organizations . . . constitute a sort of second government. In the normal democratic process the people elect their representatives in the parliament, who then presumably express the will of the people.. . . In Sweden the people also elect their representatives in the organizations, who then push for the interests of their members.. . ."

Associational participation has repeatedly been found to relate quite strongly to political participation in many Western societies (Berry, 1970:358; Palma, 1970:194; Nie et al., 1969; Verba and Nie, 1972:174–208), although none of these studies has included Sweden. The Swedish data reported here are taken from a survey conducted in Gävle, Sweden, in 1972. Located approximately a hundred miles north of Stockholm, Gävle is the capital of its län, or region. The economic base of this community of eighty thousand people has traditionally been shipbuilding and shipping, but it is also a railroad and trucking center. Interviews were conducted with a randomly selected sample of adult residents in the community. Back translation by several persons fluent in both Swedish and English was used to ensure that the Swedish-language questions were equivalent to their English counterparts.

For this analysis, respondents in both Indianapolis and Gävle are counted as a member of an association if they so identify themselves, regardless of their formal membership status in that association. They are considered to be actively involved in an association if they attend its meetings at least once a month. This fairly stringent definition of active involvement is intended to provide a clear conceptual distinction between passive and involved participation in the activities of the association, in contrast to Verba and Nie's (1972:176) reliance on respondents' self-classification as either passive or active members.

All relationships reported as statistically significant are at the .05 probability level, using the F-test.

Association Participation

Although Alexis de Tocqueville's (1961:141) often-quoted observation that "Americans of all ages, all conditions, and all dispositions, constantly form associations," has never been fully realized, interest associations of many diverse types pervade American society. The *Encyclopedia of Associations* (Fisk, 1973), for instance, lists over forty thousand national nonprofit associations in this country at the present time, and this figure might well be over one hundred thousand if it also included local groups of all kinds. Several recent studies using national samples (Hausknecht, 1962; Hyman and Wright, 1971) have discovered that membership in such associations is not as widespread as once assumed, with about one-third of the population belonging to no organizations and another third belonging to just one. Nevertheless, it does appear that the United States is at least as much a "nation of joiners" as most other industrialized societies (Curtis, 1971), and Almond and Verba's (1963:302) data indicate that associational participation is generally more extensive in this country than in Britain, Germany, Italy, or Mexico.

A frequently mentioned exception to this comparative generalization, however, is Sweden, which is often described as totally saturated with interest associations—or, in Swedish, *genomorganiserad,* meaning "thoroughly organized." As expressed by David Jenkins (1968:74); "It is taken for granted that every Swede belongs to whatever organizations are appropriate to his station in life and that if something is to be accomplished, it will be done through these bodies." Richard Tomasson (1970:242), meanwhile, writes that "among modern societies, only the other Scandinavian countries approach Sweden in the development of organizational life, but here again Sweden is the most advanced. . . ." He estimates that the eight million Swedes have over nine million memberships in interest associations, which is one of his primary reasons for labeling Sweden the "prototype of modern society."

Thus far, however, there have been no studies published in English that attempted to test these assertions concerning Sweden.[1] The initial focus of this chapter, therefore, is on rates of membership and attendance in voluntary associations in Indianapolis and Gävle, both overall and within seven categories of associations.

Overall Participation Rates

The most complete data for the United States as a whole (Verba and Nie, 1972:41–42) indicate that in 1967 about 62 percent of the adult population belonged to at least one interest association (including labor unions and church-sponsored groups, but not churches themselves), 39 percent

---

1. Some years ago, Hans Zetterberg (1959) wrote a paper on organizational participation in Sweden but reported only that 51 percent of all Swedes belonged to at least one association, exclusive of churches, unions, and cooperatives. Sten Johansson's recently completed Low Income Study in Sweden, based on a national sample survey, does contain some information on associational participation, but none of the reports from this study (e.g., Johansson, 1971) has yet been translated into English.

belonged to two or more associations, and 40 percent were active in some way in at least one organization. Our 1968 Indianapolis findings are quite similar: 61 percent of these respondents reported belonging to at least one association, 32 percent mentioned two or more associations, and 31 percent said they attended monthly meetings of at least one organization. In Gävle in 1972, as expected, participation rates were somewhat—though not greatly—higher than in Indianapolis: 79 percent of this sample belonged to at least one interest association, 46 percent belonged to two or more, and 36 percent were monthly attenders of at least one organization. More detailed data on overall membership and attendance rates for Indianapolis and Gävle are given in Table 5.1.

These data reveal that, although the Gävle respondents belonged to and attended more associations than did people in Indianapolis, neither of these differences is particularly large. This is especially evident in the case of organizations attended, where the difference between the two sample means is only .16 organizations. In other words, although the Swedes are nominal members of somewhat more interest associations than the Americans, if we take into account only those associations that people attend regularly, half of this difference disappears. Thus, in terms of active participation, the Swedish respondents do not appear to be notably more involved in interest associations than the Americans.

Participation by Type of Association

To explore further this difference in nominal memberships between the American and Swedish respondents, let us divide their associations into seven different categories: (1) labor unions (which in Sweden includes

Table 5.1
**Membership and Attendance Rates in Interest Associations
in Indianapolis and Gävle**

Number of Associations	Membership Indianapolis	Gävle	Monthly Attendance Indianapolis	Gävle
None	39%	21%	69%	62%
One	29%	34%	22%	24%
Two	14%	22%	6%	9%
Three or more	18%	24%	3%	5%
Mean	1.3	1.7	0.4	0.6
S.D.	1.7	1.4	0.8	0.9
N	750	388	750	388

white-collar and many professional as well as blue-collar associations); (2) business, professional, civic, scientific, etc.; (3) political (other than parties); (4) educational, cultural, youth serving, charitable, ethnic, etc.; (5) fraternal, veterans', men's, women's, retired, etc.; (6) recreational, sports, hobby, social, etc.; and (7) church related (in the United States this does not include churches themselves, while in Sweden it does include "free" or non-Lutheran churches—which are commonly defined as special-interest associations—but not the state-supported Lutheran church). The first three categories of associations are largely instrumental in nature, the fourth category includes primarily instrumental but some expressive associations, and the last three categories consist mainly of expressive associations. Table 5.2 reports the percentage of respondents belonging to and attending (the latter computed in two ways) at least one association in each of these seven categories in Indianapolis and Gävle.

We see that most of the difference in membership rates between the two communities is caused by the fact that more than three times as many Swedes as Americans belong to labor unions. Membership in business, professional, civic, and scientific associations also appears to be considerably higher in Gävle than in Indianapolis, although this difference is at least partly due to the fact that in Sweden most professional associations also function as unions in salary negotiations. The membership rate in recreational and sports associations is also somewhat higher in Gävle, reflecting the extensive network of sports organizations existing in Sweden. In contrast, Indianapolis residents are more likely to belong to non-work-oriented organizations such as (a) educational, cultural, youth serving, charitable, and ethnic associations; (b) fraternal, veterans', men's, women's, etc., associations, and (c) church-related groups (which are virtually nonexistent in Sweden except for the "free" churches).

The picture changes considerably when we examine the rates for active participation, however. Percentages for attendance are computed here in two ways: (1) the percent of all respondents attending monthly meetings of at least one organization in a category, and (2) the percent of members belonging to organizations in a category who attend monthly meetings of at least one of those organizations. The first figure is an absolute measure but is influenced by the proportion of the total sample who belong to each type, whereas the second figure is relative and in effect holds constant differences in membership rates between the two communities.

People in Gävle are four times more likely than those in Indianapolis to attend union meetings regularly, but this is because more of them

Table 5.2

Membership and Attendance Rates in Seven Types of Interest Associations in Indianapolis and Gävle[a]

Type of Association	% of Respondents Belonging to at Least One		% of Respondents Attending at Least One		% of Members Attending at Least One	
	Indianapolis	Gävle	Indianapolis	Gävle	Indianapolis	Gävle
Labor union	17	59	3	13	18 (130)	22 (229)
Business, etc.	11	24	4	5	32 (88)	20 (93)
Political	3	1	1	1	36 (25)	67 (3)
Educational, etc.	30	21	10	12	34 (220)	56 (80)
Fraternal, etc.	21	7	7	4	32 (159)	54 (28)
Recreational, etc.	21	27	13	15	62 (160)	57 (105)
Church related	11	2	6	2	63 (78)	83 (12)

[a]The N's for % of respondents who belong to each type of association and who attend each type of association are 750 in Indianapolis and 388 in Gävle. The N's for each % of members attending are given in parentheses.

belong to unions. The proportion of union members who regularly attend meetings is almost the same in both communities, however. In the business, etc., category, the absolute attendance rates are virtually identical in the two samples despite the higher membership rates in Gävle, so that the proportion of members who attend meetings is considerably greater in Indianapolis. The reverse situation occurs in both the educational, etc., and fraternal, etc. categories. About as many Swedes as Americans attend such organizations despite their lower membership rates, so that the proportions of members who are active in these two types of associations are greater in Gävle than in Indianapolis. In the recreational, etc., category the two communities are roughly similar on both attendance measures. A larger percentage of Americans than Swedes attend church-related groups, but in proportional terms people who belong to such groups are more likely to attend them in Gävle than in Indianapolis.

In short, the overall generalization that the Swedish respondents belong to somewhat more interest associations than the Americans grossly oversimplifies the actual situation. Most of this membership difference, we have discovered, occurs because so many more Swedes than Americans belong to labor unions, while the proportion of active union members is about the same in both communities. In contrast, the Swedish respondents are less likely than the Americans to belong to educational, etc., fraternal, etc., and church-related associations, although in each of these three categories the proportion of members who actively attend meetings is higher in Gävle than in Indianapolis. Different types of organizations thus display sharply contrasting membership and attendance patterns in these two societies.

Political Participation Mobilization

Organizational involvement is often said to be especially important in democratic societies because of its effects on individuals' participation in politics. Involvement in interest associations of all kinds, regardless of whether or not they have any links with the political system, tends to mobilize individuals into active political participation. As expressed by Almond and Verba (1963:321), "the organization member, compared with the nonmember, is likely to consider himself more competent as a citizen, to be a more active participant in politics, and to know and care about politics." Regardless of the underlying social-psychological dynamics of this process, associational involvement is without doubt highly associated with political participation (Berry, 1970:53–63; Erbe, 1964; Milbrath, 1965: 130–33; Nie et al., 1969; Verba and Nie, 1972: 174–208). Moreover, there is some evidence to support the contention that the causal process flows from associational to political participation (Maccoby, 1958; Olsen, 1972), at least among the general population if not among political elites.

Our concern here will be to answer several interrelated questions about the nature of this relationship in both Indianapolis and Gävle. (1) How strongly do both membership and attendance rates in interest associations correlate with four types of political activity: discussing politics,[2] voting turnout,[3] partisan activities,[4] and government contacts?[5] (2) What are the net effects of associational membership and attendance on each type of political activity, apart from the effects of compounding variables such as age, education, occupation, and income?[6] (3) What are the relative effects of passive versus active association participation on each type of political participation? (4) Is membership related to political activity within each of the seven categories of interest associations? Data pertaining to the first three of these questions from both communities are reported in Table 5.3.

Basic Relationships

In answer to the first question about zero-order relationships, we see that in both communities the number of interest associations to which one belongs is moderately correlated with all four types of political activity, but particularly with contacting government officials. The coefficients for Indianapolis are all somewhat higher than the corresponding figures for Gävle (especially in the case of voting turnout), but these relationships

2. The political discussion index for Indianapolis takes into account frequency of talking about politics with friends, relatives, neighbors, and coworkers. For Gävle it is based only on political discussions with friends.

3. In Indianapolis, the voting turnout index is based on the last two presidential elections, the last congressional and the last local ballots, and on whether one is currently registered. In Gävle the index is based only on the last two parliamentary elections.

4. The party activities index for Indianapolis includes questions about attending party meetings, doing volunteer work for a party or candidate, and holding any kind of position within a political party. The index for Gävle included only the first two of these party activities.

5. In both communities the government contacts index measures frequency of writing, telephoning, or personally visiting any government officials.

6. The only previous research that examined both organization membership and attendance in relation to different types of political activity was done by Verba and Nie (1972:200) but they did not compute either zero-order or partial coefficients; so it is impossible to compare their results with these data.

Table 5.3
Zero-Order and Partial Relationships between Association Membership and Attendance and Four Types of Political Activity in Indianapolis and Gävle

Association Participation	Political Activities							
	Indianapolis				Gävle			
	Political Discussion	Voting Turnout	Partisan Activities	Government Contacts	Political Discussion	Voting Turnout	Partisan Activities	Government Contacts
Number of Associations								
Belonged to								
r	.28	.29	.29	.41	.21	.15	.29	.31
β^a	.15	.15	.24	.29	.12	.09	.21	.23
Attended monthly								
r	.18	.23	.20	.28	.18	.08	.34	.26
β^a	.09	.10	.13	.17	.12	NS	.28	.20
Dummy Variables								
Belong to 0								
Mean score	.8	2.6	.3	.5	1.7	4.9	.9	.1
Belong to 1; attend 0								
r	.24	.17	.06	.17	NS	NS	NS	NS
β^a	.19	.14	.06	.12	NS	NS	NS	NS
Mean score	1.4	3.3	.5	.9	1.6	5.1	.8	.1
Belong to 1; attend 1								
r	.19	.19	.07	.12	.36	NS	.25	.15
β^a	.11	.17	.08	.08	.31	NS	.23	NS
Mean score	1.3	3.6	.6	.8	2.9	5.0	2.1	.3
Belong to 2+; attend 0								
r	.30	.21	.11	.26	.28	.11	.11	.22
β^a	.16	.13	.10	.12	.21	.14	NS	.17
Mean score	1.8	3.7	.8	1.3	2.5	5.4	1.4	.5
Belong to 2+; attend 1								
r	.33	.33	.20	.37	.15	NS	.19	.18
β^a	.21	.26	.22	.26	NS	NS	.16	.16
Mean score	1.9	4.1	.9	1.6	2.1	5.2	1.5	.4
Belong to 2+; attend 2+								
r	.34	.31	.22	.37	.33	.16	.47	.47
β^a	.18	.25	.23	.24	.24	.16	.40	.36
Mean score	1.9	4.1	1.0	1.8	2.6	5.6	3.0	.9

[a]Controlling age, education, occupation, and income

133

suggest that the political mobilization process may likely occur within interest associations in both societies. The correlations for number of associations attended monthly are somewhat lower than for membership (except for partisan activities in Gävle), which suggests that in general political mobilization may be affected more by breadth than by depth of association participation.

In response to the second question, all but one of these relationships remain significant after the effects of age, education, occupation, and income have been held constant (associations attended is not significantly related to voting turnout in Gävle). In Indianapolis, the betas for attendance are all considerably smaller than for membership, but this contrast is less evident in Gävle. These findings suggest that the political mobilization process is not just a spurious consequence of other factors such as age or socioeconomic status.

Membership versus Involvement

The third question arises from the work of Verba and Nie (1972:184–86), who argue that once the effects of other compounding variables are removed, sheer number of memberships has no effects on political participation. Only the number of active memberships has any political effects under these controlled conditions, they maintain. To determine more precisely the relative importance of organizational membership versus attendance in mobilizing individuals for political activity, the respondents in both Indianapolis and Gävle were divided into six categories of associational participation: (1) belong to no associations (I., 292; G., 80); (2) belong to one association but do not attend it (I., 147; G., 98); (3) belong to one association and attend it (I., 71; G., 36); (4) belong to two or more associations but attend none of them (I., 74; G., 62); (5) belong to two or more associations and attend one of them (I., 95; G., 57); (6) belong to two or more associations and attend two or more of them (I., 65; G., 55). Each category (except the first) was then treated as a dummy variable, and three measures were computed for each of the four political activities: (a) zero-order correlation coefficients for categories 2 through 6 (in each case in conjunction with the first category); (b) partial beta coefficients for categories 2 through 6 while controlling education, occupation, and income; and (c) a mean score for each of the six categories.

The data from Indianapolis are contrary to Verba and Nie's generalization in several respects. First, all of the coefficients (both r's and β's) for those persons with just one inactive membership (category 2) are significant, which indicates that even this minimal amount of passive participation is definitely related to, and may have direct consequences for, several types of political activity. Second, among persons with one active membership (category 3) the coefficients are not significantly higher (and in some cases are lower) than the corresponding figures for nonattenders (category 2). Third, the coefficients for those who belong to two or more associations but attend none of them (category 4) are in every case higher than the corresponding figures for persons with one active membership (category 3). Fourth, there are no significant differences between the coefficients for the last two categories (5 and 6), indicating that multiple association attendance has no more political effects than attendance at just one organization. In sum, these data from Indianapolis show that membership in interest associations appears to be considerably more important than regular attendance in mobilizing people to participate in several kinds of political activities, even with socioeconomic status taken into account.

The situation is not so clear-cut in Gävle, however. Inactive membership in one association (category 2) has no significant effects on any forms of political activity. Active membership in one organization (category 3) is significantly related to political discussion and partisan activities, but not to voting turnout or government contacts (with socioeconomic status controlled), which suggests that attendance may be of some importance in these areas. However, multiple memberships but no attendance (category 4) has significant net effects on political discussion, voting turnout, and government contacts, which indicates that multiple inactive membership may mobilize people for politics in Gävle. Membership in several organizations and attendance at one of them (category 5) produce still a different pattern, with significant net effects only on partisan activities and government contacts. Finally, multiple membership and attendance (category 6) have quite noticeable effects on all four types of political activity. These findings appear to be saying that in this Swedish community both extensive and intensive association participation are generally related to political involvement, which is more in accord with Verba and Nie's generalization, although multiple memberships by themselves also appear to produce some mobilization effects.

One possible—although quite speculative—reason for the discrepancies (total in Indianapolis and partial in Gävle) between these findings and those of Verba and Nie may lie in the fact that their criterion for "active" membership was merely self-designation by the respondents, whereas this study required monthly attendance for active status. This difference suggests that political mobilization occurs only when individuals are involved enough in their organizations to think of themselves as active, as opposed to merely nominal, members, but that activity at the level of monthly attendance is not necessary for this process to occur.

Mobilization by Type of Association

The fourth question raised at the beginning of this section asked whether or not the observed relationships between association membership and the four kinds of political activity occurred within each of the seven types of organizations described previously. Moreover, do these relationships within organizational categories remain significant when age, education, occupation, and income are held constant? Table 5.4 gives the zero-order *r*'s and the partial betas relevant to this issue for both Indianapolis and Gävle.

Although there is considerable variation in the patterns of relationships in these two communities, several broad generalizations emerge from the data in Table 5.4. (1) The basic relationship between organizational membership and political participation occurs in all of the seven categories of associations with at least some political activities. (2) The large majority of these relationships remain statistically significant with age and socio-economic status controlled. (3) In Indianapolis, union membership has the least effects on political participation, whereas in Gävle membership in "free" churches is least relevant for politics. (4) Membership in political and educational, etc. associations has the most effects on political participation in both communities (with the exception of voting turnout in Gävle). (5) In Indianapolis, partisan activity is less related to association membership than the other three political activities are (which is partly due to the small number of people involved in political parties in this community), whereas in Gävle voting turnout is least related (which is partly due to the extremely high levels of voting in Sweden).

Conclusions

The main findings of this analysis of American and Swedish voluntary association participation and political activity can be stated as a series of generalizations.

1. Contrary to many impressionistic observations, Swedes in the Gävle sample are only slightly more likely than Americans in Indianapolis to belong to and attend interest associations.

Table 5.4

Zero-Order and Partial Relationships between Membership within Seven Categories of Associations and Four Types of Political Activity in Indianapolis and Gävle

(Coefficients for each category of associations are based on the percentage of respondents belonging to any organization within that category. N's for each category in each community were given in Table 5.2.)

	Political Activities							
	Indianapolis				Gävle			
Categories of Associations	Political Discussion	Voting Turnout	Partisan Activities	Government Contacts	Political Discussion	Voting Turnout	Partisan Activities	Government Contacts
Labor union								
r	.08	NS	NS	NS	.12	NS	NS	.12
β^a	.09	NS	NS	NS	.09	.11	NS	.11
Business, etc.								
r	.21	.11	NS	.25	.10	.14	.09	.16
β^a	.09	NS	NS	.13	NS	.12	NS	.12
Political								
r	.25	.10	.25	.19	.10	NS	.18	.23
β^a	.22	.07	.25	.14	.10	NS	.18	.23
Educational, etc.								
r	.16	.21	.13	.28	.16	.12	.28	.24
β^a	.06	.07	.14	.19	.09	NS	.20	.17
Fraternal, etc.								
r	.12	.17	.19	.12	NS	.11	.10	.08
β^a	.07	NS	.17	NS	NS	NS	NS	NS
Recreational, etc.								
r	.15	.19	NS	.20	.12	NS	.15	.11
β^a	NS	.11	NS	.10	NS	NS	.10	NS
Church related								
r	NS	.16	.09	.18	NS	NS	.10	NS
β^a	NS	.06	.06	.10	NS	NS	.08	NS

^{a}Controlling age, education, occupation, and income

137

2. The main difference between these two communities in association participation rates is due to much higher membership, but not attendance, by Swedes in labor unions.

3. Participation rates vary widely among the other types of interest associations in both communities, but no overall patterns are discernible.

4. Membership in virtually all types of interest associations is related to several kinds of political activities, regardless of one's socioeconomic status, and hence acts to mobilize people for political involvement.

5. Membership is as important as—or perhaps even more critical than—attendance in this mobilization process, especially in Indianapolis.

6. With slight variations, this mobilization process takes place within all types of voluntary associations in both the American and Swedish communities.

In more general terms, we can conclude from this analysis that the political mobilization process appears to occur in most types of interest associations with most forms of political activity in at least two different societies. In contrast to the findings of Verba and Nie, however, these data indicate that in Indianapolis, and to a lesser degree in Gävle, active membership to the extent of monthly attendance at meetings is not necessary for the mobilization process to operate. Sheer number of memberships by itself may lead to political participation, even with age and socioeconomic status held constant. It is rather interesting that this conclusion confirms an assertion made by Almond and Verba (1963:322) a number of years ago: "Membership in some association, even if the individual does not consider the membership politically relevant, and even if it does not involve his active participation, does lead to a more competent citizenry."

6. *Social Participation and Voting Turnout*

Political democracy assumes that citizens will exercise their franchise on election day. Yet millions of people in the United States regularly fail to vote. Presidential elections typically attract only about 60 percent of the voting-age population; off-year congressional elections generally draw less than 50 percent; and separate state and local elections usually have even lower turnouts. Why so many people fail to vote is a critical problem for democratic political theory and for understanding political participation.

A compound index of voting turnout was one of the measures of political participation utilized in the previous two chapters, but none of those analyses examined actual turnout rates in specific elections. In this chapter, therefore, we explore rates of voting turnout in three different national elections: (a) the 1966 congressional election, which was the last national election prior to the Indianapolis survey; (b) the 1964 presidential election; and (c) the 1960 presidential election.[1]

---

*Adapted by permission from Marvin E. Olsen, "Social Participation and Voting Turnout: A Multivariate Analysis," *American Sociological Review*, vol. 37, June 1972, pp. 317–33.

---

1. Survey questions on voting always evoke bias—in this case toward overreporting voting rates, especially in earlier elections—but there is no simple technique for eliminating this bias. The following three questions were used to elicit reports of voting turnout: "Did you vote in the 1966 congressional elections, when we elected members of the U. S. House of Representatives?" (Indiana did not elect a U. S. Senator in 1966); "Did you vote in the 1964 presidential election, when Johnson ran against Goldwater?" and "Did you vote in the 1960 presidential election, when Kennedy ran against Nixon?" If the respondent said no, he was asked if he was registered to vote in that election and, if not, if he was eligible to register at that time.

This research is based on the social mobilization theory of political participation discussed in chapter 2, but it focuses on the role of social participation in voluntary associations, community events, church activities, and interpersonal interaction as mobilizers of voting turnout. The analysis proceeds in three stages: (a) determining relationships between voting turnout and various measures of social participation, both separately and in combination; (b) exploring the relevance of the social participation thesis as a causal argument; and (c) examining the relationships between social participation and voting turnout while holding constant the effects of other known voting correlates, using multivariate techniques.

The social participation thesis predicts the following research hypotheses:

Hypothesis 1: Participation rates in voluntary associations will be positively related to voting turnout, whatever the nature of the association.

Hypothesis 2: Participation rates in community and church activities will also be positively related to voting turnout, and these relationships will remain significant when voluntary association participation is held constant.

Hypothesis 3: Participation rates in interpersonal interaction will be related to voting turnout; but holding constant participation in voluntary associations, churches, and community affairs will eliminate these correlations.

Correlations between rates of social participation and voting turnout indicate covariation between these two factors but say nothing about causation. The argument that one variable causes another is always a logical inference based on available evidence and cannot be directly tested. We can, however, ask what evidence exists for making a causal inference and evaluate its relevance and adequacy. This kind of inquiry thus focuses on a logical "expectation" rather than a statistical hypothesis. In this chapter we shall examine evidence for inferring a causal sequence from social participation to voting turnout.

Finally, voting turnout is known to correlate with a wide range of other variables in addition to social participation. Hence the social participation thesis is valid only if correlations between voting turnout and voluntary association, community, and church participation remain significant after holding constant the effects of all other compounding variables. These additional correlates of voting turnout can be placed in four categories: (a) demographic location, including age, sex, marital status, and religion; (b) socioeconomic status, as indicated by educational, occupational and income levels; (c) political contacts, including parents' political activities, interpersonal political discussion, mass media news exposure, and party mailings and visits, and (d) political orientations, such as party identification, political interest, and political efficacy. Each of these sets of variables influences voting turnout differently, and persuasive arguments for the importance of each set have been advanced. This research, however, is concerned with these variables primarily as compounding factors in relation to the basic relationship between social participation and voting turnout.

Previous Research

Every voting turnout study that has included a measure of associational participation has found these two variables to be fairly highly correlated.[2] But most of this research has been straightforward descriptive analysis, attempting neither to (a) relate the empirical correlation to any theoretical argument or (b) perform multivariate analysis examining the relationship while holding constant other variables. Of the few multivariate analyses of voting turnout, some have been quite narrow in scope (Lazarsfeld, 1944,[3] and Connelly and Field, 1944[4]), others have examined only a single explanatory variable (Glenn and Grimes, 1968[5]), and still others (Erbe, 1964;[6] and Alford and Scoble, 1968[7]) have used voting turnout as only one among many variables in composite indexes of overall political participation, so that their results do not apply directly to the act of voting.

---

2. Among the better known of these works are the following: Berelson et al., 1954:336–37; Campbell et al., 1952:29 and 1954:70–73; Hastings, 1956; Lane, 1959:45–62; Lipset, 1960:179–219; Lazarsfeld et al., 1944:40–51; and Zimmer and Hawley, 1959.

3. Lazarsfeld found that controlling for level of political interest eliminated the relationship between voting turnout and education, income, age, and religion (but not for sex), thus suggesting that interest in politics is an intervening factor between these independent variables and voting.

4. In this study, with level of income controlled, the voting rate became the same for all educational levels except college graduates for whom it remained higher.

5. Whereas most previous studies had found that voting rates declined after age sixty, they demonstrated that this decline is due largely to lower education levels and a preponderance of females among the old. With these two variables controlled, the voting turnout rate in their sample did not begin to decline until age eighty.

6. He found organizational participation more highly correlated than either socioeconomic status or political efficacy with overall political participation; but in multiple correlations SES evidenced a slightly stronger partial relationship than did participation, while efficacy became nonsignificant.

7. This research, which examined relationships between some twenty independent variables and a combined index of political participation, showed that education, voluntary association activity, and home ownership were the most basic and strongest predictors of overall participation. (These predictor effects were approximately equal.)

The present research, in contrast, treats voting turnout as a single dependent variable within a complex, multivariate theoretical framework.

Research Design

Data for this analysis were taken from the 1968 Indianapolis survey described previously.

Whereas many earlier voting studies computed the proportion of the total sample voting in an election, this research *expresses the voting rate for each election as a percentage of the number of persons eligible to vote in that election,* and omits those made ineligible by residency requirements and/or age. Thus, the category of "nonvoters" includes only eligible but unregistered persons, and registered persons who did not vote. Hence the population base differs for each election: for 1966 it is 651 of the sample of 750; for 1964 it is 649; and for 1960 it is 592.

The social participation independent variables were operationalized as follows.

Voluntary Association Participation Index: For each voluntary association (including labor unions but excluding churches) to which a person belonged, he received one point for membership, two points if he attended at least half the meetings, and three points if he had ever held office or served on a committee.

Church Participation Index: Points were awarded similarly for church membership, frequency of attendance at services, and membership and participation in church-sponsored groups.

Community Participation Index: Points were given for frequency of participation in public community events and communitywide service projects.

Friends Interaction Index: Based on the number of one's close personal friends in the Indianapolis area, frequency of joining them for informal activities, and membership and activities in informal friendship groups.

Neighbors Interaction Index: Based on the number of people in the immediate neighborhood addressed on a first-name basis, and frequency of talking with them. The remaining independent variables will be described as they appear in the analyses.

All the analyses reported here were performed with the Multiple Classification Analysis computer program, which provides zero-order (eta), partial (beta), and multiple (R) correlation coefficients with nominal and ordinal data. These coefficients are roughly analogous to Pearsonian r's, and eta and R can be interpreted, when squared, as the proportion of total variation explained by the predictor variable(s). And although squared betas cannot be interpreted in terms of variation explained, they do indicate what the strength of an observed relationship between two variables would be if the compounding effects of all other variables in that analysis were eliminated. It is therefore legitimate to compare the relative sizes of various beta coefficients. The program uses an additive model and assumes that none of the predictor variables are highly intercorrelated, but it does not assume a linear model or designate the direction of relationships. In this analysis, only coefficients of .10 or larger are viewed as substantively as well as statistically significant.[8]

Findings for Social Participation

Hypothesis 1

To test Hypothesis 1, we first correlate the Voluntary Association Participation Index with voting turnout in the 1966, 1964, and 1960 elections. The resulting zero-order (eta) coefficients are .30, .30, and .32, respectively—all of which might be described as moderately strong. These coefficients, as well as the percent of respondents in each category who voted in each election, are reported in Table 6.1 in the three left-hand columns of the top row. (These percentages must be examined to see if the relationship is monotonic, since the coefficients do not assume a linear model.)

The hypothesis also states that the above relationship should occur among all types of voluntary associations. Consequently, all the organizations to which respondents belonged were coded into one of twelve categories, as follows: labor union, fraternal association, veterans or patriotic association, business or civic association, educational association, youth-serving association, cultural association, nationality or ethnic association, sports or hobby group, professional or scientific association, social or recreational association, and charitable or welfare association. With one exception, voting was significantly related to participation in each kind of organization, with coefficients ranging between .12 and .18. The exception was labor unions, in which participation was uncorrelated with voting turnout. This finding is easily interpreted, however, since for many workers union membership is not voluntary, but is required for

---

8. Statistical significance at the .05 level with these data requires a coefficient of between .08 and .10, depending on the N.

Table 6.1

Zero-Order, Partial, and Multiple Relationships between Social Participation Variables and Voting Turnout in the 1966, 1964, and 1960 Elections

	Zero-Order Relationships: Actual Voting Rates and Correlations			Partial Relationships: Adjusted Voting Rates and Correlations		
	1966	1964	1960	1966	1964	1960
Voluntary Association Participation Index[a]						
None	56%	69%	72%	61%	74%	76%
Low	64	77	81	67	79	82
Moderate	79	94	96	74	89	91
High	93	95	98	84	87	91
Eta/Beta	.30	.30	.32	.18	.16	.18
Community Participation Index[a]						
None	52%	66%	69%	61%	72%	76%
Low	64	78	79	67	78	83
Moderate	76	84	93	77	89	91
High	86	96	95	79	89	87
Eta/Beta	.28	.30	.30	.14	.17	.13
Church Participation Index[a]						
None	46%	61%	71%	53%	68%	75%
Low	63	74	76	65	76	77
Moderate	75	89	90	74	87	89
High	85	92	93	78	84	89
Eta/Beta	.28	.30	.29	.18	.17	.17

144

Friends Interaction Index[a]						
None	52%	62%	66%	63%	70%	74%
Low	72	79	84	75	81	85
Moderate	67	83	87	70	83	86
High	79	90	91	68	83	83
Eta/Beta	.18	.24	.23	NS	.11	NS
Neighbors Interaction Index[a]						
None	53%	64%	67%	64%	76%	78%
Low	67	82	84	69	85	86
Moderate	74	83	87	70	79	84
High	74	86	90	69	79	84
Eta/Beta	.16	.18	.20	NS	NS	NS
Multiple Correlation R (Voluntary Association, Community, and Church Participation only)				.36	.38	.38
Social Participation Combined Index[a]						
Low	45%	59%	61%			
Moderately low	68	79	84			
Moderately high	77	87	91			
High	80	93	94			
Eta	.40	.40	.41			

[a]All of these indexes contain six categories (eight for the Combined Index), and the eta and beta coefficients are based on the full range of these categories, but for ease of presentation in this table each index has been collapsed to four categories.

145

employment. Apparently the political mobilization process occurs only in truly voluntary organizations. We could speculate that the process doesn't occur in other semivoluntary or nonvoluntary organizations such as prisons, mental hospitals, or the military; but our data do not permit a test of this possibility.[9]

From these findings, we conclude that Hypothesis 1 is confirmed: participation in truly voluntary associations is positively and somewhat strongly related to voting turnout, regardless of the nature of the organization. Notice, moreover, that the coefficients for the combined Voluntary Association Participation Index are much stronger than the figures for any specific kind of association, the highest of which was only .18. This suggests that social participation effects on voting are cumulative. The greater the number of one's organizations, the more likely one will vote. Indeed, a simple count of the number of organizations to which respondents belonged correlates with the three elections at .27, .26, and .26, respectively.

Hypothesis 2

Hypothesis 2 states that participation in community and church activities will also be related to voting turnout, even with voluntary association participation controlled. Voting percentages and correlation coefficients for these variables are shown in the second and third rows of Table 6.1. The zero-order (eta) coefficients for both factors (given in the table's three left-hand columns) are approximately the same as those for voluntary associations—around .30.

The three right-hand columns in the table report the partial (beta) relationships between voting and each predictor variable, simultaneously holding constant the effects of the other four predictor variables. Under these extensive controls, the coefficients for voluntary association, community, and church participation all decline in strength, but they remain statistically significant. In other words, each measure of social participation affects voting turnout separately, and no observed zero-order relationship is spurious. Hypothesis 2 is therefore verified.

---

9. Despite these negative findings for labor unions, unions were kept in the overall Voluntary Association Participation Index on the theoretical grounds that all discussions of pluralistic theory have included them. Thus an adequate test of this thesis must take them into account. Leaving unions in the index had the effect of reducing the observed correlations, since participating in these organizations does not contribute to the tendency for voting turnout to increase with association participation. Conversely, were we to exclude unions from the index, the observed correlations with voting turnout would be even higher. Further research might explore this distinction between union and nonunion associations—or more generally, between economically and noneconomically oriented associations.

Hypothesis 3

Hypothesis 3, concerning interpersonal interaction, can be investigated with the data in rows four and five of Table 6.1. The zero-order coefficients for interaction with both friends and neighbors are significant but not strong, ranging from .16 to .24. When all the other participation measures are held constant, however, five of the six partial coefficients for these variables become nonsignificant, and the remaining one is very low. In short, neither interpersonal interaction index appears to explain significant amounts of variation in voting rates, once participation in more formal voluntary associations, community activities, and church events has been accounted for. It may be—though these data cannot test the possibility—that personal friendships occurring within more formal settings do affect political mobilization in some way. But we can at least infer that personal friendships do not, by themselves, influence voting turnout. Consequently, Hypothesis 3 can be accepted; and we shall discard the Friends Interaction Index and Neighbors Interaction Index from further analyses.

The multiple correlations in Table 6.1 are therefore based only on the voluntary association, community, and church participation indexes. Since these multiple R's are all much larger than any beta coefficient for their components, it is clearly preferable to use all three factors together to predict voting turnout, rather than any one alone.[10] Finally, for convenience, these three variables were combined into a single Social Participation Combined Index, as shown in the last panel of Table 6.1[11] Comparison of the eta coefficients for this index with the corresponding multiple R's based on its component variables reveals that the Combined Index predicts voting turnout slightly more strongly, and hence does reflect the overall dimension of social participation.

---

10. As an alternative measure of community participation, we examined length of residency in Indianapolis—a variable that most studies have found to correlate with voting. Length of residency is moderately related to voting turnout, as follows: 1966, .23; 1964, .18; and 1960, .15. However, these coefficients are not as high as those obtained with the Community Participation Index; and when the two measures are simultaneously related to voting, the resulting partial correlations for residency are much lower than those for the participation index. In fact, the observed relationship between community residency and voting turnout appears to be largely a spurious consequence of the fact that older people (who tend to vote regularly) are also more likely to have lived in the community longer. The beta correlations for community residency drop to .14, .16, and .14, respectively, with age held constant. With the three major social participation indexes added as controls, these relationships for community residency become nonsignificant.

11. The procedure used in constructing this Combined Index—as well as all the other combined indexes—was to sum a respondent's scores from the component variables, and then group these into eight categories as nearly equal in number of cases as possible.

Causal Inference Argument

We have now determined that three measures of social participation—in voluntary associations, community affairs, and church events—correlate independently with voting turnout. But which causes which? How relevant is the social participation theory as a causal explanation of voting turnout? Though causation cannot be directly tested, it can be inferred with some confidence if, in addition to covariation and a reasonable theoretical causal explanation, we can demonstrate temporal sequence between the presumed cause and effect. In this case, what evidence have we that social participation precedes voting?

Though we didn't solicit their life histories, we did ask respondents for the year when they joined their current voluntary associations. Regrettably, we did not gather comparable data for community and church participation, which will limit this analysis. Nevertheless, if we can show that people do belong to voluntary organizations prior to voting, we will have some additional evidence for inferring causation from social participation to voting turnout.

Data

Since the 1960 election is so remote from the 1968 data on voluntary associations, we shall here examine only the 1966 and 1964 elections, in three analyses.[12] The first pertains to each respondent's "most important" association. (If a respondent belonged to only one, this automatically became his or her most important organization; if two or more, the respondent was asked to identify the one most important to him or her.) Of the 310 respondents voting in 1966 who had a "most important" organizational membership in 1968, 94 percent had belonged to the association at least one year prior to that election. Of the 354 respondents voting in 1964 who had a "most important" organizational membership in 1968, 91 percent belonged before the election.

The second analysis includes only respondents belonging to two or more organizations, and it pertains to their "second-most-important" association. A total of 173 persons voted in 1966 and named a second

---

12. We omitted the 1960 election because all data on voluntary associations pertain to organizations to which respondents currently belonged. Those who had been members of an association in 1960 but had either changed organizations or dropped out before 1968 would have been counted as nonmembers in the 1960 election and that would clearly have distorted the findings. This distortion could also occur with the 1964 and 1966 elections, but the shorter time spans involved for them should prevent its frequent occurrence.

organization, while 198 did so for the 1964 election. In both cases, 88 percent belonged to their second organization prior to the election in question.

The third analysis pertains to the "third-most-important" organization among persons with three or more memberships. Of the 101 people with a third association who voted in 1966, 92 percent had joined prior to that election. Of the 111 people with a third association who voted in 1964, 90 percent were members before the election.

Argument

These findings support the causal argument that social participation tends to influence voting turnout in a temporal sequence, though two possible biases (in addition to the omission of data for community and church participation) should be noted: First, the data for both organizational participation and voting pertain only to the past few years, and many respondents may have begun voting long before joining any voluntary associations. Even so, we can argue that voluntary association participation may continually reinforce the habit of voting and hence influence current voting turnout, whatever the initial causes. Second, these analyses are limited to persons belonging to at least one voluntary association. Since organizational participation tends to increase with age and SES, we may have introduced bias by looking disproportionately at older and higher-status persons, who also tend to vote more regularly. However, as the next section shows, controlling for age and SES does not eliminate the relationship between voluntary association participation and voting, so that the effects of any such bias cannot be great.

Additional support for this causal argument is provided by Maccoby (1958). He examined the relationship of membership in one voluntary association (concerned with developing a publicly sponsored community recreation program) with voting turnout in two primary elections—one held before the organization was formed and the other two years after. The organization took no part in the second campaign, and its objectives had no ties with election issues. Nevertheless, among nonvoters in the first election, participants in this association were much more likely than nonparticipants to vote in the second election: 66 percent to 39 percent, respectively. Moreover, the voting rate rose to 80 percent among those who had become highly involved in association activities. These findings are fairly compelling, since the research design approximated a controlled experiment.

Based on both our and Maccoby's data, we conclude that it is tenable to infer a causal sequence from social participation to voting turnout, in accordance with our initial expectation.

Findings for Compounding Variables

Previous studies of voting turnout have found that it correlates with a host of other social, economic, and political variables.[13] And since many of these factors are also related to social participation, their effects must be held constant before we can claim that social participation has independent effects on voting turnout. This section therefore examines these compounding variables, both separately and in combination with social participation, to investigate our general expectation that the basic relationship between social participation and voting turnout will remain significant under extensively controlled conditions. To keep the discussion manageable, many of the findings will be briefly summarized without reporting the supporting data.

Demographic Variables

Past research has established that men tend to vote more often than women, whites more often than blacks, middle-aged and older people more than the young, married persons more than unmarried ones, Jews more often than gentiles, and Catholics more than Protestants. These demographic variables of sex, race, age, marital status, and religion were therefore related to voting turnout in the three elections.

As expected, men in this sample vote slightly more often than women, but the differences are statistically nonsignificant. With respect to race, blacks appear to have voted slightly more often than whites, but again the differences are nonsignificant.[14] Age is moderately correlated with voting turnout (mean eta for the three elections = .22), with the relationship

---

13. These studies include the following: Alford and Lee, 1968; Buchanan, 1956; Campbell, Converse, Miller, and Stokes, 1960; Campbell, Gurin, and Miller, 1954; Connelly and Field, 1944; Dahl, 1961; Glaser, 1958, 1960, and 1965; Glenn and Grimes, 1968; Hastings, 1956; Janowitz and Marvick, 1956; Karlsson, 1958; Key, 1958; Lazarsfeld et al., 1944; Lipset, 1960; Miller, 1952; Olsen, 1970; Orum, 1966; and Ranney and Epstein, 1966. For an extensive bibliography of studies dealing with all forms of political participation published through 1964, see Milbrath, 1965.

14. In a separate paper (Olsen, 1970), I examined voting turnout and other kinds of participation among blacks, with socioeconomic status and age held constant. Under these controlled conditions, voting rates among blacks are considerably higher than among whites of comparable statuses, and the differences are significant in the 1964 and 1960 presidential elections.

remaining monotonic up to age seventy and declining only slightly up to age eighty. Married persons vote more extensively than single people, but the rates for the divorced and widowed are as high as those for married people. All three of these latter correlations are quite weak, and they become nonsignificant with age controlled. Religious preference (coded conservative Protestant, liberal Protestant, Catholic, and no preference[15]) correlates moderately with voting (mean eta = .22). The interesting finding here, however, is that liberal Protestants tend to be as active as Catholics, while both conservative Protestants and persons with no religious preference vote much less often.

Since the correlations between voting turnout and sex, race, and marital status were all weak or nonsignificant, and since further analyses showed these variables to have no effects on any other relationship in this study, we shall discard them here. Age, however, remains significantly related to voting with all other compounding variables controlled, as we shall see later. The same is not true of religion. Though controlling for age has no effect here, holding constant the variables of education, occupation, and income reduces all three relationships for religion almost to nonsignificance. And when the three social participation indicators are also added as controls, the three relationships become statistically nonsignificant. (Controlling religion does not affect the correlations for the social participation measures at all.) Hence the observed differences in voting rates among the religious preference categories are apparently spurious, and the religion variable can be discarded. Of the original five indicators of demographic location, only age remains as a significant independent predictor of voting participation.

Socioeconomic Status

All previous voting research has found that the higher a person's socioeconomic status—as shown by educational level, occupational status, and annual income—the more likely is he or she to vote. Our data support these

---

15. The sample was not large enough to permit analysis of each separate Protestant denomination, but preliminary examination of the data indicated that voting rates among the denominations varied too greatly to justify combining them into a single "Protestant" category. Hence the compromise decision was reached to dichotomize Protestant churches into the categories of "conservative"—including the Pentecostal churches, Church of Christ, Disciples of Christ, Nazarene Church, and all Baptists—and the more "liberal" churches of Methodists, Presbyterians, Episcopalians, Congregationalists, and community churches. Because only six Jews fell into the sample, they could not be analyzed separately and were discarded from all analyses involving religion.

generalizations for all three elections (mean eta for education = .26, occupation = .21, and income = .19).[16] When each of these variables was examined while holding constant the other two, education and occupation remained significantly related to voting turnout (though the coefficients for occupation were quite low), but income became nonsignificant. Moreover, the occupation correlations also became nonsignificant when the three social participation measures, as well as education, were held constant. (The relationships for the social participation measures were not substantially affected when either income or occupation, or both in combination, were used as controls.) Hence we shall retain only education as an indicator of socioeconomic status.

Political Contacts

This variable set is composed of four indexes measuring the respondent's exposure to the political system: Parents' Political Activities Index,[17] Political Discussion Index,[18] Mass Media News Exposure Index,[19] and Party Contacts Index.[20] All four indexes were found to have moderate to relatively strong correlations with voting turnout (mean eta for parents' participation = .20, political discussion = .27, political news exposure = .33, and party contacts = .37). However, the coefficients for parents' participation became nonsignificant when the other measures were simultaneously controlled. This finding does not necessarily mean that the degree of parents' political activity does not influence their chil-

16. The respondent's education was measured by total number of years of schooling completed, including technical and vocational training. Occupation of the head of the household was classified as "low manual" (all semiskilled, domestic service, and unskilled jobs), "high manual" (skilled workers, public service workers, and foremen), "low nonmanual" (clerical and sales workers, and managers and owners of businesses with less than five employees), and "high nonmanual" (owners and managers of larger businesses, technicians, and all professionals). Family income was the total gross income in 1967 before taxes.

17. Constructed from questions on whether or not the respondent's father and mother had political party preferences, the frequency with which the respondent's parents discussed politics while the respondent was growing up, whether they usually voted, whether they belonged to any political organizations, and whether they ever did volunteer work for a party or candidate.

18. Based on frequency of talking about political topics with personal friends, neighbors, relatives, and coworkers.

19. Points were given for frequency of watching national network news broadcasts on television, listening to local news broadcasts on television and radio, reading national and international news in newspapers, reading editorials and columnists in newspapers, and reading political articles in magazines.

20. Based on the frequency with which the respondent received mail from a political party and whether or not it was read, the number of times a party worker had called at the respondent's house and for how long, and other personal contacts with people active in politics.

dren's later voting participation, but that these effects apparently operate indirectly, through more immediate factors such as exposure to the mass media or reading party literature. Nevertheless, this variable is not relevant here, since controlling it does not affect the relationships between social participation and voting turnout. Hence we discard it.

The correlations for political discussion also decline markedly when the other political contacts measures are controlled, but they remain barely significant because persons who never discuss politics score lower than all other respondents. (There are no major voting rate differences among any of the other categories of political discussion.) While we cannot drop this variable, its importance is minimal.

Political contacts via the mass media and political parties are much more relevant for voting turnout, with the latter correlating more strongly than the former under simultaneous control (mean beta for party contacts = .24, mass media = .18). These findings suggest that house-to-house canvassing and other political leg-work are still quite important in getting out the vote.

As a summary measure of this political contacts dimension, a Political Contacts Combined Index was constructed from the variables of political discussion (dichotomized), political news exposure, and party contacts, using the same procedure as with the Social Participation Combined Index.[21] This index correlated with voting turnout in the three elections as follows: 1966, .41; 1964, .41; 1960, .37. This combined index, rather than its separate components, will be used in subsequent analyses.

Political Orientations

The three indexes in this set—Political Interest,[22] Party Identification,[23] and Political Efficacy[24]—measure a person's various cognitive and evaluative orientations toward the political system. Political interest and party

---

21. Since the only significant difference on the Political Discussion Index lies in the distinction between those who do and don't discuss politics with others, this index was reduced to a dichotomy. Because the maximum score on this index becomes 1, it contributes much less to the Political Contacts Combined Index than the other two indexes.

22. Constructed from a series of questions on how interested the respondent was in political issues and activities in Indianapolis, in Indiana, at the national level, and in foreign affairs.

23. Points were given for having a party preference in national politics, having a preference in local politics, and for being able either to describe some difference between the two major parties or tell why in the respondent's opinion they did not differ.

24. Measured with the political efficacy scale devised by Campbell, et al. (1954), but focused on national politics.

identification were found to exert approximately equal, and rather strong, effects on voting turnout (mean eta for political interest = .43, party identification = .41), but the political efficacy correlations were much lower (mean eta = .16). With all three indexes simultaneously related to voting, the partial coefficients for the first two remain fairly high and roughly equivalent (mean beta for political interest = .32, party identification = .28). Those for political efficacy become nonsignificant, however, so that this index was discarded. The remaining two indexes of political interest and party identification were then added together to form a Political Orientations Combined Index.

Multivariate Analyses

We can at last gather the remaining control variables in a series of multivariate analyses, to evaluate our expectation that the relationship between voting turnout and social participation will remain significant under extensively controlled conditions. We will also be able to determine the independent effects of each compounding variable on voting turnout, holding all other variables constant.

The control variables to be included in this analysis are age, education, the Political Contacts Combined Index (based on the separate indexes for political news exposure, party contacts, and political discussion), and the Political Orientations Combined Index (based on the indexes for political interest and party identification). To measure participation in organized social activities, we shall use the Social Participation Combined Index, which is based on the separate indexes for voluntary association, community, and church participation.

Before combining all these variables in a single analysis, let us briefly examine three subsets that yield interesting findings. First, when just age and education are simultaneously related to voting, the partial (beta) coefficients for both are slightly higher than their original zero-order (eta) coefficients, as follows: for age, mean eta = .22, mean beta = .27; for education, mean eta = .26, mean beta = .33. This occurs because both age and education are positively related to voting, but negatively related to each other (eta = −.25). Hence controlling for one enhances the other's positive correlation with voting turnout. (These effects do not occur when education is replaced by occupation or income, since both correlate positively with age.) This interactive effect of age and education can be viewed as meaning that young and poorly educated persons are quite unlikely to vote, while older and highly educated persons are very likely to go to the polls—but that neither type exists in great numbers in the total population. For the majority, age and education pull in opposite directions, partly cancelling out each other's effects on voting turnout.

Second, when education (as an indicator of socioeconomic status) and the Social Participation Combined Index are simultaneously related to voting, we can answer the oft-debated question, What are the relative effects of socioeconomic status versus social participation voting turnout? Some previous studies have favored socioeconomic status, others social participation, and still others have found their effects on political partici-pation to be approximately equal.[25] Our data clearly favor social par-ticipation: for the three elections, the mean beta for social participation with education controlled = .35, while that for education with social participation controlled = .14. (The results are almost identical when a Socioeconomic Status Combined Index, based on education, occupation, and income, is used in this analysis.) This finding should not be interpreted to mean that education (or socioeconomic status) is unimportant as an influence on voting, but that many of the effects of this dimension on voting are conveyed indirectly through participation in voluntary associ-ations, community events, and church activities—all of which relate directly and strongly to education.

Third, since the political dimensions of contacts and orientations are highly interrelated (eta = .51), we must ask whether each affects voting turnout independently. When these variables are joined in a multiple correlation, the resulting mean beta coefficient for political contacts with orientations controlled = .24, while the mean beta for political orientations with contacts controlled = .40. Thus both dimensions exert separate effects on the decision to vote, though political orientations is a noticeably better predictor.

We can now bring all of these voting correlates together in a single analysis. We note first that all four remaining control variables are at least moderately correlated with social participation: age, .20, education, .41, political contacts, .45, and political orientations, .37. Consequently, hold-ing constant the effects of these variables will doubtless reduce the relationships between social participation and voting turnout. But by how much? Conversely, when simultaneously controlled, will all the com-

25. Erbe (1964) found socioeconomic status to have a slightly higher partial correlation with political participation than voluntary association participation. Nie, et al. (1969) reported a somewhat higher zero-order correlation for organizational participation than for socioeconomic status with political participation, based on data from five nations. Alford and Scoble (1968) believed the effects of these two factors to be roughly equal.

pounding variables remain significantly related to voting? For answers, let us examine the data in Table 6.2, which joins the Social Participation Combined Index, age, education, the Political Contacts Combined Index, and the Political Orientations Combined Index in multiple correlations with voting turnout rates in the three elections.

Several conclusions can be drawn from these data:

1. Even under these extensively controlled conditions, social participation remains relatively strongly related to voting turnout. Thus our general expectation is verified and the social participation thesis is supported. The mean beta for this index from the three elections is .22, which is surpassed in magnitude only by the figures for political orientations.

2. Age remains moderately related to voting turnout, though the beta for the 1966 election is higher than the figures for the other two elections, which suggests that age has more impact on voting in Congressional than Presidential elections.

3. Education is significantly but extremely weakly correlated with voting in the 1966 and 1960 elections, while the 1964 figure becomes nonsignificant. Once again, we interpret this finding to mean that education (or more broadly, socioeconomic status), does not directly affect voting turnout, but rather that its effects are transmitted indirectly through other related factors.

4. All partial coefficients for the Political Contacts Combined Index remain significant, but not strong; the mean beta = .13. Note that the original eta coefficients for this index (1966 = .41, 1964 = .44, 1960 = .40) were slightly higher than those for the Social Participation Combined Index (1966 = .40, 1964 = .40, 1960 = .41) in two of the elections, but that in Table 6.2 social participation has become a considerably stronger voting predictor than political contacts. (Three separate analyses, using just age, education, and political orientations as single control variables, showed that each reduces somewhat the relationship between political contacts and voting, and that their effects are cumulative.)

5. Last, the Political Orientations Combined Index remains quite strongly related to voting under these controlled conditions (mean beta = .36), especially in the 1964 and 1960 presidential elections. At this point, political orientations seem to predict voting turnout better than social participation, but presently we shall question this interpretation.

Before leaving Table 6.2, we should also note that the multiple coefficients obtained from these correlations are all relatively strong for social science research with ordinal data. These multiple R's of .56, .59, and .58 for the three elections (the corresponding R^2's and .31, .35, and .34)

Table 6.2
Partial and Multiple Relationships of Age, Education, Social Participation Combined Index, Political Contacts Combined Index, and Political Orientations Combined Index with Voting Turnout in the 1966, 1964, and 1960 Elections.

		Adjusted (Partial) Voting Rates and Correlations		
		1966	1964	1960
Social Participation Combined Index				
Low		52%	68%	69%
Moderately low		67	78	83
Moderately high		75	83	87
High		77	89	91
	Beta	.22	.20	.24
Age				
21–29		48%	65%	72%
30–39		67	81	83
40–49		71	80	83
50–59		76	84	85
60 and older		82	87	89
	Beta	.25	.17	.12
Education				
0–8 years		62%	79%	79%
9–11 years		67	80	87
12 years		70	79	83
13–15 years		70	82	86
16 or more years		80	82	86
	Beta	.11	NS	.10
Political Contacts Combined Index				
Low		68%	75%	80%
Moderately low		65	81	84
Moderately high		67	80	84
High		74	84	85
	Beta	.10	.15	.14
Political Orientations Combined Index				
Low		48%	55%	61%
Moderately low		70	86	89
Moderately high		78	89	93
High		78	89	88
	Beta	.29	.40	.39
Multiple R		.56	.59	.58

indicate that we are explaining approximately a third of the variation in voting turnout rates with all predictor variables combined.[26]

26. This multiple correlational analysis was repeated using all the separate variables rather than the combined indexes for social participation, political contacts, and political orientations. The results were essentially equivalent to those reported in Table 6.2, in that all these variables remained significantly related to voting turnout.

Discussion and Conclusions

The main empirical findings of this research are as follows: (a) Participation in voluntary associations correlates with voting turnout at mean eta = .31. This relationship occurs with all kinds of organizations except labor unions, which suggests that the political mobilization process occurs only in truly voluntary organizations. (b) Participation in community events and church activities are also both related to voting, with mean etas for both of .29. Moreover, all three of these social participation measures remain significantly related to voting with the other two factors controlled. The Social Participation Combined Index, based on all three measures, correlates with voting turnout with a mean eta of .40. (c) Measures of informal interaction with friends and neighbors correlate only weakly with voting, and both relationships become nonsignificant with the above measures of participation in more formal settings held constant. (d) Among respondents belonging to one or more voluntary associations who voted in the 1964 and 1966 elections, almost all belonged to these organizations before the election. These data provide some basis for inferring causation from association participation to voting turnout. (e) Among the other voting correlates examined in this study, the factors of (1) age, (2) education, (3) political contacts via the mass media, partisan mailings, and party workers, and (4) political orientations such as party identification and interest in politics, all remain significantly related to voting turnout when simultaneously controlled. Of these four variables, political orientations has the strongest partial correlation, at mean beta = .36. (f) With the effects of these four compounding factors all held constant, the Social Particiption Combined Index remains significantly and moderately correlated with voting, at mean beta = .22. (g) Taken together, all five predictor variables produce a mean multiple correlation with voting turnout of $R = .58$ $(R^2 = .33)$.

From these findings, we conclude that participation in the activities of voluntary associations, one's community, and one's church does mobilize people to vote. In addition, the efforts of political parties and candidates to reach voters through the mass media, partisan mailings, and personal visits do have some further effects on getting out the vote—though these are minimal in comparison with the effects of social participation. Voting rates also rise steadily with age, at least until retirement, although rising educational levels among the young may in time erase many of these age differentials. Education does show a moderate relationship with voting, but the main causal process here appears to go from education to social participation to voting turnout. The other socioeconomic status indicators of occupation and income, finally, seem to be relatively unimportant for voting turnout.

Of all the variables examined in this study, the dimension of political orientations—having a party preference and being interested in politics— appears at first to be the most relevant for explaining voting. But this assumes that political orientations act as independent causal factors. It is equally plausible to argue, however, that this dimension of cognitive and attitudinal responses toward the political system acts as an intervening variable between the other predictor variables and voting. From this perspective, political orientations would be seen as providing a vehicle through which the other phenomena—especially one's social participation and political contacts—affect one's decision to vote. Such a view does not diminish the importance of political orientations in the total theoretical model, but argues that they should not be taken as initial causes.

By this reasoning, we might remove political orientations from the multiple correlations in Table 6.2. When we do so, the multiple R's are only slightly reduced, so that mean $R = .49$ ($R^2 = .24$). This finding indicates that political orientations may in fact be operating mainly as an intervening variable, since removing it does not reduce the multiple correlations too greatly—though it does have some small independent effects on voting (or at least effects that are independent of the other predictor variables examined here). In this multiple correlation, the mean partial beta coefficients for the remaining variables are as follows: social participation = .27, political contacts = .19, age = .21, education = .14. Thus with political orientations omitted as an independent causal variable, the dimension of social participation becomes the most important predictor of voting turnout.

To conclude, let us return to the theory of social participation as an explanation of voting turnout, which is the central concern of this study. This theoretical explanation, derived from the mobilization version of social pluralism theory, argues that active involvement in voluntary, special-interest, nonpolitical organizations—including voluntary associations, community activities, and churches—tends to bring individuals into contact with political issues, actors, and affairs, and provides them with information and skills necessary for voting and other kinds of political participation. Partially as a result of this stimulation, the individual gives greater attention to political messages from the mass media, party workers, and other sources, and also develops stronger party identification and political interest. All of these factors then combine to propel individuals to the polls. The main import of this argument is that we must look beyond the political system for many of the crucial causes of political participation. In addition to the commonly examined nonpolitical factors of age and education, we must give special attention to the individual's involvement in organized social activities which may have little or no formal connection with politics. The obvious prior question—which awaits further research—is what factors lead people to join and become involved in voluntary associations and similar activities? The social participation theory by itself provides only a partial explanation of voting turnout, but the results of this study indicate that it must be given serious attention if one wishes to understand why people go to the polls on election day.

7. Three Routes
to Political Party
Participation*

Political parties constitute the organizational backbone of the political system in all democratic nations, and they provide a major channel for the exercise of influence on political affairs. Yet as we have seen in previous chapters, only a small minority of the population in the United States participates in any way in party activities. One crucial way of eliminating mass powerlessness in modern societies, therefore, would be to involve more citizens in political parties. This chapter explores several ways in which that might be accomplished.

Previous Research

Participation in political party activities has been investigated by numerous researchers in recent years, but most of these studies have examined only party leaders such as precinct committeemen and county chairmen (Bowman and Boynton, 1966; Eldersveld, 1964; Hirschfield et al., 1962; Ippolito, 1969; Keefe and Seyler, 1960; Monroe, 1971; Patterson, 1963). A few studies have focused on volunteer party workers (Holt and Turner, 1968; Marvick and Nixon, 1961) or party members (Berry, 1970; Duverger, 1963), but virtually none have covered the full range of party participation. Moreover, most of this previous research has dealt with the motivations or incentives that lead people to party involvement (Bowman et al., 1969; Conway and Feigert, 1968; Holt and Turner, 1968; Ippolito,

---

*Adapted by permission from Marvin E. Olsen, "Three Routes to Political Party Participation," *The Western Political Quarterly,* vol. 29, December 1976, pp. 550–62.

1969; Marvick and Nixon, 1961; Monroe, 1971), and has given little attention to social factors that might stimulate participation in party affairs. Those few studies that have given serious attention to social variables have generally not attempted to carry their analysis beyond reporting zero-order relationships (Bowman and Boynton, 1966; Patterson, 1963).

The literature on general political participation, meanwhile, says very little about party activism. Lane (1959) did not distinguish among any of the various types of political activity. Key (1964) gave only brief attention to party activists, noting simply that they tend to have above-average education, occupations, and incomes. Milbrath (1965:18) included several different forms of party participation in his "hierarchy of political involvement," but did not specifically examine any of these activities. Alford (1968) identified attendance at political meetings as one of four basic types of political participation, but he then combined it with the other types in a single composite index.

The only research that examines a wide variety of party activities and relates them to several social variables through multivariate analyses is Verba and Nie's *Participation in America* (1972). One of four basic "modes" of political participation in their model is "campaign activity," as indicated by contributing money to a party or candidate, attending political meetings, doing volunteer work for a party or candidate, belonging to a political club, and trying to persuade others how to vote. It should be noted, however, that (a) the last two of these measures do not pertain to political parties, and (b) none of the measures involves holding party leadership positions. Although Verba and Nie's concept of "campaign activity" is therefore not strictly comparable to the usual notion of party participation, the results of their analyses will be compared with the findings of this study wherever relevant.

The research reported in this paper goes beyond previous studies of party activism in three aspects: (a) To encompass the full range of party activity, it examines three different levels of increasing involvement – attending meetings, doing volunteer work, and holding a party office – which are combined into a Party Participation Index. (b) To explain rates of party participation, it examines and tests six alternative causal arguments incorporating a wide variety of predictor variables. (c) To provide an overall picture of the ways in which individuals become involved in party affairs, the relevant predictor variables are combined in a path model, and multiple regression analysis is used to identify three alternative party involvement process. The data for this analysis are taken from the Indianapolis survey described in Chapter 3.

Party Involvement Levels

Participation in political party affairs can be conceptualized as occurring at three levels of increasing involvement:

Level 1: *Party attendance*. These people limit their party activities to occasionally attending party events. In response to the question "Have you ever attended a meeting, rally, dinner, or convention of a political party?" 8 percent of the respondents said once, 6 percent said twice, and 16 percent said three or more times for an average of 0.67 times.[1]

Level 2: *Volunteer party work*. In addition to attending party events, these people also do volunteer campaign work for their party or its candidates. Responses to the question "Have you ever done any sort of volunteer work for a political party or candidate?" were distributed as follows: one campaign, 6 percent; two campaigns, 4 percent; three or more campaigns, 9 percent; mean, 0.41 campaigns.[2]

Level 3: *Party leadership*. These highly involved partisans serve on party committees or hold party offices, as well as attending meetings and working in campaigns. When asked "Have you ever served on a committee or held any kind of office in a political party?" 1 percent of the respondents replied once, 2 percent replied twice, and 3 percent replied three or more times, for a mean of 0.13 times.[3]

The questions used to measure each of these participation levels unfortunately did not specify when each activity was done — whether recently or long ago. This gave older people an advantage, since they would have had more time to engage in these activities on a repeated basis. To minimize this bias as much as possible, each item — and hence each level of participation — was dichotomized as "never done" or "ever done" as follows: ever attended a party meeting, 30 percent; ever done volunteer work, 19 percent; ever held a party position, 6 percent. As expected, these three items are highly interrelated, with the following product-moment

---

1. Verba and Nie (1972: 31) found that only 19 percent of the respondents in their national sample had attended at least one political meeting, but the question was restricted to the last three years.

2. Verba and Nie (1972: 31) found that 26 percent of their respondents reported having done volunteer work in at least one election.

3. To test the possibility that party leaders might also occupy leadership positions in several other areas of community life, thus constituting a relatively closed set of multidimensional elites, the computer was instructed to identify all party leaders who were also college graduates, had professional or managerial occupations, held leadership positions in two or more voluntary associations, and scored in the top quintile on a community activity index. This search produced one person from among the 45 party leaders in this sample. When the criteria were lowered to only 13 or more years education, one associational leadership, and the top third of the community activities distribution, only three more people emerged. Quite clearly, political party leaders are not multidimensional elites.

correlations: attend meeting and volunteer work, .86; attend meeting and hold position, .95; volunteer work and hold position, .94.

Implicit in the descriptions of these levels of party involvement is the proposition that they form a unidimensional scale. To test this possibility, the three items were subjected to Guttman scaling techniques. The resulting coefficient of reproducibility was .96, minimum marginal reproducibility was .82, and the coefficient of scalability was .79. Thus we can describe these three levels of party participation as forming a stepwise pattern in which party workers also attend meetings and party leaders also attend meetings and do volunteer campaign work.

As a composite measure of partisan involvement, the three items were combined to form a Party Participation Index by summing the number of "ever done" scores for each person. On this index, 65 percent of the respondents scored 0, 19 percent scored 1, 10 percent scored 2, and 5 percent scored the maximum of 3 points, with a mean index score of .55 and a standard deviation of .87. The three component items are correlated with the index as follows: attend meetings, .84, do volunteer work, .82, and hold party position, .66.[4]

Theoretical Arguments

The existing literature on party participation suggests six alternative but not mutually exclusive theoretical arguments to explain why people become involved in political party activities. Although some of these causal theses are merely implicit — rather than explicit — in the work of the writers cited in the following paragraphs, in all cases the empirical relationships underlying the theoretical arguments have been extensively documented.

Political Socialization

Although all previous research on political socialization supports Milbrath's (1965:43) generalization that "family experience has a profound impact on a person's . . . activity level in politics," most of this work has not dealt specifically with party activism. A theoretical rationale for the importance of parental political involvement in promoting party participation is found in the idea of the politicized family, "in which political

---

4. An alternative Party Involvement Index was also constructed by summing the number of times a respondent had done each of the three party activities. It is not utilized in this paper because it is biased in favor of older people and ignores the unidimensional feature of the Party Participation Index. Nevertheless, when all of the analyses were repeated with the Party Involvement Index, the results were almost identical to those reported here for the Party Participation Index.

matters receive both substantial and sustained attention, and in which skills in the analysis of public issues are supplemented by examples of adult political participation (Marvick and Nixon, 1961:209). Children growing up in such a family will presumably learn (often at a very early age) to be interested in and concerned about political affairs. They internalize the norm that political activity is important and acquire social skills that facilitate involvement in politics. As adults, they are then quite likely to carry on the patterns of political participation learned in childhood. Empirical support for this argument in relation to political parties is provided by Knoke (1972), who found parents' party preferences to be the most critical factor influencing sons' party preferences as adults. Two common indicators of a politicized family are frequent discussions of political affairs in the home and parental involvement in political groups and parties.

Intellectual Sophistication

This argument places primary emphasis on education as the main determinant of a person's involvement in politics. Building on the repeatedly observed empirical correlations between amount of education and all forms of political participation, it suggests that the greater one's intellectual capabilities and sophistication (a) the more one will know about the political system; (b) the more attention and interest one will give to politics; (c) the more complete will be one's understanding of political issues; and (d) the better prepared one will be to take part in political activities (Milbrath, 1965:68). Unfortunately, many previous studies have simply used education as one indicator of overall general socioeconomic status and have not examined the effects of education apart from those of occupation and income. From this theoretical perspective, however, occupation and income correlate with political participation only because they are so highly influenced by education, which is the crucial determining factor.

Socioeconomic Influence

All previous studies of political participation have found fairly strong correlations between socioeconomic status and whatever kinds of political activity were being investigated. Verba and Nie (1972) consequently assumed that socioeconomic status is the fundamental determinant of political involvement and employed a "standard socioeconomic model" as a baseline throughout their analyses, controlling for status whenever they computed the effects of other independent variables. Theoretically, the crucial process in this perspective is the exertion of social influence or power. The argument is that the greater one's ability to exert power in various realms of social life (and hence also the greater one's privileges and prestige), the more resources one can commit to political activities and the more likely one is to use these resources to ensure that the political system operates to one's advantage. The major indicators of one's own current socioeconomic influence are occupational status and income.

Political Communication

Whereas a socioeconomic power perspective can lead one to see the political system as an arena of conflicting interests and influences, a communication perspective can lead one to view politics as a forum for more-or-less rational discussion and debate. The more information about political affairs that one receives, the more likely one is to respond by becoming involved in partisan affairs. Previous research has discovered moderately strong relationships between most forms of political activity and (a) exposure to the mass media (Lane, 1959:238), and (b) receiving party mailings (Milbrath, 1965:39), so that both of these activities can be taken as empirical indicators of the political communication process. Obviously, however, a person's interest in political messages and the extent to which they motivate him to become involved in partisan politics will be strongly influenced by his level of education, so that education must be held constant when examining the relevance of this political communication argument.

Social Participation

Every previous study that has included any measure of associational participation has found it to be positively correlated with most types of political activities, even after socioeconomic status was controlled (Alford and Scoble, 1968; Berry, 1970; Milbrath, 1965; Nie et al., 1961; Palma, 1970; Rokkan, 1970). In fact Nie, Powell, and Prewitt state definitively that "organizational involvement is the predictor variable with the most strength. Within each of the five nations [United States, United Kingdom, Germany, Italy, and Mexico] the citizen who is an active member of social groups is more likely to be a political participant than the citizen with few or no organizational involvements." Involvement in one's community has not been as extensively investigated in relation to political participation, but several studies have indicated that length of residency in the community is related to political activity, and Alford found a moderate correlation between home ownership and his composite index of participation in politics. The causal process underlying these relationships can be explained in terms of "social mobilization" (Deutsch, 1961:493–514). The argument is that participation in organized social activities of all kinds — regardless of whether or not they are at all related to politics — tends to mobilize individuals to become more active in the political system, including parties. Social participation mobilizes an individual political activity as it (a) makes public affairs and political issues more salient and important to him, (b) brings him into contact with a wide range of people and new social relationships that broaden his sphere of activities, and (c) gives him experience in dealing with organizational activities and teaches him participation skills and norms. In this study, involvement in both voluntary interest associations and one's community are taken as indicators of overall social participation.

Civic Orientations

This final theoretical argument is quite straightforward: the stronger or more salient one's cognitive or affective orientations toward the political system, the more likely one is to become actively involved in political affairs. From this perspective, party participation is caused by such factors as interest in politics, identification with a political party, and feelings of political efficacy (Bowman et al., 1969; Conway and Feigert, 1968; Marvick and Nixon, 1961; and Monroe, 1971). These three factors, therefore, provide indicators of the presence of viable civic orientations. Social variables are taken into account in this argument only as background factors that shape one's orientations toward politics – and which consequently have no direct effects on political participation. The crucial determinant in this thesis is how one views and feels about the political system, which in turn determines the strength of one's motivation to engage in partisan activities.

Basic Relationships

The first analytic step in this research was to examine the basic zero-order relationships between party participation and all of the relevant predictor variables, as a means of evaluating the validity of the six causal arguments.

Demographic Variables

The basic demographic variables of sex, age, and race have repeatedly been found to correlate at least moderately with many forms of political activity, and hence must be taken into consideration in this analysis (Milbrath, 1965:134–41; Verba and Nie, 1972:138–73). They are not included within any of the six theoretical arguments sketched above, and cannot be said to affect party involvement in a causal sense, but to the extent that they correlate with rates of partisan participation they are useful as predictor as well as control variables. The data revealed that neither sex nor race is significantly related to party participation.[5] However, involvement in party affairs does relate directly to age, peaking at about age fifty-five and then remaining constant until age seventy, for a correlation of $r = .17$.[6]

Political Socialization Variables

Two kinds of parental political activities were investigated as indicators of the political socialization thesis: (a) the frequency with which one's parents discussed politics in the home and (b) whether or not one's parents engaged in political actions such as belonging to a political club, working for a political party, or contacting governmental officials about current issues. Since both variables correlate significantly with party participation (with r's of .24 and .21 respectively), they were combined to form a Parents' Political Activities Index, which is related to party participation at $r = .27$.[7]

Education

Number of years of schooling, including both academic and vocational study, was used as a measure of intellectual sophistication. The coefficient

---

5. This finding is consistent with the results of an earlier analysis of these same data, which found that as blacks rise in socioeconomic status, their political participation rates tend to equal or even exceed those of whites (Olsen, 1970). Verba and Nie (1972:162) report similar findings with a national sample.

6. If people under thirty are removed from the analysis of age, on the grounds that they have had only a short time in which to become involved in party affairs, the correlation for age declines somewhat in magnitude but remains statistically significant. In terms of the three items comprising the Party Participation Index, attending party meetings is most frequent among people in their mid-forties, doing volunteer work is most common among people in their fifties, and party leadership positions are most often held by people in their sixties.

7. When examined separately, both of these components continued to have separate and significant effects on party participation throughout all subsequent analyses.

for education with party participation is only $r = .15$, and detailed inspection of this relationship revealed that increasing education has virtually no effects on party involvement below the level of college graduates, who are considerably more active than all other people in political parties.

Socioeconomic Variables

Two measures of the respondent's current socioeconomic status were utilized as indicators of the socioeconomic influence thesis: (a) the occupational status of the head of the household (measured with the first digit of the Duncan Index of Socioeconomic Status; Reiss, 1961), and (b) total annual gross family income. Neither measure correlates very strongly with participation: for occupation $r = .15$, and for income $r = .11$.[8] Moreover, neither of these relationships is totally linear: party participation is slightly higher among clerical and sales workers than among managerial and professional persons, while poverty-level people are more active politically than those with incomes between $4,000 and $8,000, producing a J-shaped curve. Nevertheless, when these relationships were recomputed using multiple classification analysis (which does not assume linearity), the coefficients barely increased in magnitude: occupation became .17 and income became .12. A Socioeconomic Status Index was then constructed by combining respondents' scores for occupation and income. Its correlation with party participation is $r = .15$, or the same as occupation alone, but the relationship is monotonic.

Communication Variables

As suggested previously, two major sources of political messages are the mass media and direct party contacts. A Mass Media Exposure Index was constructed from items measuring frequency of exposure to "serious" programs (such as news, documentaries, and specials) on television and radio, number of daily newspapers read regularly, and number of nonfiction magazines read regularly. A Partisan Contacts Index was constructed from questions about frequency of receiving party mailings and being visited by party workers.[9] Exposure to political information via the mass media was found to relate moderately strongly with party participation, at $r = .25$, while the relationship for direct partisan contacts is much

---

8. Verba and Nie (1972:135) found SES to be moderately related to their measure of campaign activities ($r = .20$), but they included education in their SES index.

9. Both of these factors are separately and significantly related to party participation, at approximately equal strengths.

stronger, at $r = .39$. Joining these two variables in a multiple regression with party participation produces an $R = .40$, but the net effects of mass media exposure in this situation are almost nonsignificant (beta $= .10$), which contributed to a later decision to discard mass media exposure from the final analyses.[10]

Social Participation Variables

To measure membership and involvement in voluntary interest associations, an Association Participation Index was constructed by giving a respondent one point for each organization to which he or she belonged, a second point for regularly attending at least half the meetings, and a third point for ever having held a leadership position in the organization. This measure correlates fairly strongly with party participation, at $r = .34$.[11]

Three items were examined as indicators of community involvement, but only one of these was related to party participation: (a) the coefficient for length of residency in the community is very weak and becomes nonsignificant when age is held constant; (b) the coefficient for home ownership (owning or buying versus renting) is nonsignificant; but (c) a Community Activities Index, measuring frequency of participation in community public events, is moderately related to party involvement at $r = .24$. Taken together, the two variables of association participation and community activities produce a multiple $R = .34$ with party participation, which is identical to the coefficient for association participation alone. Hence these two social participation measures were kept as separate variables for further analyses.

Civic Orientations Variables

Following the lead of Verba and Nie (1972:133–36), three variables were used to operationalize this theoretical argument: (a) a Political Interest Index based on questions about degree of interest in local, state, national, and international political affairs; (b) a Party Identification Index, based on whether or not one identified with a political party at both

---

10. A combined Communications Index was constructed by combining the Mass Media Exposure and Partisan Contacts indexes. It was not utilized in the analysis, however, because its correlation with party participation was only $r = .38$, which is lower than the figure for partisan contacts of $r = .39$.

11. Analyses were also made with the separate measures of number of associational memberships, number of associations attended regularly, and number of associations in which the person had ever held a position. All three of these measures were significantly related to party participation (number of memberships $= .25$, number attend $= .20$, number of positions $= .29$), but not as strongly as the combined Associational Participation Index.

the local and national levels, and whether or not one perceived any issue or ideological differences between the two major parties; and (c) Political Efficacy, measured with the standard Campbell (Campbell et al., 1954) efficacy scale. Political interest has by far the strongest relationship with party participation, at $r = .39$; party identification ranks second in strength, with $r = .24$; while the figure for political efficacy is only $r = .17$. Rather interestingly, although both party identification and political efficacy are related to political interest (with r's of .33 and .30, respectively), identification and efficacy are totally unrelated to one another. When all three are combined in a multiple regression with party participation, both party identification and political interest continue to have independent predictive effects, but the partial coefficient for political efficacy become nonsignificant. Consequently, political efficacy was discarded from the analysis at this point. Taken together, political interest and party identification produce a multiple $R = .41$ with party participation, but for theoretical reasons explained below they were retained as separate variables for inclusion in the path model.

Multivariate Analysis

Statistical Controls

Since one's age and education might potentially affect many of his or her other activities, the effects of all the other predictor variables were next reexamined while holding constant these two basic factors. With a few exceptions, the resulting partial betas were identical to, or only slightly lower than, the original zero-order coefficients. In particular, controlling education does not significantly diminish the relationships for either of the communication variables, which indicates that the political communication thesis is applicable regardless of one's educational level. Conversely, holding constant the Partisan Contacts Index completely eliminates the relationships between education and party participation, suggesting that amount of education may have no direct effects on one's party activities. The most interesting finding to emerge from this analysis, however, concerns the effects of age and education on each other. Since these two factors are inversely related at $r = -.24$, holding constant either one strengthens the effects of the other on party participation, so that their partial betas are both raised to .20 (from .17 for age and .15 for education). In other words, older, well educated people are particularly likely to take part in party affairs, while younger, poorly educated people are quite likely to avoid political parties.

Because of the recurrent debate in the literature over the relative importance of socioeconomic status versus voluntary association participation in explaining political participation (Alford, 1968; Erbe, 1964), the next step in the analysis was to examine the partial relationship of each of these factors with party participation while controlling the other. The results are unequivocal. Regardless of whether education, occupation, income, or any combination of these variables is taken as an indicator of socioeconomic status, holding status constant has relatively little effect on the relationship between association and party participation. (For example, the partial beta for association participation, controlling education, remains .34, and when occupation and income are simultaneously controlled, it is still .30.) In contrast, controlling association participation reduces the relationships for all of the status variables to nonsignificance. The same results occur when community activities is substituted for association participation.

Multiple Regression

Let us now bring all the relevant predictor variables — age, parents' political activities, education, socioeconomic status, media exposure, partisan messages, association participation, community activities, political interest, and party identification — together in a single multiple regression with party participation. Several interesting findings result from this analysis: (a) Both age (beta = .14) and parents' activities (beta = .11) continue to have some — though not great — direct effects on party participation, independent of all other factors. (b) The coefficients for both education (beta = $-.08$) and socioeconomic status (beta = $-.10$) become negative, suggesting that if all else is equal, people with little education, low-status jobs, and small incomes are as likely or even more likely than others to become involved in party activities. These findings are in direct opposition to the predictions of all previous theorizing, and seriously question the usefulness of the "standard socioeconomic model" that underlies all of Verba and Nie's (1972:125–37) analyses. (c) Mass-media exposure has no significant net effects on party participation, but partisan contacts (beta = .17) does have moderate direct effects. (d) Community activities also become nonsignificant in this analysis, but association participation continues to have noteworthy net effects (beta = .20). (e) Party identification is now nonsignificant, but political interest still displays a moderately strong relationship (beta = .20) with party participation.

Looking at these findings from the perspective of our six theoretical arguments, the social participation and civic orientations theses appear to have equal explanatory power in regard to party participation, with direct effects of .20 in both cases. The political communication argument is also clearly valid, although its direct effects of .17 are not quite as strong. The political socialization thesis also remains relevant, but with very weak (.11) direct effects. The intellectual stimulation and socio-economic influence theses are apparently invalid, however, since their empirical indicators have negative rather than positive direct effects on party involvement. Taken together, all ten predictor variables produce a multiple $R = .55$ with the Party Participation Index, so that they are explaining 30 percent of the variance in this index. The variables of age, partisan contacts, association participation, and political interest contribute most of the explanatory power, however, since these four factors alone produce an $R = .53$.

Path Model

As a means of exploring the interrelationships among the various pre-dictor variables that presumably influence party involvement, our next step is to design and analyze a causal path model of political party participation. The particular pattern of causal relationships proposed here is only one of many possible models that might be constructed with these variables, but it is the most theoretically meaningful pattern in terms of causal effects among the component variables. Path analysis will not prove or disprove the validity of the overall model, but it will reveal how strongly each predictor variable affects all other variables located subsequent to it in the model.

The proposed path model is shown in Figure 7.1. Table 7.1 gives the matrices of both (a) zero-order correlation coefficients among all the variables in the model (above the diagonal); and (b) partial standardized beta coefficients obtained through least squares regression analyses (below the diagonal) for this model. All coefficients reported here are statistically significant at $p < .05$.

To construct this model, the three factors of parents' political activities, age, and education were first designated as exogenous variables, since all of them are determined early in one's life and are not affected by any other variables in the model (except for the occasional adult who returns to school as a regular student). Party identification and socioeconomic status were then taken as the initial endogenous variables. Most people form their

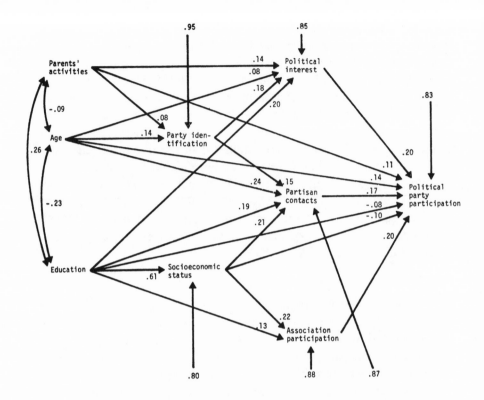

Figure 7.1.   Path Model of Political Party Participation

party identification relatively early in life and do not readily alter it (Knoke, 1972). Socioeconomic status, meanwhile, is highly influenced by factors in one's past life history — such as father's occupation and one's educational attainment (Blau and Duncan, 1967) — and also remain relatively stable through time. These two variables can be affected, however, by one's parents' political activities or by one's age or education.

The two variables of mass-media exposure and community activities were discarded from the model after preliminary attempts to include them revealed that (a) neither factor had any direct effects on party participation, and (b) except for a moderate-sized linkage between them (beta = .18), neither factor had any notable effects on any other variables in the model.

The remaining three variables of partisan contacts, association participation, and political interest then constitute a set of "immediate" or

Table 7.1
Zero-Order and Path Coefficients Among All Variables (*r*'s above the diagonal and betas below)

Variables	Parents' Political Activities	Age	Education	Socio-economic Status	Party Identi-fication	Partisan Contacts	Association Participation	Political Interest
Parents activities	—	-.09	.26	.22	.08	.25	.17	.32
Age	*	—	-.23	-.08	.14	.17	NS	NS
Education	*	*	—	.60	.12	.27	.39	.35
Socioeconomic status	*	NS	.61	—	.10	.31	.41	.31
Party identification	NS	.14	NS	NS	—	.24	.14	.31
Partisan contacts	*	.24	.19	.21	.15	—	.31	.35
Association participation	*	NS	.13	.22	*	.12	—	.26
Political interest	.14	.08	.20	NS	.18	.13	NS	—
Political Party Participation Index								
r	.27	.17	.15	.15	.24	.39	.34	.39
Direct effects	.11	.14	-.08	-.10	NS	.17	.20	.20
Indirect effects	.03	.06	.09	.08	.06	—	—	—
Total effects	.14	.20	.01	-.02	.06	.17	.20	.20

* = Not theoretically meaningful
NS = Not statistically significant

"current" endogenous variables in the model. Since there are no temporal grounds for specifying causal sequence among them, let us assume that they all occur at the present time and constitute a single "block" of variables within the path model. We can then analyze the model in three different ways, taking each of these "current" variables in turn as the last factor leading to party participation and regressing it on all the other variables in the model.

Nine features of this model are especially noteworthy. First, the three alternative analyses of the block of current variables revealed that no path exists between association participation and political interest. Regardless of which factor is taken as the final dependent variable in the model, the beta for the path leading from the other one is nonsignificant and negative ($-.03$ in both cases). This finding suggests the proposition that there are at least two relatively distinct routes through which people become involved in political parties: (a) they may become interested in politics, which *motivates* them to take part in party activities, or (b) they may become involved in voluntary associations, which *mobilizes* them for party involvement. Expressed differently, the dynamic process in the political interest route is an internal motivational "push," whereas the crucial process in the associational route is an external social "pull." Both political interest and association participation have identical paths of beta = .20 to party participation, it may be recalled, but neither factor leads to the other. Some people may follow both these routes, of course, and hence be doubly likely to participate in party affairs. (The sixty-six respondents who scored in the top third of the distributions on both variables have a mean party participation score of 1.52, compared to .24 for those in the bottom third of both distributions.) The critical point, however, is that these two routes to party involvement appear to operate independently of each other.

Second, partisan contacts have weak linkages with both association and participation (.13) and political interest (.12) when it is taken as the final variable in the model. These paths are not included in the path model in Figure 7.1, however, because the direction of the causation is not clear in either case. Since partisan contacts also have direct effects of beta = .17 on party participation, it apparently provides a third (but not independent) route through which people can become involved in political parties. In this case, individuals are *attracted* to partisan issues and party activities as a result of direct contacts by a party. This attraction may either lead directly to party participation, or it may interact with political interest and/or association involvement and thus indirectly affect party participation.

Third, as noted previously, party identification has no direct effects on party participation, but it does affect both political interest (a logical expectation) and partisan contacts (since party mailings and visitors usually go only to those people who have previously indicated a preference for that party). Political party identification is not related to either socioeconomic status or education, however.

Fourth, as also noted previously, socioeconomic status has negative effects (beta = $-.10$) on party participation, but has moderate positive effects on both partisan contacts (beta = $.21$) and association participation (beta = $.22$). The former relationship is probably due to the fact that higher status people are better known to party workers, while the latter relationship occurs because higher status people are generally more active than others in voluntary associations.

Fifth, the effects of parents' political activities on both party identification (beta = $.08$) and political interest (beta = $.14$) are rather small, as are also its direct effects on party participation (beta = $.11$). This finding suggests that the political socialization process has rather minimal long-term effects on several kinds of political participation.

Sixth, in addition to the direct effects of age on party participation (beta = $.14$), it has minor effects on party identification (beta = $.14$) and political interest (beta = $.08$), and considerably larger effects on partisan contacts (beta = $.24$). The last relationship is probably due to the fact that older people are likely to have lived in the community longer and hence be known to party workers.

Seventh, although education has small negative effects on party participation (beta = $-.08$), it has very strong effects on socioeconomic status (beta = $.61$) and moderate effects on political interest (beta = $.20$), partisan contacts (beta = $.19$), and association participation (beta = $.13$). Amount of education thus acts as a common starting point for all three of the possible routes to party involvement — motivation through political interest, mobilization through voluntary associations, or attraction through party contacts.

At the bottom of Table 7.1, in addition to the zero-order r's for each predictor variable with party participation, is reported the sum of the indirect effects that each variable exerts on party participation through all the other variables. These indirect effects of a variable, when added to its direct effects, together comprise its total effects on party participation.[12] Two additional findings emerge from this final analysis.

Eighth, the total effects of age (.20) are as large as the direct effects of both political interest and association participation. The reason for this is not readily apparent, although it might be due either to a general maturation process that leads older persons to become more concerned about public affairs, or simply the fact that older people without small children and with established careers have more free time and resources for politics.

Ninth, both education and socioeconomic status have noticeable indirect positive effects on party participation via their paths to partisan contacts and association participation, but these are offset by their negative direct effects, so that the total effects of both factors on party involvement are practically zero.

Discussion and Conclusions

Returning to the six theoretical arguments concerning why people participate in party affairs, the results of this study indicate that:

1. The political socialization thesis is relevant, but the effects of this process on adult party participation are rather minimal.

2. The intellectual sophistication argument, with its stress on education, is irrelevant except insofar as education provides a common starting point for all three alternative routes to participation in political party activity.

3. The socioeconomic influence explanation is either irrelevant or perhaps inverted as far as direct effects on involvement in parties is concerned.

4. The political communication thesis is relevant in terms of receiving partisan messages but not in terms of exposure to the mass media.

5. The social participation theory is clearly relevant and crucial in respect to voluntary association participation, which tends to mobilize people for political party involvement regardless of their interest in politics, but involvement in community affairs plays only a very minor role in this process.

6. The civic orientations argument is also relevant and important, since strong interest in political affairs tends to motivate individuals to par-

---

12. Indirect effects through linkages between partisan contacts and political interest and association participation are not included in these computations, because of the questionable causal nature of these two paths.

ticipate in party activities, but other orientations such as identification with a party or feelings of political efficacy have few or no effects on party participation.

From the perspective of practical application, these findings suggest that if party officials desire to involve more of their supporters in party activities as attenders, workers, or perhaps even leaders, they can adopt any of three tactics. First, they can attempt to increase people's interest in politics. This approach is seriously limited, however, by the fact that two principal determinants of political interest — the political involvement of one's parents and one's amount of education — have already transpired and cannot be altered. Second, they can follow the traditional practices of mailing out party literature and sending out party workers to talk with people in their homes. This direct contact does increase party involvement somewhat, in contrast to impersonal mass media communications, which do not. A third tactic is to encourage people to join and take part in all kinds of voluntary associations, regardless of whether or not these organizations have any concern with politics, and then to look for potential party activists among these organizational participants. Both of the latter two approaches will operate regardless of one's parents' activities or one's age or education, although they do involve a socioeconomic bias in that higher-status people are more likely than others to receive party messages and to participate in voluntary associations. In brief, people can be either motivated, attracted, or mobilized toward participating in political parties.

8. Organizational
Mediation Processes

The analyses of individual political participation in chapters 3 to 7 were concerned with the social factors that lead individuals to become involved in political activity in democratic societies. The theoretical focus of these chapters was the social mobilization thesis, as derived from the mobilization version of pluralist theory.

In this and the following chapter, we shift the level of analysis from individuals to organizations — particularly voluntary interest associations — as units of analysis. Our theoretical emphasis, consequently, becomes the mediation version of pluralist theory. From this perspective, the primary function of voluntary interest associations for political democracy is to act as influence channels between citizens and the government (Baskin, 1971; Dahl, 1956; Nisbet, 1962). In addition to participating directly in the political system, citizens can also indirectly influence political decisions by working through interest associations that in turn exert pressures on political leaders.

With effective sociopolitical pluralism, interest associations enact a mediating role in political processes, simultaneously (a) providing an organized route through which individuals can exert influence upward on political leaders, and (b) giving leaders an established means through which they can reach downward to large numbers of constituents

Portions of this chapter are reprinted by permission from Marvin E. Olsen, "Interest Association Participation and Political Activity," *Journal of Voluntary Action Research*, vol. 4, Fall 1974, pp. 17–33.

(Kornhauser, 1959). Political parties and other politically oriented organizations obviously perform this role much of the time, but pluralistic theory also insists that nonpolitical interest associations must at least occasionally become parapolitical actors, participating as organizations in the political system when issues involving their areas of special interest and competency are involved.

This chapter examines three basic criticisms that are frequently made of the mediation process. Although the mediation version of sociopolitical pluralism is admittedly an ideal model that no existing society presently achieves, these three criticisms strike at the heart of the theory and raise serious questions about its usefulness as a means of attaining participatory democracy. The chapter also presents some limited empirical data—drawn from the Indianapolis and Gävle surveys—that are relevant to the first two criticisms. In addition, it describes the set of organizational influence procedures through which Sweden attempts to deal with the third—and perhaps most critical—of these problems. The following chapter then analyzes the effectiveness of this Swedish system of organizational influence processes.

Political Activity within Organizations

As we saw in chapter 5, many people in both the United States and Sweden do not belong to any voluntary interest organization, and a large proportion of those who do belong are merely nominal members who do not participate at all actively in their organization(s). To the extent that this occurs, the entire mediation process breaks down at the very start. If people do not participate in such associations, they obviously cannot use these organizations as vehicles for exerting influence on the government. Even if the organizations are active in the political arena, they are at best representing only what their leaders believe to be the interests of their members or the general public, and at worst they are representing only the interests of the leaders themselves.

The first criticism of the mediation process begins by noting the relatively low levels of organizational involvement that occur in all societies, which negates the assumption of sociopolitical pluralism that most citizens will be active members of at least one interest association—and preferably two or more, to allow for crosscutting linkages. In addition, it questions the extent to which nonpolitical interest associations ever take any political actions. If these organizations fail to at least occasionally pursue their interests within the arena of politics, they cannot function as vehicles for exerting political influence. Finally, this criticism also points out that, even when interest associations are politically active, very few of their members actually participate in these activities. To the extent that these latter two arguments are valid, the political mediation process as envisioned by the proponents of sociopolitical pluralism is clearly a failure.

Previous Research

Despite widespread acceptance of pluralistic theory as an ideal model, there have been very few attempts to determine empirically how extensively interest associations actually become involved in politics. The available evidence suggests, however, that most associations rarely take any political actions. Typical of the few existing studies on this topic is Robert Presthus's (1964:264–78) investigation of decision making in two small New York towns. His sample of interest organizations was admittedly biased, since he picked those most likely to take such political actions as passing a resolution concerning a public issue, forming a committee to work on an issue, or committing organizational funds or other resources to an issue. Nevertheless, of the fifty-two organizations studied, only twenty-one had taken any such actions on any of ten recent community issues, and only three of them had been active on more than one issue. He concluded that "most community organizations in our sample are relatively passive as measured by their participation in the ten critical decisions," and he speculated that one reason for this may be that "voluntary organizations . . . often have interests that are too specialized and resources that are too limited to encourage direct participation in large-scale, community-wide decisions."

Organizational Political Actions

For additional data on this issue, let us inquire into the extent to which respondents in both the Indianapolis and Gävle surveys belonged to interest associations that were politically active. For the most part the data consist of respondents' reports of the political actions of their associations, so that we are in fact measuring their perceptions or awareness of such events, not objective rates of organizational actions. Since most members are not likely to be aware of everything their associations actually do, their reports are undoubtedly incomplete. Nevertheless, it can be argued that, if members are not aware of whatever political actions their interest associations are pursuing, these organizations are not acting as political influence channels for these members. The fact that organizational leaders may be taking political actions in the name of the organization does not necessarily mean that these interest associations are fulfilling a political mediation role.

We begin this analysis by noting that only a small minority of the respondents in either study belonged to political parties or other overtly political organizations. Party membership has no precise meaning in the United States, but if we consider donating money two or more times to be an indication of party involvement, only 14 percent of the Indianapolis respondents can be described as party supporters. When sample members in Gävle were asked directly whether they belonged to a political party, just 8 percent said yes — although this figure is probably inaccurate, since membership in most blue-collar unions in Sweden automatically enrolls one in the Social Democratic party, unless one specifically refuses membership. Other political organizations, meanwhile, enroll only 3 percent of the respondents in Indianapolis and 1 percent in Gävle.

Pluralistic theory insists, however, that all kinds of nonpolitical associations can — and must — at least occasionally enact the role of influence mediator between individuals and political leaders. Let us therefore determine how commonly this occurs in both communities.

The respondents in the Indianapolis study were asked if, in their memory, the interest associations to which they belonged had ever engaged in any kind of political action such as taking a stand on a political issue or trying to influence a political decision. Of the 1,013 nonpolitical associations to which these respondents belonged, only 18 percent (180) had ever — within the memories of the respondents — engaged in any kind of political action. Moreover, when the respondents were asked how often their politically active associations had taken such actions, they responded that more than two-thirds of these organizations (13 percent of the total) had been politically active only once, so that just 5 percent of all the interest associations to which these respondents belonged were reported to have been politically active two or more times.

In Gävle, the respondents belonged to 632 nonpolitical associations, of which they identified 25 percent (158) as ever having taken a political action. Three-fourths of these organizations (19 percent of the total) had been active only once within the memories of the respondents, so that just 7 percent of the interest associations of these Swedish respondents were known to have taken two or more political actions. In general, however, it is clear that in neither community do interest associations enter the political arena to any great extent.

Whether or not these levels of political activity by interest associations negate the theory of sociopolitical pluralism depends, of course, on how frequently they are expected to be politically active. Pluralist theory says nothing on this point beyond the general expectation that organizations will take political action whenever their particular interests or concerns are involved. Hence any assessment of the adequacy of an association's political actions should compare this rate to the frequency of occurrence of relevant issues — however they are defined by the organization. Taking the observed actions as the numerator of a proportion and the number of relevant issues as the denominator, we might then calculate a political involvement ratio for that interest association. How high must this ratio be for pluralism to operate effectively? To expect 100 percent involvement would be quite idealistic, but clearly a ratio of only 10 percent would be inadequate from the pluralistic perspective. Might we quite arbitrarily expect interest associations to take political actions in at least two-thirds of the issues that concern them if the pluralistic mediation process is to remain viable? By this criterion, sociopolitical pluralism is not functioning very adequately in either Indianapolis or Gävle.

Member Involvement in Political Actions

A more stringent approach to measuring the pluralist mediation process is to ask what proportion of association members have ever personally participated in the political actions of their organizations.

In Indianapolis, merely 6 percent of the respondents said they had ever taken part in any kind of political activity within any nonpolitical associations to which they belonged, with half of these people saying that they had done this once and half saying more than once. These low percentages are largely due, obviously, to the fact that so few organizations ever do anything political and hence never give their members a chance to become politically involved. Nevertheless, of those persons who did belong to an organization that they knew had been politically active, only 37 percent had themselves participated in such an activity. This low rate of involvement cannot be attributed to ideological factors, since 93 percent of these people viewed the political actions of their association(s) as legitimate organizational activities, and 82 percent of them said they agreed with the political position(s) taken by their association(s). Hence we can only conclude that a large majority of organizational members are not sufficiently concerned to become personally involved in political matters within their nonpolitical interest associations, even when opportunities to do this are available.[1]

Much the same situation occurs in Gävle, where 8 percent of the respondents reported some personal involvement in organizational political activities, and only one-fourth of these people had done so more than once. Among members of politically active organizations, just 32 percent said they had participated in these actions.[2] Thus we see that, although political activity is slightly more common among Swedish than among American interest associations, Swedes who belong to politically active organizations are less likely than American members of active organizations to become personally involved in these political activities.

The final step in this analysis is to determine whether political action is more common in some types of associations than others. As seen in the two left-handed columns of Table 8.1, differences do occur among the six categories of nonpolitical interest associations, but the patterns are quite similar in both communities.

Unions are most likely to engage in political actions in both Indianapolis and Gävle — although the relatively lower figure for Gävle may be due to ignorance among the respondents, since almost all unions in Sweden do in fact take public (not necessarily partisan) stands on many issues. The second highest rate of political activity in both communities occurs among business and professional associations, which share with unions an instrumental concern with the economic system. Next in this ranking of political activity in both communities come fraternal, veterans', and similar associations, whose concerns with promoting their members' special interests might frequently involve them in politics. Not surprisingly, educational, welfare, and similar organizations are rather unlikely to take political actions, while recreational/sports and church-related groups avoid politics almost entirely. The two right-hand columns of the table, finally, show the percentage of all members of the organizations within each category who

---

1. Personal involvement in political activities within interest associations in Indianapolis was relatively unrelated to the sociodemographic characteristics of the members. The only significant relationships were weak correlations with education ($r = .10$), occupation ($r = .09$), and income ($r = .07$), plus a slight tendency for political involvement to be most common among people in the fifty to fifty-nine age bracket.

2. The only significant relationship between personal involvement in organizational political activities and any sociodemographic characteristics in Gävle was a tendency for men to be more involved than women ($r = .28$).

Table 8.1
Organizational Political Actions and Member Involvement in Them within Six Categories of Nonpolitical Interest Associations in Indianapolis and Gävle

Categories of Interest Associations	Organizational Political Actions—% of Members Who Say That Their Association Has Ever Taken Any Kind of Political Actions		Individual Participation in Organizational Political Actions —% of Members Who Have Ever Taken Part in Any Such Actions		Number of Members	
	Indianapolis	Gävle	Indianapolis	Gävle	Indianapolis	Gävle
Union	42%	31%	5%	10%	130	229
Business, etc.	31	28	8	6	88	93
Educational, etc.	13	11	4	4	220	80
Fraternal, etc.	23	18	7	7	159	28
Recreational, etc.	4	6	2	2	160	105
Church related	5	8	3	8	78	12

have personally participated in political activities within these organizations. These figures are uniformly low across all types of interest associations in both communities, telling us that personal involvement in organizational political actions is relatively rare in both communities.

On the basis of both the Indianapolis and Gävle data, therefore, we are led to conclude that the first criticism of the pluralist mediation model has considerable validity. Political activity by interest associations is not a common practice in either community, and the fraction of the population that attempts to use these organizations as channels for exerting influence on the political system is almost minute in both cases. Interest associations are not functioning as influence mediators for citizens in either community.

Internal Organizational Oligarchy

The second criticism of the pluralistic mediation model argues that, even if individuals do actively participate in interest organizations that attempt to exert influence on government, most ordinary members find it impossible to have any significant effects on the policies or actions of their organizations. If an organization is large and powerful enough to be capable of exerting influence in the political arena, it is almost certain to have a hierarchial authority structure and to be largely or entirely controlled by a small set of elites—or oligarchy—occupying the top positions in this structure. Consequently, most members cannot use these organizations as vehicles for making their own interests and preferences known to political leaders. At best, therefore, pluralism exists only to the minimal extent of organizational elites competing with one another and attempting to promote their own special interests. This pattern of pluralistic elitism may prevent the government from becoming overly monolithic, but in no way does it promote participatory democracy.

The "Iron Law of Oligarchy"

The classical study of internal organizational oligarchy is Robert Michels's (1966) analysis of the German Social Democratic party at the beginning of the twentieth century. He reasoned that, if internal participatory democracy was at all possible in large organizations, it should occur in those parties that were thoroughly dedicated to democratic principles in their own functioning as well as throughout the total society.

His research revealed, however, that in reality these organizations were highly oligarchic, from which he concluded that oligarchy is inevitable in all large and complex organizations: "Who says organization, says oligarchy" (Michels, 1966:365).

Among the many reasons Michels offered to explain this tendency toward oligarchy are the following:

1. Large size and an elaborate division of labor within an organization necessitate centralized coordination and control if the organization is to function effectively and achieve its goals.

2. Collective decision making on complex organizational matters can only be accomplished with speed and efficiency by a small set of elites.

3. Incumbents of leadership positions tend to become functionally indispensable as they develop skills and experience in running the organization, so that other members feel they cannot afford to vote them out of office.

4. Over time, leaders build up legitimate rights to their offices and extensive webs of interpersonal influence, both of which further increase their power in the organization.

5. Through continued performance of their leadership functions, elites acquire dominant control over organizational finances, communications, disciplinary agencies, and other internal activities, all of which they can then use to their own advantage.

6. Elites are normally more unified than other members, and hence can effectively thwart or absorb (coopt) potential challengers to their authority positions.

7. Most rank-and-file members tend to be indifferent and apathetic toward the organization and its activities and are only too happy most of the time to leave the problems of leadership to those who are willing to assume them.

The "iron law of oligarchy" may not be quite as inescapable as Michels presumed, but it is a serious problem with which all large interest organizations must contend. This tendency is perhaps most critical in highly centralized and bureaucratized organizations, but it also plagues those with more decentralized authority structures if the power of top administrators is not severely restricted. To the extent that oligarchy prevails in any organization, it negates the fundamental influence-mediation process upon which the pluralistic model rests.

The Swedish Consumers' Cooperative Movement

To test Michels's thesis in a contemporary Swedish setting, Gail Garinger (1968) examined the Swedish Consumers' Cooperative Movement. This organizational network consists of approximately two hundred fifty local consumer cooperative associations which are organized into twenty-four regional organizations and a national Cooperative Federation (Kooperative Förbundet, or K.F.). The total movement has over a million and a half members representing about half the households in Sweden, and in terms of total sales it ranks as the largest business enterprise in the country.

From its inception over one hundred years ago, the movement has been strongly dedicated to the principle of membership control, and each local association holds an annual meeting at which members (or their elected representatives) formulate basic policies and elect representatives to the regional and national governing bodies. In the words of Nils Elvander (1966:78), "No popular movement has devoted so much attention to the problem of the participation of its members as has the Consumer's Cooperative Movement."

The ideal of membership participation and control has continually clashed with the utilitarian requirement of economic efficiency within the movement, however. As it grew in size and attempted to compete more effectively with private businesses, its goals moved steadily away from popular involvement toward operational efficiency, so that most members today regard the movement as nothing more than an economic enterprise. As described by Elvander:

> Most persons today join a cooperative society simply because they reside near a cooperative store and because they wish to take advantage of the low prices and the annual dividend; they are totally uninterested in the cooperative ideology and never attend any meetings. [1966:80]

One of the respondents in Garinger's study (the Education Director for K.F.), meanwhile, remarked that

> The time is past when members went to the meetings to tell the representatives their personal desires, etc. Likewise, there was a time when the members actually worked for the movement. However, today a much greater precision is required. Therefore, we need an administrative body that takes over these tasks. This is what is meant by efficiency.

Unfortunately, it has brought about a shift from direct to indirect to perhaps no democracy.

To achieve administrative and economic efficiency, responsibility for directing and operating the cooperative movement has been steadily shifted from the local associations to the national organization (K.F.), which is largely controlled by a board of full-time paid directors. Moreover, during the past twenty years K.F. — while not formally aligned with the ruling Social Democratic party — has become directly involved in numerous governmental actions and programs. The result has been that fewer and fewer people are involved in making decisions and establishing policies for the total cooperative movement. The following statements by two respondents in this study express that fact quite pointedly:

> There are only some — an elite — who can understand the organization's business — who can control the complexity of the organization's affairs.
> We say that the members are to make the decision, but sometimes this isn't the case. It is a dictatorship instead.

An outside observer, Wilfred Fleisher, is even more despairing of the fate of democracy in the movement:

> The leadership is in the hands of seven top directors. They are the real "bosses" of the Cooperative Movement. They direct its business, determine its growth, and plan its future. They themselves would deny it. . . . They would stress that the movement was built from the bottom up and that they are trustees for the cooperative rather than leaders of the movement. But the fact is that the Cooperative Movement, like all big business enterprises, is run from the top down and that the "Big Seven," who sit on the Board of Directors, are the driving power in the movement. [1956:81]

Garinger concluded her study with the following observation:

> The Consumers' Cooperative Movement, an organization with two not entirely compatible goals, has increasingly over time chosen as its primary goal the achievement of material gains for members. The normative involvement of leaders has shifted from a concern with participatory democracy to a concern with economic efficiency. These

shifts have been evident in an examination of the goals themselves and in an examination of the power structure of the organization. . . . All of this has spelled a concentration of power in the top of the organization, now an embodiment of the "Iron Law of Oligarchy."

It appears that, if any large organization is to achieve effectively its operational goals — and thus be capable of enacting the pluralistic role of an influence mediator in relation to government — it must invariably be largely or totally controlled by a small set of oligarchical elites.

An Apologetic Argument

Given this pervasive trend toward oligarchy in interest organizations, does it not negate any possibility of realizing the pluralist mediation model? The answer to that question depends largely on one's conception of pluralism. If one's concern is only to establish a check on the power of central government by enabling interest organizations to influence political decisions, then the existence of oligarchy within those organizations is irrelevant. In fact, it may even be beneficial, since a highly centralized organization will generally be more capable than a relatively decentralized one of acting readily, decisively, and forcefully within the political arena. As expressed by Seymour Martin Lipset (1959:431):

> Institutionalized democracy within private governments is not a necessary condition for democracy in the larger society, and may in fact at times weaken the democratic process of civil society. The various secondary associations independent of the state which Tocqueville saw as necessary conditions of a democratic nation have been in both his day and ours largely one-party oligarchies.

Conversely, according to this argument, control of an organization by members who are promoting their own particular interests may severely limit the operational flexibility of the organization and its ability to bargain and compromise with other organizations in the political process:

> Integration of members within a trade-union, a political party, a farm organization, a professional society, may increase the chances that members of such organizations will be active in the group and have more control over its politics. But extending the functions of such organizations so as to integrate their members may threaten the larger political system because it reduces the forces making for compromise and understanding among conflicting groups. [Lipset, 1959:433]

This apology for oligarchy, as formulated by Lipset and accepted by Presthus (1964) and others, in effect reduces the pluralistic model to the notion of "pluralistic elitism" as propounded by Dahl (1956). These theorists are content to label a political system as pluralistic — and democratic — provided only that all political decision-making power is not concentrated in the hands of a single, small set of dominant elites. In short, they equate pluralism and democracy with an established set of political checks and balances between government and private-interest organizations.

This entire argument crumbles, however, if one conceives of pluralism as a mediation process through which citizens utilize their interest organizations as channels for exerting influence on the government. From this perspective, internal organizational oligarchy thoroughly negates any possibility of realizing the pluralist ideal of popular democracy, for the bulk of ordinary members will then find it impossible to make their voices heard even within their own organizations, let alone in the national political arena.

Organizational Influence on Government

The third criticism of the pluralist mediation model asserts that, even if individuals participate in and control their interest associations, most such organizations are incapable of performing an effective mediating role between citizens and the government. With a few notable exceptions, private-interest organizations are quite weak politically in relation to the national government and hence cannot normally exert significant influence on national decision making. This theme has been expressed in several different ways, as seen in the following three arguments.

The Power Elite Argument

Numerous social critics, following the lead of C. Wright Mills (1956), have maintained that contemporary industrialized-bureaucratized societies such as the United States and Sweden are dominated by a small but extremely powerful elite class. We will briefly examine Mills's original thesis, even though many other writers, such as William Domhoff (1970), Ralph Miliband (1969), and Roland Huntford (1971), have added subtle variations to his central theme. The U.S. "military-industrial-political" complex, according to Mills, is becoming increasingly unified through functionally interdependent relationships, interpersonal linkages and career mobility routes, and a common set of cultural values and ideologies.

As its resources and functional importance for society have steadily expanded, this elite class has extended its lines of influence and control throughout society. Consequently, the "middle levels of power" — in which Mills placed most interest organizations — have steadily diminished in influence on the national scene. Although they may still appear to be carrying out the "pluralist game" of political debate and compromise, these middle-level political actors are dealing only with minor technical and procedural details, not basic policies, which are largely determined by the power elite outside the political system. Indeed, argued Mills, intermediate organizations are steadily being coopted by the power elite to carry out its policies and programs.

Many aspects of Mills' work have been severely criticized, especially his failure to demonstrate convincingly that national economic, political, and military elites are indeed closely unified into a single "ruling class," and that the "middle levels" no longer exercise significant power in American society. In both cases, he presented virtually no empirical evidence to substantiate his critical charges, so that they remain merely speculative hypotheses, not verified conclusions.

Regardless of the applicability of Mills' charges to the United States at the present time, however, he has pointed to a potentially serious limitation to pluralistic theory. To the extent that there is a tendency in contemporary societies for sociopolitical power to become increasingly centralized — for whatever reasons and in whatever forms — does not this trend reduce interest organizations to mere pawns of the ruling class? The answer to this question remains evasive; the charge may be valid, but not necessarily so. Growth in the amount of power being exerted at the "center" of society does not necessarily imply diminution of power throughout the rest of society. All parts of the total power system could be growing concurrently, so that both the central elites and interest organizations might be expanding their power capabilities. Quite clearly, extreme concentration of power in the hands of a few elites would eliminate pluralism, but on the other hand a society could remain pluralistic while experiencing rapid and enormous growths of governmental power. The key factor here is the ability of special-interest organizations to mediate between individual members and the national government, serving as a vehicle through which people could collectively influence political decisions and policies. And that in turn would depend considerably on the manner in which these organizations interacted with the government.

The Influence Leverages Argument

This second argument has also been discussed by several writers, but we shall draw on V. O. Key, Jr. (1963), who presented the case quite cogently. What kinds of power resources can private, special-interest organizations possibly command that would begin to compare with those of the national government, and hence provide adequate leverages for exerting meaningful influence on national political decisions? Conversely, what assurance does pluralist theory offer that governmental leaders will respond (or even listen) to private interest associations? Ideally, organizational leaders could commit or threaten to withhold the votes of their members as a means of exerting influence on politicians, but in practice this is rarely possible.

> Most pressure organizations as they deal with the government . . . gain not the slightest leverage from the vote of their members. Even if the votes could be delivered, they are too few to have an effect one way or another. . . . Mass-membership organizations may have within their circles millions of voters; yet data on the way people behave in their voting make it plain that a theory of standing alliance with parties and politicians more nearly explains the electoral basis of group strength than does a theory of intimidation by group threats to move their members one way or another come the next elections. [Key, 1963:519]

To explain why politicians at least sometimes listen to organizational leaders, Key suggests that two factors may be operating: (a) Governmental consultation with organizations is a traditional ritual that the public expects the government to perform, and which politicians therefore carry out to avoid the possibility of being labeled as "biased" or "autocratic." In short, these consultations are just a meaningless ritual to placate the public. (b) Through this process of consultation, politicians ensure that organizational leaders will not at a later time become too critical (at least in public) of the final decision, and will likely even support it enthusiastically since they "helped to shape it." In short, these consultations are a process of cooptation of organizations by the government. If governmental officials consult with organizations for either of these reasons but are not influenced by them, pluralism will exist in form but not in substance.

How, then, can private special-interest organizations make the government take account of their wishes and act on them — at least to some degree some of the time? Key's entire argument rests on the assumption that organizational influence attempts are not particularly desired by politicians, will be resisted as far as possible, and will be heeded only when they cannot be avoided. It also assumes that organizations have neither the legal right to influence political decision making nor any formally established procedures for doing so. But what if the political system of a society explicitly recognized this as a legitimate, legal right (and obligation) of organizations, and provided them with established influence channels leading to the heart of the political decision-making process? Once again, we are led to the crucial importance for pluralism of the procedures through which private organizations interact with the government.

The Political Access Argument

The third of these arguments holds that it is not possible in a pluralistic society for all interest organizations to acquire adequate access to political decision-making processes. As expressed by Joseph Gusfield (1962) and others, some organizations—especially those that challenge the basic structure or legitimacy of the political system—are often excluded from participation in this system. In the contemporary United States, for instance, could groups such as the Black Panthers or the Communist Party ever hope to be seriously consulted by the federal government? Meanwhile, would not many other small or narrowly focused organizations be permanently limited to the role of "veto groups" that could occasionally impede or block adoption of certain public policies but would play no active part in the formation of policies and programs (Riesman et al., 1951:242–54)?

In sharp contrast to these relatively powerless groups, the argument continues, would stand a few giant and immensely powerful organizations representing industrial, business, or other dominant interests in the society. The government might well listen seriously to them and continuously take their interests into consideration when debating legislation, but these organizations represent only the elites of society, not the masses of people. Indeed, their interests might often coincide so closely with those of governmental leaders that they might properly be considered part of the ruling "establishment" or class. Again, some theorists would maintain that such a condition of "pluralistic elites" satisfies the basic requirements of sociopolitical pluralism, but gross inequality would obviously exist among organizations in their influence capabilities.

To the extent that these conditions exist in contemporary societies such as the United States and Sweden, we must seriously question the feasibility of pluralism as a means of democratizing political decision making. If we take seriously the idea that sociopolitical pluralism calls for at least rough equality of opportunity among all social organizations in political processes, extreme organizational-influence inequality must be prevented. Is this possible in contemporary industrial societies? Although pessimists might be inclined to argue "never," there is at least theoretically a way out of this inequality impasse. If procedures could be devised that ensured all organizations — whatever their goals or size — open and equivalent routes for exerting influence on political decision making, then presumably none should be seriously and permanently disadvantaged if they wished to participate. The amount of influence any organization actually exercised might certainly fluctuate considerably through time and over various issues, but the organization would always be guaranteed opportunities for entering the political arena. For the third time, we are confronted with the fact that the viability of sociopolitical pluralism depends on the nature of the relationships between private interest organizations and the government.

Swedish Influence Procedures

The central thrust of the three criticisms of the pluralist mediation model is that, in modern societies, most private-interest organizations are quite weak in relation to the national political system, so that they are normally incapable of performing an effective influence-mediating role between the people and the government. This suggests that the pluralistic model, as commonly envisioned, is seriously incomplete, in that it fails to specify any procedures through which interest organizations might carry out the influence-mediation process. Specification of organizational operating procedures might at first seem to involve us in minor practical details, but without some idea of how organizations are to go about exercising influence on government, pluralist theory remains open to all three facets of this crucial criticism.

To fill this theoretical gap, let us turn to Sweden for an operating example of a complex set of organizational influence procedures.[3] Our purpose in this discussion and the research reported in the following

---

3. Norway and Denmark both have sets of influence procedures that are quite similar to Sweden's, but in both cases these were largely patterned after practices that were first developed in Sweden.

chapter is not to test the total pluralist model, but rather to ask how it might be elaborated in light of the Swedish experience. Most observers of Swedish politics have been highly impressed with the role of private-interest organizations as influence mediators in this system, and they have given considerable attention to the influence mechanisms that presumably bring interest organizations into the center of Swedish political decision making.

Formal Influence Procedures

Unlike the United States, where interest associations are considered to lie entirely outside the formal governmental structure, Sweden has eight relatively formal procedures through which such organizations can interact directly with various governmental organs, thus becoming integral parts of the political system. Briefly, they are as follows:

1. Initiatives (*initiativ*)— initiating questions, requests, or topics to the government for consideration.

2. Planning councils (*planeringsråd*)— having representatives on the policy advisory councils of the various governmental departments.

3. Investigative commissions (*offentliga utredningar*)— having representatives on commissions appointed to investigate problems or issues of public concern, or consulting with these commissions.

4. Commentaries (*remissyttranden*)— submitting written comments on commission reports or proposed legislation.

5. Riksdag membership (*medlemskap i Riksdagen*)— getting organizational leaders or spokesmen elected to the parliament.

6. Riksdag committees (*Riksdags utskott*)— consulting with parliamentary committees in writing or in closed hearings.

7. Administrative agency boards (*styrelser i ämbetsverk*)— having representatives on the governing boards of administrative agencies.

8. Administrative agency consultation (*ämbetsverken*)— consulting directly with operating units of administrative agencies.

Each of these procedures is described in more detail in the following paragraphs.

Initiatives. Of these eight procedures, initiating proposals for new governmental policies or legislation is the least formalized and the most diffuse. Legally, anyone— private individuals, small groups, business firms, municipalities, or political parties, as well as all special-interest organizations— can request the cabinet or a particular department or the Riksdag to consider any topic. At first glance, it may appear that most initiatives originate within governmental departments or administrative agencies, but further investigation often reveals that "the original impulse or demand for reform can often be ultimately traced to the Riksdag, organized interests, or the press. . . ." (Swedish Institute, 1970a). Nils Andrén (1968:181) describes the process this way: A bill may "originate with one or more interested private individuals, a voluntary organization, or a local authority. The matter may be discussed in small groups before it reaches the public through oral presentation to larger groups and through the press. Eventually the discussion has reached such proportions that the matter is ripe for presentation to the Government." Whatever the exact route of this process, however, "taking initiatives to the government" is one means by which interest organizations in Sweden can make their voices heard at the very inception of a political issue.

Planning Councils. During the 1960s, several governmental departments established top-level planning councils to advise the minister and his staff on broad, long-range policy issues. These include the Economic Planning Council, the Industrial Policy Council, the Educational Planning Council, the Environmental Advisory Committee, the Employment Committee, and the Industrial Location Committee. These councils normally include two to four representatives of the major labor-market organizations (i.e., union confederations and employers' and industrial organizations), selected by the departmental minister, not the organizations themselves. This selection practice, plus the limited number of organizational members on the councils and the fact that the councils are solely advisory and have no decision-making power, all severely limit the effectiveness of this procedure as an influence channel for private organizations (Elvander, 1966:203–5). Nevertheless, the councils provide a route through which at least a few of the most powerful organizations can potentially affect basic governmental policies.

Investigative Commissions. Prior to drafting any major legislative proposal, an investigative or royal commission — *utredning* in Swedish, which literally means unraveling or disentangling — is appointed to study the topic thoroughly and submit a written report to the government. In recent years, there have typically been around five hundred commissions at work at any one time, so that "practically all important questions which are brought before Parliament have at one time or another been studied in a royal commission, the report of which is made public well ahead of the bill which is presented to Parliament" (Heckscher, 1958a:166). The thoroughness and extensiveness of this investigative process is illustrated by

Richard Tomasson (1970:24) with this example: "Many of the commissions publish reports of their investigations that run to thousands of pages. For example, the Commission on Higher Education, appointed in 1955, published seven volumes between 1957 and 1963, totalling almost three thousand pages of dense text." Over one hundred commission reports are published annually by the government.

The composition and size of the commissions vary with their tasks, but on important or controversial issues the commission is likely to have ten to fifteen members, including members of the Riksdag (from all four major political parties), representatives from several relevant national organizations (primarily labor-market organizations, but not always), and perhaps individual scientific or technical experts (Vinde, 1971:26). In addition to having their representatives sitting as members of these commissions, interest organizations can also attempt to influence their reports in three other ways: writing letters or sending other documents to the commissions, testifying before their hearings, or requesting to appoint technical experts to work with the commissions as nonvoting consultants. As expressed by Christopher Wheeler (1975:41): "Interest groups place a high priority on gaining access to such commissions in their efforts to influence public policy. At this early stage in the decision-making process, when positions are still highly flexible in many cases, groups have great opportunity for influence."

Commentaries. The Swedish Constitution specifies that all reports of investigative commissions must be submitted to affected governmental agencies for examination and comments (*remissyttranden*), but over the years the practice has developed of including large numbers of interest organizations and local officials in this process. Most of the governmental departments maintain lists of organizations to whom they routinely send requests for comments on commission reports, but any interested individual, group, or association may obtain a copy of any report and submit a commentary on it. This *remiss* process enables all interest organizations, regardless of whether or not they participated in preparing the initial commission report, to examine it, express their reactions to it, and propose minor or major alterations in it (Andrén, 1968:186–87; Vinde, 1971:27–28). "These opportunities for public authorities and interest organizations to make their views known on forthcoming Governmental legislative proposals are widely taken advantage of, which means besides the material contained in the reports, the Government is provided with yet another source of information regarding the reactions of various groups in the society to planned measures" (Meijer, 1969:115).

If these objections are excessively critical, the proposal may be dropped at this point. Otherwise, a formal bill may be prepared for submission to the cabinet or the Riksdag (Jenkins, 1968:78–79). Attached to this bill, as background information, will be the official report of the investigative commission and summaries or digests of all the commentaries received on it. "For interest groups the *remiss* stage offers a chance to make known their criticism both of the general principles and specific details of a proposal. As the policy is still in the formulating stage, the opportunities for influence are great" (Wheeler, 1975:43).

The presumed benefits of this combined process of investigative commissions and *remiss* statements are summed up by the Swedish Institute (1970b) in these words: "This method is cumbersome and often time-consuming. It is, however, considered to be a very valuable form of democratic government. The parties of the opposition, directly taking part in the preparation of political decisions, are given a chance to influence the Government before it takes its position. The work method described [here] fosters compromise and 'middle-way' decisions. The fact that different ideologies and groups may make their voices heard at an early stage is also believed to lead ultimately to the taking of wiser decisions."

Riksdag Membership. A more traditional means through which interest associations seek to influence political decisions is by getting some of their members — especially organizational leaders — elected to the Riksdag. This procedure is certainly not unique to Sweden, except perhaps to the extent that it is recognized as a legitimate practice and actively encouraged by the political parties. "Since parties are eager to bring forward candidates with more important group attachments, all major groups can count on having spokesmen in one or more parties. . . ." (Heckscher, 1958a:165). Some observers feel that this procedure is of major importance for interest organizations: "They also have considerable weight in the Riksdag, since many officers and members of organizations are also members of the Riksdag. The power thus exerted is truly immense" (Jenkins, 1968:79).

Balanced against this assertion, however, is the fact that parliamentary debate on bills is of relatively small importance in the Swedish political system. "Except when the matter at issue is politically controversial, parliamentary debate is considerably less important as a preliminary to legislation than in most other democratically governed countries" (The Swedish Institute, 1970a). Indeed, some writers maintain that the Riksdag has virtually no independent power apart from the cabinet: "The Riksdag has given up the practice of writing new legislation; since about 1920 it has restricted itself to requesting the government [i.e., the cabinet] to prepare bills on matters which in the Riksdag's judgment require action, and to approving, amending, and rejecting governmental bills...." (Rustow, 1955:174–75).

Riksdag Committees.   To the extent that the real work of the Riksdag is done in committees, it would seem important for interest organizations to have input into committee deliberations. This is accomplished in two ways: (a) organizations can send written statements concerning pending bills to a committee, or the committee may request such commentaries from at least the major organizations (these are also called *remissyttranden*); (b) organizational representatives may be requested to testify before closed hearings of the committee (Heckscher, 1958a:166–67). Written statements are submitted by organizations to Riksdag committees with some regularity, but they usually pertain to relatively minor or technical points. "As a rule, Riksdag committees concentrate on motions to amend or on points where they recommend changes [to government bills]" (The Swedish Institute, 1970a). The second practice is used only infrequently. "Three factors may be suggested as explanations: The bureaucratic tradition of the Riksdag, with emphasis on written procedures, the inevitable practice of closed committee sessions, and the thorough investigation of opinions and interests, without any secrecy, before the presentation of Government propositions" (Andrén, 1968:98).

Administrative Agency Boards.   In the Swedish political system, program administration is carried out by some seventy specialized administrative agencies that are functionally autonomous from the governmental departments that supervise them. Responsible to the Department of Health and Social Affairs, for instance, are the Board of Social Welfare, the Board of Pensions, the Board of Insurance, the Labor Market Board, and several others (Heckscher, 1958a:168). "The Cabinet formulates the general instructions that govern the activity of these agencies, makes the higher-level appointments, and passes on budget requests before they are incorporated in the appropriation bill that goes to the Riksdag. But within such wide limits, the agency heads ... are generally free to interpret the statutes and decrees for whose application they are responsible" (Rustow, 1955:176).

Each agency is headed by a director-general, but most of the larger ones also have a governing board that includes the bureau chiefs and representatives of several interest organizations — especially the major labor-market confederations. The authority of these boards varies considerably among the different agencies, from purely advising to final decision making. But in any case, at least a few of the most powerful interest organizations are able, through their representatives on these boards, to make their views and positions known to administrative agency officials.

Administrative Agency Consultation. Below the level of the governing board in an administrative agency, considerable consultation can occur between particular operating bureaus or offices in the agency and their counterparts in many of the major interest organizations. "In all matters affecting the interest of a group there is both official and unofficial cooperation with administrative organs, who may ask a group . . . to state its views officially or ask informally for its advice." Conversely, "whenever an organization finds that the administration is about to decide a question of interest to them, it will as a perfectly normal thing and without attempt at dissimulation demand consultation, and this is invariably granted" (Heckscher, 1958a:168).

Much of this consultation concerns fairly narrow practical and technical practices or problems (Elvander, 1966:235), but this procedure brings interest organizations directly into contact with the day-to-day administration of governmental programs. Although any one such consultation may be of quite minor importance, cumulatively these contacts may enable an organization to exert considerable influence on an agency. Moreover, "in negotiating with government agencies, [interest organizations] are in a position of strength, and the agencies know that lack of cooperation on their part will frequently lead organizations to appeal over their heads to political authorities, who are as likely (or perhaps more likely) to follow the advice of organizations as that of civil servants" (Heckscher, 1958a:168–69).[4]

Informal Influence Procedures

Whereas the eight influence procedures discussed above are all considered to be established, permanent parts of the total political process, other procedures used by interest organizations are not formalized in that sense. Three of these more informal procedures are described below.[5]

4. For an illustration of the use of this procedure by the National Environment Protection Board, see Lundqvist (1973).

5. Another informal procedure, occasionally employed as a last resort by organizations when they feel that they have exhausted all other possibilities, is to send a delegation to meet directly with one or more departmental ministers (*uppvaktningar i departement*). It is utilized primarily by local governments rather than interest organizations, however.

Private Meetings.   The best example of this procedure is the meetings held monthly between the Board of the Swedish Confederation of Trade Unions (LO) and leaders of the Social Democratic party to work out common positions and policies on impending issues. Other organizations meet with Riksdag members from all four of the major political parties, commonly once or twice a year at an elaborate dinner. The purpose of these meetings is for the organizations to present their views on current topics to political leaders — although they usually refer to this as an "educational" rather than "influence" process.

Public Opinion Formation.   Virtually all interest organizations attempt to influence public opinion in some way, from distributing pamphlets to sponsoring conferences. At least some of this effort will presumably be directed at political issues, in hopes that an aroused and concerned public will in turn bring pressures to bear on politicians to take desired stances on these issues. This public opinion formation approach is particularly important for smaller and less powerful groups, who lack the resources and direct access to government of the major labor-market organizations. But all organizations use it to a considerable extent, especially as a prelude to initiating a proposal to the government.

Personal Contacts.   Over time, as organizational leaders and politicians interact frequently, they come to know each other personally and to build up webs of personal friendships and contacts. These can be used as highly effective, if sometimes indirect, channels for exerting influence. This process undoubtedly occurs in all societies, but many observers claim that it is especially pervasive in Sweden, where the total number of people involved in this "influence network" is quite small (probably no more than a few hundred at the maximum), and virtually all of them are located in Stockholm. In addition to the eight formal influence procedures, David Jenkins (1968:82) maintains that "an equally forceful — perhaps even more forceful — channel of influence is the system of informal contacts that develop between the state organs and the organizations whose area of specialization they are dealing with. This occurs through the day-to-day contacts necessary for carrying out the business at hand, but also through get-togethers of a more social character."

Conclusion

Pluralist theory does not specify any processes through which interest organizations are to exert influence on political decision making, and hence can be severely criticized as an unattainable ideal. In an effort to put the pluralist ideal into practice, however, Sweden has developed a set of eight formal influence procedures and several informal techniques that interest associations can utilize when interacting with the national government. Numerous writers have praised this Swedish organizational influence system as an example of functioning pluralism, but with the exception of Nils Elvander (1966, 1972b), none of them has seriously questioned the effectiveness of this system. The study reported in the following chapter asks whether or not these influence procedures — as evaluated by the top organizational and governmental leaders in Sweden — actually enable private-interest organizations to perform an influence-mediating role between the people and the government in Sweden.

9. Sociopolitical Pluralism
in Practice

We saw in the previous chapter that a major deficiency in traditional pluralist theory is a failure to specify operational procedures through which interest organizations could effectively influence governmental policies and decisions. We also saw, however, that Sweden has developed a set of formal procedures and several informal techniques for bridging that theoretical gap. This chapter reports the results of research conducted in Sweden to evaluate the functional effectiveness of those Swedish influence processes. The study does not attempt to assess the overall applicability of sociopolitical pluralism to modern industrial societies, but it does seek to determine whether or not the Swedish system of organizational influence procedures provides a viable model for other nations to emulate as a means of putting pluralist theory into practice.

Swedish Interest Organizations and Politics

Virtually every observer of Sweden has commented on the vast number of interest groups and associations that pervade this society. Frederic Fleisher (1967:40–41), for instance, writes that "Sweden has become an organized society. . . . Swedes belong more to organizations than any other people in the world. . . . Of Sweden's . . . eight million inhabitants, over 90 percent who earn a living belong either to an industrial, a white-collar, a professional, or an employer's union. Virtually all the farmers market their products through the farmers' cooperatives. Over one-third of the households belong to a consumers' cooperative." And

Richard Tomasson (1970:242) comments that: "Among modern societies, only the other Scandinavian countries approach Sweden in the development of organizational life, but here again Sweden is the most advanced. . . . "[1]

Given this high level of organizational development, it is not surprising that interest associations play a central role in the Swedish political system. In the words of Nils Andrén (1968:22–23):

> The public authorities recognize the organizations as representatives of the sections of the nation they claim to speak for. The state not only listens to the views of these bodies but also seeks their advice. Many important decisions are preceded by conferences between the organizations and Cabinet ministers. Proposed legislation is submitted for comment not only to the relevant administrative authorities, but also to the organizations most concerned before the proposal is finally drafted for presentation to the Riksdag. In the democratic process of government by discussion, the organizations, therefore, play a very important part. Thanks to their importance as recruiting agencies for democratic leadership, the organizations always have spokesmen in the Riksdag. It is not unusual for representatives of trade and industrial associations to serve on government boards and commissions and in some cases the organizations have even undertaken tasks that are in reality governmental administrative duties.

Some writers, such as Jane and Andrew Carey (1969:471), argue that the role of interest organizations is as powerful as that of political parties in the Swedish system: "Of equal political importance with the parties are the powerful privately formed organizations. These great organizations, which constitute a kind of 'extraconstitutional power balance system,' are in some ways a part of the political process, with membership overlapping that of the political parties and with pressures criss-crossing between the two." This situation may weaken the role of the parties and the Riksdag in the political process, as pointed out by Nils Stjernquist (1966:130), but he agrees with the Carey's (1969:472) assertion that these organizations "provide a means by which the interests of different groups within the society are accommodated, and offer ways other than through the ballot for a citizen to make his influence felt." This thesis that interest or-

---

1. Tomasson (1970:ch. 8) devotes an entire chapter to organizations and provides the most extensive description of Swedish interest organizations available in English.

ganizations in Sweden constitute a second political system, paralleling the normal political process of elections, has also been noted by David Jenkins (1968:86):

> The organizations' machinery does, in effect, constitute a sort of second government. In the normal democratic process the people elect their representatives in the parliament, who then presumably express the will of the people through their management of the government. In Sweden the people also elect their representatives in the organizations, who then push for the interests of their members. . . . The second government may, indeed, be more powerful than the first one, but it would be difficult to say that it is any less responsive to the will of the people as a whole, especially since the existence of equally powerful organizations expressing opposite points of view means that they act as a check on one another's opportunities to abuse their power.

This idea of interest organizations acting as a check on governmental power is of course the essence of sociopolitical pluralism.

An American observer might easily jump to the conclusion that the role of interest organizations in Swedish politics is analogous to that of pressure groups or lobbies in the United States, but this analogy is only superficial. Whereas pressure groups in the United States are essentially outside the formal machinery of government, in Sweden "it is not for the most part a question of making great exertions to bring influence to bear; the organizations are firmly locked into the country's political, social, and economic machinery" (Jenkins, 1968:78). Indeed, it has been argued that: "It would seem that 'the pressure groups' in Sweden should not really be called by that name. The organizations form regular parts of the democratic system itself. Not only are they involved in the public debate; but they also play a responsible part in actual administration at all levels. . . ." (The Swedish Institute, 1970b). American-style exertion of political pressure through such tactics as lobbying and writing letters to legislators does occur in Sweden but is of minor importance. "This is not due to any superior moral attitude on the part of organizations, but chiefly to the fact that these activities are largely unnecessary in a system where the opportunities for open participation are as great as in Sweden" (Heckscher, 1958a:168).

The principal outcome of this sociopolitical system, as seen by many writers, is a stable balance of power. "The Swedish Government," writes

Gunnar Heckscher (1958a:170), "has been characterized by the term 'politics of compromise.' Indeed, there is hardly any point at which this term seems more definitely warranted than with regard to interest organizations; an equilibrium is maintained chiefly through the willingness of each of them to make concessions in order to achieve important results, rather than using force in order to gain all or nothing."

Nils Andrén also states this argument quite forcefully:

> The fundamental nature of large interest organizations is that of class or group warfare instruments. Their primary task is to maintain the interests of their members, such as workers, employers, consumers, producers, etc., against other groups and against public authorities and even against society itself. If any of these groups were to dominate to such an extent that its members could too obviously and too grossly provide for themselves at the expense of other groups, it would mean a serious menace to harmony and stability as well as to democracy itself. It is evident that some organizations are more influential than others, but on the whole Organized Sweden . . . presents a picture of considerable mutual understanding. This understanding is founded both on mutual appreciation among the organizations of each other's strength and on the knowledge that one-sided measures and demands can provoke effective counteractions. . . . In this way there is a balance of interest within the whole society, marked both by the tension between the conflicting interests of different groups and by the understanding that the well-being of all groups and of the society as a whole is a condition for the well-being of each individual group. [1968:240–41]

Recent studies of the Swedish political system (Elvander, 1966, 1972b; Wheeler, 1975) have demonstrated that this argument concerning the influence of interest organizations on political decision making in Sweden is undoubtedly true for the large labor union confederations such as the Swedish Confederation of Trade Unions (LO) and the Central Organization of Salaried Employees (TCO). But it may not be applicable to the entire spectrum of interest organizations in Sweden, as is often asserted (Heckscher, 1958b; The Swedish Institute, 1970b).

The Research Design

The data for this study were obtained through personal interviews with fifty top Swedish organization and government leaders in 1972. The organizations and governmental units they represented are described in the following paragraphs. The procedures followed in conducting these interviews are also discussed.

Interest Organizations Studied

The thirty-one interest organizations represented in this study are all national in scope, and in general they are the most important private organizations in Sweden. They can be divided into the two main categories of economic ("labor-market" in Swedish) and noneconomic ("idealistic" in Swedish) organizations, according to whether they are directly involved in the business/labor market or whether their main concerns are outside that realm. The sixteen economic organizations can in turn be subdivided into five "labor" organizations (composed of persons who participate in the labor market as individuals) and eleven "business" organizations (representing various kinds of business firms and concerns). The fifteen noneconomic organizations can be similarly subdivided, on the basis of their primary goals, into nine "member-serving" organizations (primarily performing services or providing benefits for their own members) and six "public-serving" organizations (mainly concerned with informing, helping, or changing the larger society).

Several of the organizations studied are actually confederations of numerous independent nationwide associations with specialized but broadly similar concerns, as in the case of the Swedish Confederation of Trade Unions, which is composed of thirty-seven national unions, and the Swedish Sports Federation, representing fifty-one national associations for different sports. These confederations, rather than their component associations, were utilized in the study because it is they who interact directly with the government, in the name of all their member organizations. These organizations are listed and described below.[2]

Labor Organizations

LO   Swedish Confederation of Trade Unions *(Landsorganisation i Sverige)*. A confederation of thirty-seven national craft and other unions, with a total membership of 1,600,000 (about 95 percent of all wage workers); it is the largest and most powerful interest organization in Sweden and has very close ties with the Social Democratic party.

---

2. Many of the organizations are known in Sweden by initials derived from their Swedish names. In the remaining cases, the initials listed here were constructed from the Swedish name.

TCO   Central Organization of Salaried Employees *(Tjänstemännens centralorganisation).* A confederation of twenty-three national white-collar (primarily clerical and technical) unions, with a total membership of over 600,000 (about 40 percent of all white-collar workers); it is the second-largest and second-most-influential interest organization in Sweden but maintains strict political neutrality.

SACO   Central Organization of Swedish Professional Workers *(Sveriges akademikers centralorganisation).* A confederation of thirty-one national professional associations, with a total membership of about 100,000 (about 75 percent of all workers with university degrees); it functions both as a labor market and a professional organization, with strict political neutrality.

SAC   Swedish Workers Central Organization *(Sveriges arbetares centralorganisation).* An organization of manual workers, with about 20,000 members, based on syndicalist principles.

HGRF   National Association of Tenants[3] *(Hyregästernas riksförbund).* Composed of about 350,000 renters of apartments and concerned primarily with rent agreements and rights of tenants; it is politically neutral but shares many goals with the Social Democratic party.

Business Organizations

SAF   Swedish Employers' Confederation *(Svenska arbetsgivareföreningen).* A confederation of forty-four employer organizations in most (but not all) sectors of the economy, representing a total of about 25,000 firms; it is politically neutral but partial toward the Conservative party.

SIF   Swedish Federation of Industries *(Sveriges industriförbund).* An association of over 4,000 of the largest industrial firms which seeks to promote and protect their interests; it has in the past cooperated fairly close with the Conservative party.

SHIO   Swedish Organization of Crafts and Small Industries *(Sveriges hantverks- och industriorganisation).* A confederation of forty-

---

3. Strictly speaking, the National Association of Tenants is not a labor organization, since it does not deal with employee income issues. However, its membership does overlap heavily with those of the labor organizations; it seeks to protect and promote their economic interests; and its members are economically disadvantaged in relation to the Property Owners Association in the same sense as are employees in relation to employers.

five national associations of craft, trade, and small-to-medium-sized industries, with about 30,000 members; it is politically neutral but has common interests with the Liberal and Conservative parties.

SAEF General Export Association of Sweden *(Sveriges allmänna exportförening)*. An association of approximately 1,300 firms engaged primarily in foreign exporting.

SGF Swedish Wholesalers' Federation *(Sveriges grossistförbund)*. An association of most of the major importers and wholesale merchants in Sweden.

SKF Swedish Retailers' Federation *(Sveriges köpmannaförbund)*. An association of most of the private retail chains and major stores in Sweden.

SFRF Swedish Association of Insurance Companies *(Sveriges försäkringsbolags riksförbund)*. Composed of all the major insurance firms in Sweden.

SBF Swedish Association of Banks *(Svenska bankföreningen)*. An association of all the national banks in Sweden.

SFF Swedish Property Owners Association *(Sveriges fastighetsägareförbund)*. Long composed primarily of owners of rental property, it has recently been gaining members among owners of private residences.

LRF National Union of Farmers *(Lantbrukarnas riksförbund)*. With over a million members, this organization is composed of both individual farmers and many agricultural producer cooperatives; it has informal links with the Center (formerly Agrarian) party.

KF Cooperative Federation *(Kooperativa förbundet)*. The national confederation of about 250 local and specialized rental cooperatives which operate over 3,500 stores and represent close to 1.5 million people; it originated from the same ideology as the Social Democratic party.

Member-Serving Organizations

ABF Workers' Education Association *(Arbetarnas bildningsförbund)*. Operates over 60,000 study circles, enrolling approximately

600,000 persons, plus a variety of other educational programs; it is closely allied with the Social Democratic party, as well as LO.

SRIF   Swedish Sports Federation *(Sveriges riksidrottsförbund)*. A confederation of fifty-one national associations for various sports, representing 1,700,000 members; it is politically neutral but cooperates fairly closely with the government.

KAK   Royal Automobile Club *(Kungliga automobilklubben)*. The oldest of the three major automobile associations in Sweden.

SLF   Swedish Medical Association[4] *(Sveriges läkarförbund)*. Represents most physicians in Sweden.

SAS   Swedish Bar Association *(Sveriges advokatsamfund)*. Represents most lawyers in Sweden.

HFHS   Swedish Housewives Association *(Husmodersförbundet Hem och Samhälle)*. An association of about 44,000 women, concerned with issues related to homemaking and family life.

FBF   The Fredrika Bremer Association *(Fredrika-Bremer-förbundet)*. The oldest of the womens' rights organizations in Sweden; it has about 11,000 members.

SFS   Swedish United Student Union *(Sveriges förenade studentkårer)*. A confederation of thirty-five local student unions at all the universities and other schools of higher education in Sweden, and technically representing all students in these institutions; it is politically neutral.

SUL   National Council of Swedish Youth *(Sveriges ungdomsorganisåtioners landsråd)*. A confederation of fifty-two associations for youth and secondary school students.

Public-Serving Organizations

RFSU   National Association for Sexual Education *(Riksförbundet för sexuell upplysning)*. Concerned with disseminating sex education, birth control information and supplies, and "naturalistic" sexual attitudes throughout the population.

---

4. SLF is part of SACO and functions both as a labor union and as a professional association. In this research, it is treated as a professional association because the SLF respondent felt that the latter activities were more predominant and hence answered the questions from this perspective.

KRUM National Association for Penal Reform *(Riksförbundet för krim-inalvårdens humanisering)*. Concerned with humanizing the penal system, and eventually abolishing prison.

RFHL National Association for Help to Addicts and Drug Abusers *(Riks-förbundet för hjälp åt läkemedelsmissbrukare)*. Concerned with both educating the public about drugs and helping addicts overcome their problems.

RMH National Organization for Mental Health *(Riksorganisationen för mental hälsa)*. Concerned with both educating the public about mental health problems and helping people with such problems.

IOGT The International Order of Good Templars — The National Order of Templars *(IOGT-NTO)*. The largest of the twenty-nine national temperance organizations in Sweden; it is concerned with promoting temperance attitudes and values in the general public, as well as in the Riksdag.

CAN Swedish Council for Information on Alcohol and Other Drugs *(Centralförbundet för alcohol- och narkotikapplysning)*. An educational and public informational association concerned with alcohol and drug abuse; it is supported by all the temperance organizations and cooperates quite closely with the government.

Government Units Studied

Seventeen government units were also included in the study, to provide a view of the influence process from the "receiving" as well as the "sending" end. Interviews were conducted in ten of the twelve departments in the Swedish government at that time, excluding only the Foreign Affairs and Defense departments because they are not directly involved in the organizational-governmental influence process.[5] In the Swedish government structure, however, departments are solely policy-making bodies. Program implementation, administration, and other operational duties are assigned to separate administrative boards that report to the relevant departments but function with relative autonomy. There are presently over seventy such boards, but most of them deal only with quite

5. The Cabinet Office, comprised of the Office of the Prime Minister and several ministers without portfolio, is sometimes listed as an additional department, as is also the Organization Department, which provides financial and administrative services to the other departments; but neither of these were included in this study.

narrow or highly technical matters. Seven of the most encompassing and functionally important boards were included in the research, since they interact regularly with interest organizations on many diverse topics. Because the titles of these departments and boards are fairly self-explanatory, the listings below do not include descriptive statements.[6]

Governmental Departments

DJUS   Department of Justice *(Justitiedepartementet)*

DSOC   Department of Health and Social Affairs *(Socialdepartementet)*

DCMN Department of Communication and Transportation *(Kommunikationsdepartementet)*

DFIN   Department of Finance *(Finansdepartementet)*

DEDU Department of Education *(Utbildningsdepartementet)*

DAGR Department of Agriculture *(Jordbruksdepartementet)*

DCOM Department of Commerce *(Handelsdepartementet)*

DINT   Department of Interior (Labor and Housing) *(Inrikesdepartementet)*

DIND   Department of Industry *(Industridepartementet)*

DPLN   Department of Physical Planning and Local Government *(Civildepartementet)*

Administrative Boards

BWEL National Board of Health and Welfare *(Socialstyrelsen)*

BEDU National Board of Education *(Skolöverstyrelsen)*

BAGR National Board of Agriculture *(Lantbruksstyrelsen)*

BTRD   Board of Trade *(Kommerskollegium)*

BLBR   National Labor Market Board *(Arbetsmarknadsstyrelsen)*

BHOS National Housing Board *(Bostadsstyrelsen)*

BPLN   National Board of Town and Country Planning *(Statens Planverk)*

---

6. None of these governmental units are identified by initials in Swedish. Hence the initials given here, which are used in this report merely for reporting convenience, are derived from the English rather than the Swedish names in all cases.

Interview Procedures

The respondents in this study were all directors or other top officials in these interest organizations and governmental units. They were asked to respond as knowledgeable individuals who had gained considerable personal experience with the Swedish organizational influence system, however, and not as a spokesperson for their particular organization or office. With two exceptions, one person in each interest organization and governmental unit was interviewed. If the purpose of this research had been to describe the precise actions and policies of each interest organization and governmental unit, it would have been necessary to interview many people within each setting. This research was designed, however, to evaluate the functional adequacy of the Swedish organizational influence system as a whole; it was not concerned with the role of specific organizations or offices within that system. Hence the respondents were selected from a wide range of interest organizations and governmental offices merely to ensure that they would reflect a wide diversity of experiences.

In the interest organizations, interviews were conducted with the director or general secretary whenever possible (in nineteen of the thirty-one organizations). If this person was not available, the interview was held with an assistant director (in ten organizations) or some other top functionary such as a director of research. Multiple interviews were conducted in the two major labor organizations, the Swedish Confederation of Trade Unions (LO) and the Central Organization of Salaried Employees (TCO), because of their large size and functional dominance in the labor market.[7]

In seven of the governmental departments the respondent was the under secretary *(Statessekreterare),* while in the remaining three cases some other high-ranking official was interviewed. In the administrative boards the desired respondent was the director general, but in four of these seven cases the interview was instead held with the person in charge of research or planning.

The interviews were guided by a set of standardized questions, but supplementary comments were always solicited. Most of the respondents volunteered considerable information beyond that called for by the formal questions, and all of the statements quoted in this report came from those spontaneous comments. It is important to keep in mind, moreover, that all

---

7. In LO, interviews were conducted with three top officials, although the director was not available for an interview. In TCO, interviews were conducted with the director and with the head of the Federation of Civil Servants.

of the findings reported here are subjective perceptions and judgments, not objective measurements, although these evaluations were made by people in leadership positions who were quite knowledgeable about their organization or office and the ways in which interest organizations seek to influence political decision making in Sweden. Although there is no way of determining the validity of the information obtained in these interviews, there is no reason to believe that they reflect any kind of systematic bias, especially since there was such consistent agreement across many different kinds of organizations and governmental units. All but three of the interviews were conducted in English, since the respondents were fluent in that language.

Data Utilized

Three kinds of data are reported in this chapter: (a) quantitative figures (means and percentages) from the interviews with the fifty organizational and governmental leaders, (b) comments made by these respondents in the course of the interviews, and (c) findings from Nils Elvander's (1966) earlier study of Swedish labor-market organizations,[8] plus some data from a few other writings on this topic.

The Total Influence System

Our concern in this section is to answer the question, In the eyes of Swedish organizational and governmental leaders, how effective is their total system of influence linkages between interest organizations and the national government? We shall examine the respondents' attitudes toward the overall system, the different kinds of roles they perceive organizations enacting within this system, and their views concerning the distribution of influence among various types of organizations within the system.

Attitudes toward the System

In general, all of the respondents — both in interest organizations and in government offices — were moderately well satisfied with the overall

8. Elvander's work, which can be translated as *Interest Organizations in Today's Sweden*, is the only other large-scale empirical study of this topic that has been conducted. However, his research was restricted to eighteen labor-market (labor and business) organizations (all but one of which are included in the present study) and only five influence procedures. In addition, Elvander (1972b) recently completed a more intensive examination of the role of the major labor-market organizations in twelve different decisions concerning Swedish tax policy that have occurred since 1945. The other references cited in this chapter present some empirical data taken from governmental records, personal observations, and other sources, but none of them constitute a full-scale study of the total influence system.

influence system. They were asked, "If we think of all eight influence procedures together as constituting a process through which interest organizations can influence the political system, which one of the [following] terms . . . best describes the overall adequacy of this influence process, in your opinion?" Six respondents said "somewhat inadequate," twenty-three said "fairly adequate," eighteen said "generally adequate," and one said "totally adequate." No one chose the responses of "wholly inadequate" or "rather inadequate." The average response by interest organization leaders was "fairly adequate," while the average response by government officials was midway between "fairly" and "generally" adequate.

When pressed to give reasons why they valued this influence system, respondents gave statements such as these:

This system provides a way of making democracy work.[SACO][9]

These procedures ensure democracy, by restraining the power of the bureaucracy. [LO]

This is a way of bringing together all the interests connected with a question and promoting objectivity. [SBF]

These procedures make it possible to have all concerned groups active in seeking solutions to common problems. Practically everyone in the country has the opportunity to influence political decisions. [DEDU]

Evident in these statements are the arguments that pluralism provides a means of (a) facilitating citizen participation in political decision making, (b) promoting political stability, and (c) achieving better solutions to major social problems. The "ideology of pluralism" is obviously widespread among the organizational and governmental leaders of Sweden!

At the same time, however, many of the respondents reported that there are serious weaknesses or limitations in the Swedish organizational influence system. Perhaps the most fundamental of these is the assertion that the government ultimately controls the political system, regardless of whatever the organizations do. Several of the governmental respondents were quite explicit on this point:

---

9. All quotations by respondents cited in this chapter are identified by the initials of the organizations or governmental units given above.

> We have to maintain good relationships with organizations. They can always have their say, but we always decide. [BAGR]

> It is difficult for small and new organizations to have influence because they don't understand how government operates. The government must maintain social controls over organizations, which they often don't accept. [DSOC]

> This entire system can easily be manipulated by the government to support its own positions. [DINT]

> By consulting . . . with relevant organizations about current problems and proposals, we can make them feel responsible for our decisions. [BEDU]

The last statement, it should be noted, goes beyond the idea of government control to suggest that governmental agencies may be more or less intentionally utilizing this influence system as a way of coopting organizational leadership into supporting — or at least not publicly criticizing — governmental decisions and policies.

Concurrently, several of the interest organizations — especially business associations whose political stances are sharply at variance with the then ruling Social Democratic party — were extremely critical of the government as being "closed minded" and unwilling to consider ideas that conflict with established party ideology:

> We have enough contacts at all levels, and the system structure is adequate. But too many times the government doesn't listen to our ideas or experience. This is a problem of the government, not the system. (SIF)

> If used properly, these procedures could be very useful for organizations. They were once a very good instrument for obtaining various views and achieving common understandings. But this is no longer true. Politicians today are not very open to outside views. (SAF)

> If we take a stand against the political position of the government, they don't hear us. [SFF]

More broadly, the paradox of organizational support for a system that is seen as largely ineffective for exerting political influence was concisely stated by another organizational leader:

> We want to maintain these procedures because they give us a broad
> perspective on current problems and ideas of how to go about influ-
> encing the government in other ways. But as direct influence procedures
> themselves, they are relatively worthless. [SKF]

These comments (and many others similar to them) point to a possible
fundamental weakness in the Swedish influence system. Despite all the
legal statutes supporting this system and the procedural guarantees built
into it, interest organizations that oppose the government apparently believe that they are ineffective in exerting any meaningful influence on
political decision making. To the extent that this is true, coupled with the
prior assertion that the government ultimately controls the political system, the apparent conclusion is that the Swedish system of formal influence procedures is failing to give interest organizations any real leverage
on political decision making. The system does provide several channels
through which organizations can speak to the government, but it may not
give many organizations — even quite large and powerful ones such as the
Swedish Employers' Confederation and the Swedish Federation of
Industries — enough political "clout" to ensure that a hostile government will listen to them seriously and take their interests into account in
formulating political policies. Access to political decision makers is not
the same as influence on decision making, which is the goal of the
pluralistic model. In short, it may be that this Swedish "influence" system
is in fact no more than an elaborate communication (and perhaps even
cooptation) system.

Organizational Influence Roles

To test the above thesis, the respondents were asked about the kind of
role they saw their organization (if they were an organization leader) or
interest organizations in general (if they were a governmental official)
playing within the political system. The question was worded as follows:
"Which of these roles best describes your organization's activities in
relation to the state as it tries to exert political influence: a partisan seeking
your own particular goals; an expert consultant on technical questions; a
participant in program planning; a formulator of basic governmental policies; or a decision maker for the government?" Rather significantly, the
Swedish Confederation of Trade Unions (LO) was seen as an actual
decision maker, because of its close ties with the Social Democratic party,
but no other organization was given that status and only a few of them were
described as policy formulators. Most of the respondents selected the

partisan, expert, or program-planning roles, although some interesting variations occurred.

For instance, labor organizations were described as primarily concerned with obtaining benefits for their own members, whereas business organizations were seen to be acting mainly as expert consultants on technical matters. Member-serving noneconomic organizations were also viewed principally as partisan actors, while public-serving noneconomic organizations were described as seeking to be program planners but actually functioning largely as expert consultants. Most governmental officials, meanwhile, viewed most interest organizations as partisan actors seeking their own particular goals.

The tendency for respondents from business organizations to describe themselves as merely technical advisors on business matters was especially pronounced. Presumably because their interests and goals were generally quite opposed to those of the then-ruling Social Democratic party, leaders of business organizations were very careful to separate their nonpolitical technical consultative roles from all political issues and activities, as seen in these statements:

> Technical and political questions are distinct. We have considerable influence on purely technical questions, because of our extensive resources. But on political questions we play mainly an informational role; the Social Democratic party has its own well-established policies that differ sharply from ours, and we can't influence policy decisions. . . . Moreover, we believe that industry must work within society for the good of society, not as partisans seeking its own goals. . . . We don't want a corporate society in which industry rules. [SIF]

> We try not to act politically as a pressure group, but to remain wholly technical in our dealings with the government. We are far from the positions of the government on most questions. [SFRF]

In short, most of these respondents — and especially those from business organizations — view interest organizations (with the exception of LO) as only marginal participants in the Swedish decision-making system. They may either pursue their own partisan goals or advise the government on technical matters, but they are not seen as actively involved in the political system as program planners, policy formulators, or actual decision makers. To the extent that this is true, the Swedish organizational influence system is not operating as the prevailing ideology and most current descriptions of the system would have us believe. In the next section we shall investigate this possibility further by inquiring into the amounts of political influence the respondents attributed to different kinds of interest organizations.

Distribution of Influence among Types of Organizations

To measure the amount of influence seen to be exerted by each organization through each influence procedure, respondents were asked: "Within your organization's particular area of concern, how much influence does the organization normally exert on political activities through taking initiatives? . . . through planning councils? . . . through investigative commissions?" and so on.[10] They responded in terms of a six-point influence scale: 0, no influence *(inget inflytande)*; 1, slight influence *(litet inflytande)*; 2, some influence *(något inflytande)*; 3, moderate influence *(ganska stort inflytande)*; 4, considerable influence *(stort inflytande)*; 5, great influence *(mucket stort inflytande)*. Four features of this procedure should be noted: (a) it asked the respondent to reply only in terms of issues within his or her organization's sphere of concern, and not in terms of any vague notion of all public issues; (b) it asked the respondent to make an overall evaluation across all these issues relevant to his or her organization, rather than thinking of only one or two specific issues; (c) it required making subjective judgments, based on personal experiences, concerning amounts of influence exerted, rather than trying to measure influence in any objective manner; but (d) we can assume that the "influence scale" does provide ordinal (or ranking) measurement points that have essentially the same relational meanings to all respondents, in the sense that everyone presumably considered "slight influence" to be more than "no influence," and so on up the scale.[11]

Numerical scores representing the perceived amounts of influence exerted through each of the eight formal procedures by the various types of organizations are reported in Table 9.1. (Separate figures for LO [Swedish Confederation of Trade Unions] are reported in this table because of its dominance in relation to all other interest organizations in Sweden. The figures for "all labor organizations" include LO.)

---

10. The corresponding question for governmental officials was worded in terms of the influence of all interest organizations on that particular governmental department or agency, within its sphere of normal concerns.

11. For an intensive analysis of the influence activities of one specific interest organization (TCO), see Wheeler (1975).

Table 9.1
Amount of Influence Exerted through Each Formal Procedure

(For organizational respondents, the data pertain just to their own organization; for governmental respondents, the data pertain to all organizations in relation to their own office.)

	Initia-tives	Plan-ning Councils	Investi-gative Com-missions	Commen-taries	Riksdag Member-ship	Riksdag Commit-tees	Adminis-trative Boards	Adminis-trative Consul-tation	Average
					Mean Influence Scale Scores (0 = none, 1 = slight, 2 = some, 3 = moderate, 4 = considerable, 5 = great)				
LO	5	2	5	5	3	2	5	2	3.6
All labor organizations	3.2	1.8	3.4	3.2	1.8	1.8	2.8	2.6	2.6
Business organizations	2.4	2.3	3.3	3.0	1.0	1.7	2.4	3.2	2.4
Member-serving organizations	2.2	0.9	2.6	3.2	1.6	1.3	1.6	2.0	1.9
Public-serving organizations	2.7	1.2	2.7	2.8	2.2	1.7	0.7	2.2	2.0
Governmental departments	3.0	2.4	3.8	4.0	*	*	*	*	3.4
Governmental agencies	2.6	*	2.1	2.9	*	*	2.8	3.1	2.9
All economic organizations	2.8	2.3	3.4	3.1	1.3	1.8	2.6	3.1	2.5
All noneconomic organizations	2.4	1.0	2.7	3.1	1.8	1.6	1.2	2.1	2.0
All interest organizations	2.6	1.7	3.0	3.1	1.5	1.7	2.0	2.6	2.3
All governmental units	2.8	2.4	3.3	3.5	*	*	2.8	3.1	3.2

*These procedures are not relevant to governmental departments/agencies.

Looking down the right-hand column of this table, at the average influence scores across all eight procedures, we note first that both labor and business organizations fall midway between "some" and "moderate" influence (with scores of 2.6 and 2.4, respectively), so that the overall average for all economic organizations is 2.5. In contrast, both member-serving and public-serving organizations rate only "some" influence (scores 1.9 and 2.0, respectively), so that the overall average for all noneconomic organizations is just 2.0. Finally, it is interesting to see that governmental respondents in general, and especially those in the departments, attribute considerably more influence to organizations (average score = 3.2) than the organizational leaders give themselves credit for (average score = 2.3). Despite the subjective nature of these data, it is quite clear that, relative to one another, the various interest organizations differ greatly in the amounts of political influence they exert through these eight formal procedures. It is also evident that, in general, most organizational leaders perceive their level of influence as being rather low, since neither "some influence" nor "moderate influence" imply that organizations are seen as having major impacts on political decision making in Sweden.

To the extent that significant inequality does exist among Swedish interest organizations in their ability to influence politics, these disparities appear to hit hardest at new and small organizations as they attempt to gain access to the influence system. The following comments are typical of many of the responses given to the question, "If an organization that had not previously taken part in . . . these procedures wanted to be consulted, how difficult or easy would it be for the organization to become involved? . . ."

Small and special groups carry no political weight. No matter how good or reasonable their ideas, they don't get a hearing. . . . The major organizations take the whole representation in most commissions and boards, and other organizations have no opportunity to gain any representation. . . . We're getting a kind of feudal system in this country.[BHOS]

It is considered good policy for the government to listen to all organizations. But it is difficult for small organizations to have influence, and it's getting continually more difficult. [DAGR]

It depends on the existing political attitudes; if the organization is seen as extreme, it will have many difficulties; if seen as moderate, it will have a much easier time making itself heard. [IOGT]

It is difficult for many organizations to gain access to this process because there are so many very large organizations in Sweden that small or new organizations tend to be ignored. [KF]

Gaining access can be rather difficult for small and new organizations. Everything is already so established. (SUL)

In addition to emphasizing the twin themes of influence inequality among organizations and the difficulties encountered by new and small organizations in attempting to enter the influence process, these comments — especially the last two — introduce a further aspect of this situation. "Everything is already so established," said the last respondent. At the time of this study, the Social Democratic Party had been in power for almost forty years and was unquestionably the core of an extensive and dominant Establishment in Sweden. This was not, however, a military-industrial complex. It centered, instead, around the labor movement, of which the two main (but intertwined) branches are the Social Democratic party and the Swedish Confederation of Trade Unions (LO). Roland Huntford has described the power of the "Social Democratic Movement" in these words:

Since the party has enveloped the State, it is the party . . . who is the ruler of the country. Party is perhaps a misnomer; more correctly it is the Labour movement. This is a huge, variegated organization which, in its control and penetration of society, resembles the Soviet Communist party and, in its desire to be all things to all men, is like the Catholic Church.

The Swedish Labour movement has two heads: the Social Democratic party and the trade unions. Dividing the leadership and sharing duties, they are fused into a monolithic structure with rigid discipline and tremendous strength. The party conducts parliamentary business and administers the government; the unions provide the money, maintain ideological control of the working classes and deliver their votes at election time. [1971:135–36]

In addition to sharing ideological views and pragmatic goals, the party and the unions are directly linked through their memberships, since members of LO trade unions are collectively and involuntarily enrolled in the local Social Democratic group if the majority of the members of the union local so vote (Tomasson, 1970:35). More than two-thirds of all party members are presently affiliated through trade unions in this manner (Andrén, 1968:27). Other types of linkages are also pervasive between these two sides of the movement: "LO has provided financial support to the Social Democratic press, most of which has not been self-supporting, has officially supported the party in its journals, and has actively campaigned for and financially supported the election of Social Democrats. At the top there is an informal council of the party and LO leaders that meets regularly" (Tomasson, 1970:35).

Many of the respondents in this study made similar remarks about LO, of which the following three are typical:

> LO is the only organization that is actually a decision maker in a direct sense. [BHOS]

> When evaluating the influence of interest organizations on the government, you must exclude LO, which is almost synonymous with the government. [SLF]

> One organization — LO — dominates the situation. It has direct links to the party and the government. [SACO]

Besides LO, a number of other interest organizations are also more-or-less linked into the Social Democratic Movement. These are the Cooperative Federation (KF), the Workers' Education Association (ABF), the National Association of Tenants (HGRF), the Swedish United Student Union (SFS), and the National Association for Sexual Education (RFSU). Although there is considerable variation in the closeness with which these other organizations are part of the movement, they all identify strongly with its basic philosophy, and their memberships overlap extensively with that of the Social Democratic party.[12]

---

12. The ways in which the activities of these "subsidiary" organizations support the goals and actions of the Social Democratic party are described in considerable detail in Huntford (1971).

Let us therefore reexamine the data in Table 4.1, classifying all organizations as either movement[13] or nonmovement. The resulting mean influence scores are as follows:

Procedures	Movement Organizations	Nonmovement Organizations
Initiatives	4.0	2.2
Planning councils	1.7	1.5
Investigative commissions	3.6	2.8
Commentaries	4.1	2.9
Riksdag membership	2.7	1.2
Riksdag committees	2.0	1.4
Agency boards	2.9	1.8
Agency consultation	2.8	2.7
Overall average	3.0	2.1

On all of the eight influence procedures, the mean score for movement organizations is higher than for nonmovement organizations, and the two overall average scores are almost a full rank apart. Organizations that are part of this movement are thus seen as being significantly more powerful politically than all other organizations.

Finally, to carry this thesis one step further, it might also be argued that within the movement there is a small inner circle of people — a "dominant clique" or "power elite" — that in reality makes most of the crucial policy decisions. Although this research did not specifically attempt to discover whether or not such a "mini-power elite" actually exists in Sweden today, two of the respondents suggested that this was indeed the case:

> There is a general tendency in Sweden to centralize the decision-making process more and more. The number of people influencing decisions is steadily declining. [SAEF]

> The same people meet together in different circumstances, boards, committees, etc. Perhaps 20-30 people are in all the various councils, commissions, boards, and committees dealing with education, for example. . . . The system is too small and closed. We meet the same persons in many different contexts, and they come to have perhaps too much influence, especially as these relationships become quite personal. This is not corruption, but a very closed system in which a few people have very overriding influence. [BEDU]

---

13. In this computation, the scores for LO are weighted double, because of its extreme importance within the movement.

A similar statement is also attributed by Huntford (1971:105) to an official of one of the major Swedish central organizations: "Sweden's a small country, and the whole bureaucratic establishment's also very small—not more than two or three hundred rule the country, and we all know each other. We've got a contact network behind the scenes, and it's there we really work. You might say that we rule by a kind of licensed intrigue." Sweden is apparently no exception to the general tendency for power to become increasingly centralized at the national level in contemporary industrialized-urbanized-bureaucratized societies.

Specific Influence Procedures

In this section our focus shifts from the total Swedish system of influence procedures to evaluating each of these procedures in detail. More specifically, we shall compare the perceived effectiveness of each of the eight formal procedures relative to one another, evaluate the operational adequacy of each of these procedures, and then examine the three informal techniques of private meetings, public opinion formation, and personal contacts.

Relative Effectiveness of the Procedures

How useful are the various formal influence procedures believed to be in relation to one another? Let us begin by referring back to Table 9.1, which reported mean scores for the amount of influence exerted via each procedure. A definite pattern can be seen in the summary figures for all interest organizations in the bottom panel of the table: investigations and commentaries are perceived to be the most effective procedures, with average influence scores of "moderate" (3.0 and 3.1); initiatives and agency consultation rank next in effectiveness, with scores midway between "some" and "moderate" (both 2.6); and the other four procedures — planning councils, Riksdag membership, Riksdag committees, and agency boards — are all seen as relatively ineffective, with average influence scores of "some" (2.0) or less. This basic pattern occurs among both economic and noneconomic interest organizations, although three procedures — investigations, agency boards, and agency consultation — score higher than average among economic organizations (3.4, 2.6, and 3.1, respectively) and lower than average among noneconomic organizations (2.7, 1.2, and 2.1, respectively). Essentially the same pattern also occurs among governmental units, except that all their scores are higher than the corresponding figures for interest organizations;

and agency boards (2.8) score as high as initiatives (2.8) and almost as high as agency consultation (3.1).

From these findings, we can tentatively conclude that two procedures, investigations and commentaries — which are certainly the most discussed and most distinctive features of the Swedish influence system — are seen as being the most effective channels for enabling organizations to influence the government, and that this perception is generally shared by most organizational and governmental leaders. The two second-ranking procedures, initiatives and agency consultation, meanwhile share the common characteristics of being less structured and more interpersonal than the other influence channels. Of the remaining four procedures, two center on the Riksdag, which has relatively little power itself in the Swedish political system, and two involve representation on policy boards that in many cases are not very powerful.

It is interesting to compare these findings with the results of Nils Elvander's (1966:252–55) 1965 study of Swedish interest organizations. He asked the heads of the twenty-two largest economic organizations (all but one of which are included in the present study) to rank order their organization's amount of influence through five different channels: investigations, commentaries, drafting bills in the departments,[14] the Riksdag (he did not differentiate between membership and committees), and the administration (he did not differentiate between governing boards and direct consultation). The resulting overall rankings were as follows: (1) commentaries, (2) investigations, (3) administration, (4) drafting bills, and (5) Riksdag. Moreover, when he repeated this question with reference to each of sixteen different kinds of political, economic, and social issues and then summed the ranks across all these areas, the resulting average rankings were nearly the same: (1 and 2) investigations and commentaries (virtually tied and sharply divided from the others), (3) administration, (4) Riksdag, and (5) drafting bills (the decline of this factor is the only significant difference between the two sets of rankings). Elvander (1966:252) summarized these findings with the observation that "It is noteable that commentaries and investigations are consistently regarded as the most important channels."[15] This generalization is clearly consistent

---

14. In this present research, this technique was considered to be a form of informal, personal consultation rather than a formal influence procedure, since there are no established guidelines for its use and it does in fact normally involve persons in the departments calling on people they know in the major organizations to respond informally and off-the-record to drafts of proposed bills.

15. All quotations from Elvander's book *Intresseorganisationerna i Dagens Sverige* given here are my own translations.

with the results of the present research, as are also Elvander's placement of contacts with administrative agencies at the next level of importance and his conclusion that the Riksdag is a relatively unimportant channel of influence for organizations.

A second way of evaluating the relative effectiveness of the various influence procedures is to determine which ones are seen as most and least important by the respondents. Each person was asked, "In general, which one of these eight procedures is the most effective means by which your organization can exert influence on the political system?" The question was then repeated for the second most effective procedure. [16] The resulting first and second choices are shown in Table 9.2. (In some cases there were multiple first and/or second choices.)

Scattered throughout this table are several interesting findings. Even more pronounced here than in Table 9.1 is the tendency for labor organizations to place heavy emphasis on the use of initiatives. Respondents in business organizations, meanwhile, gave approximately equal weight to initiatives, investigations, agency boards, and agency consultation. Hence, the combined figures for all economic organizations show initiatives in first place, investigations and the two administrative agency procedures essentially tied for second place, commentaries in third place, and the remaining procedures with no points at all. Leaders of member-serving organizations, in contrast, had a strong preference for commentaries over all other procedures, while leaders of public-serving organizations showed only a very slight preference for initiatives. The combined figures for all noneconomic organizations thus place commentaries in first place, initiatives in second place, agency consultation in third place, investigations in fourth place, and the rest of the procedures with few or no points. The overall figures for all interest organizations are as follows: (1) initiatives, 27 points; (2) commentaries, 21 points, and agency consultation, 20 points; (3) investigations, 17 points; (4) agency boards, 12 points; (5) planning councils and Riksdag membership and committees, few or no points.

The responses of governmental leaders to this question are not fully comparable with those of organization leaders, since the full range of procedures is not relevant for any of the governmental units. Within the options available to them, however, a clear difference emerges between departments and agencies. Departmental respondents stressed primarily

---

16. With governmental leaders, the question was phrased in terms of all organizations in relation to that governmental unit.

Table 9.2

First and Second Choices of Most Effective Influence Procedures

(For organizational respondents, the data pertain just to their own organization; for governmental respondents, the data pertain to all organizations in relation to their own office.)

Number of First Choices/Number of Second Choices
(Total points = 2 for first choices, 1 for second choices)

	Initiatives	Planning Councils	Investigative Commissions	Commentaries	Riksdag Membership	Riksdag Committees	Administrative Boards	Administrative Consultation
LO	1st		2nd	2nd			2nd	
All labor organizations	4/0 8 pts.	0/0 0 pts.	0/3 3 pts.	0/1 1 pt.	0/0 0 pts.	0/0 0 pts.	1/1 3 pts.	1/1 3 pts.
Business organizations	4/1 9 pts.	0/0 0 pts.	2/5 9 pts.	2/2 4 pts.	0/0 0 pts.	0/0 0 pts.	3/2 8 pts.	4/2 10 pts.
Member-serving organizations	1/3 5 pts.	0/0 0 pts.	0/3 3 pts.	5/1 11 pts.	1/0 2 pts.	0/0 0 pts.	0/1 1 pt.	2/0 4 pts.
Public-serving organizations	2/1 5 pts.	0/0 0 pts.	0/2 2 pts.	1/2 4 pts.	1/0 2 pts.	1/0 2 pts.	0/0 0 pts.	1/1 3 pts.
Governmental departments	2/2 6 pts.	1/0 2 pts.	2/4 8 pts.	6/3 15 pts.	*	*	*	*
Governmental agencies	1/2 4 pts.	*	0/2 2 pts.	0/1 1 pt.	*	*	5/1 11 pts.	2/2 6 pts.
All economic organizations	8/1 17 pts.	0/0 0 pts.	2/8 12 pts.	2/3 5 pts.	0/0 0 pts.	0/0 0 pts.	4/3 11 pts.	5/3 13 pts.
All noneconomic organizations	3/4 10 pts.	0/0 0 pts.	0/5 5 pts.	6/3 15 pts.	2/0 4 pts.	1/0 2 pts.	0/1 1 pt.	3/1 7 pts.
All interest organizations	11/5 27 pts.	0/0 0 pts.	2/13 17 pts.	8/6 21 pts.	2/0 4 pts.	1/0 2 pts.	4/4 12 pts.	8/4 20 pts.
All governmental units	3/4 10 pts.	1/0 2 pts.	2/6 10 pts.	6/4 16 pts.	*	*	5/1 11 pts.	2/2 6 pts.

*These procedures are not relevant to governmental departments/agencies.

commentaries, to a much lesser extent investigations and initiatives, and hardly at all their own policy councils. Administrative agency respondents, however, placed great importance on representation in their governing boards, followed by consultations and initiatives, and attributed virtually no importance to investigations or commentaries.[17] Quite clearly, governmental personnel differed among themselves and from organizational leaders in their perceptions of the relative importance of the various influence procedures.

With two sets of data from this present research plus Elvander's findings before us, let us pull this material together into a few conclusions about the relative effectiveness of the various influence procedures. First, it is evident that these eight procedures fall into two broad categories in terms of effectiveness: The first set, comprising the more effective influence mechanisms, includes initiatives, investigations, commentaries, and agency consultation. The less-effective means make up the second set, which includes policy councils, Riksdag membership and committees, and agency boards. That division comes through in all three sets of data.

Second, taking initiatives is extremely important for some kinds of organizations — particularly labor associations, and to a lesser extent public-serving groups — but not for others. The overall status of this procedure is somewhat ambiguous, therefore, since it ranks third in Table 9.1 and first in Table 9.2. Perhaps the best way of resolving the difference is simply to say that initiatives are probably at least as important as any other procedure.

Third, investigations and commentaries are believed to be relatively effective means for exerting political influence — although it must be remembered that their preeminence is only in relation to the other procedures and does not necessarily imply any degree of operational adequacy in an absolute sense. Economic organizations tend to view investigations as considerably more effective than commentaries, while noneconomic organizations favor commentaries (and for many of these organizations this is the only available influence channel other than the nebulous process of trying to influence public opinion). Governmental leaders — especially those in the departments — prefer commentaries over investigations by a considerable margin.

---

17. Administrative agencies do not use these latter two procedures anywhere near as frequently as do the governmental departments, but all of the agency respondents said that they did at least occasionally appoint investigative commissions and subsequently send the reports out for commentaries.

Fourth, there are some grounds for arguing that the less-structured procedures — initiatives and agency consultation — are presently usurping the preeminence of investigations and commentaries. Direct consultation with administrative agencies is particularly important for business organizations, since in this context they can enact their preferred role of expert consultant without becoming embroiled in political conflicts.

Fifth, organizational representatives on the governing boards of administrative agencies have more influence than do representatives on the policy councils of the departments, although governmental leaders in the agencies are more convinced of the importance of board representation than are organizational leaders. No one sees departmental policy councils as providing a viable influence channel.

Sixth, both membership in the Riksdag and testimony before its committees are viewed by nearly everyone (with the exception of the temperance associations) as almost totally ineffective as influence routes for organizations.

Overall, these findings concerning the relative effectiveness of the various influence procedures undoubtedly reflect the importance of the various stages in the policy-making process in any parliamentary political system. That is, inputs from the general public (initiatives) are necessary to begin the process in regard to some issue, formulation of governmental policies (investigations and commentaries) is the crucial stage, formal legitimization of the final policy (Riksdag approval) is largely a pro forma matter, and implementation of the policy (administrative agency consultation) becomes increasingly critical in a highly bureaucratized system.

Operational Adequacy of the Procedures

The various influence procedures have been found to differ considerably in their perceived effectiveness relative to one another. As yet, however, we have no basis for assessing the operational adequacy or inadequacy of each procedure in a more absolute sense. In the eyes of these respondents, which procedures — if any — are actually functioning as viable channels for upward flows of influence from interest organizations to the government? To make these evaluations, we turn to comments made by the respondents concerning both the benefits and the problems they had experienced with each procedure.

Initiatives. Elvander's (1966: 170) study of Swedish interest organizations concluded that it was impossible to ascertain the extent to which proposals by organizations lay behind propositions presented to the cabinet and the Riksdag, due to the fact that the origins of these propositions are rarely publicly reported. This theme of the "hidden effects" of initiatives was also mentioned by several respondents in this research.

Nevertheless, there was widespread agreement that this procedure was of considerable importance, especially for labor organizations:

> Taking initiatives to the government is extremely important for LO. We try to develop our own positions with the government, rather than follow other organizations' stands. [LO]

> Taking initiatives is the most valuable procedure for us. There are many different ways in which an organization can exert indirect pressures on various government agencies and departments, encouraging them to take desired actions. [SACO]

Moreover, as we saw in the previous section, this process of initiative taking ranked first among organizational leaders as the most important influence procedure for their organization. Hence, there can be no doubt that initiative taking is a functionally viable and useful way for organizations to influence the government. But why is this so?

Most of the organizational leaders who commented more extensively on the use of initiatives indicated that they were beneficial and effective primarily because they involved informal personal contacts with governmental officials and/or an opportunity to mold public opinion:

> LO takes initiatives through monthly meetings between governmental officials and the LO Board, as well as through informal discussion, which is one of the most important means of exerting influence. . . . Making initiatives through formal documents is much less common.[LO]

> Initiatives are an effective way of exerting influence because they often involve personal contacts, rather than just written documents. This is especially true on technical questions. [SFF]

> Initiatives are very important to our organization, even if the process is rather indirect, because they provide a way of getting publicity and affecting public opinion. [KRUM]

The governmental respondents, meanwhile, generally agreed that organizations did not make anywhere near as much use of initiatives as they might, and that most such interactions with organizations were in fact instigated by government offices:

> Our agency often takes the initiative in contacting organizations; this is more common than organizations taking the initiative, especially on technical questions. [BEDU]

> It would be profitable for me to have much more influence from the organizations, if they would simply take the initiative, especially through small, informal meetings. [DCOM]

In his recent study of twelve critical tax decisions, Elvander (1972b) agreed with this contention that many organizations are quite passive in taking initiatives: "As a rule, the actual initiatives for tax reforms have come from the government. . . . "

Overall, it would appear that this process of initiative taking is quite highly regarded by most organizational leaders and is generally welcomed and encouraged by governmental officials. Unstructured and indirect though they may be, initiatives apparently do provide a workable channel through which interest organizations can influence the government, primarily because of the personal contacts and publicity involved in this process.

Planning Councils. Several respondents stated quite explicitly that these councils are essentially vehicles for communication, not decision making:

> Our planning council is more a forum for informal discussion than for policy formation. [DFIN]

> These councils are not used as widely now as in the past; they are presently used mainly for outward communication from governmental departments to the organizations. [DIND]

> These councils are not important for LO. We have more direct methods of exerting influence. The councils are not very influential; they are mainly just information and discussion groups. LO has some influence in the councils, but they have no influence on the government. [LO]

A further factor limiting the adequacy of these councils as influence channels for organizations is the fact that only a few of the major organizations (LO, TCO, SAF, SIF, etc.) have representatives on the councils, and they are selected by the departments themselves. All other organizations have no access to these councils.

As a result of his research, Elvander (1966:206) concluded that: "The planning councils hitherto have not had any great importance as channels for organizational influence on governmental policies. They are not centers of power; important decisions are conceived and prepared elsewhere." The findings of this present study fully support his conclusion that the councils are basically powerless. Mechanisms such as these for facilitating direct communication between policy makers in the governmental departments and leaders of the major economic organizations can certainly be useful for all concerned, but they must not be mistaken for influence channels — which they clearly are not.

Commissions. There is no doubt that organizational and governmental leaders in Sweden generally think that the practice of appointing investigative commissions to study and make recommendations on all major public issues is highly desirable. In Table 9.1, we saw that, of all the influence procedures, investigations had the highest average perceived influence score (3.4) among economic organizations, and nearly as high a score (3.0) among all interest organizations. On the basis of these data alone, we might well conclude that Swedish investigative commissions are functioning quite satisfactorily.

When the respondents were pressed for more specific evaluations of the operational usefulness of investigative commissions, however, it quickly became apparent that there are actually many serious problems with this process that are rather widely recognized. The following paragraphs describe the most critical of these problems.

1. Investigative commissions operate very slowly, often taking several years to prepare a final report. If the initial conditions that prompted the appointment of a commission were at all pressing, the problem may have become extremely serious (or else been resolved in some way) before even this preliminary stage of the legislative process is completed. Some of the more cynical respondents also agreed with Andrén's (1968:183) suggestion that appointing an investigative commission is a convenient way for the government to push aside an unwanted issue and avoid having to make a decision on it: "It is all too easy to bury an unpleasant matter in

a commission — at least for some years." In addition, since each commission is appointed on an ad hoc basis (there are no permanent investigative commissions), most commissions spend a great deal of time at first developing operating procedures, becoming acquainted with their task, and otherwise settling down to work. Typical comments along these lines were that

> The major problem with these procedures is the time involved; it often takes months or years for an investigation to submit a report and then *remiss* statements to be written on it. (KF)

> Investigations often take far too long. The government sometimes conducts investigations rather than making decisions. (SUL)

2. Considerable ambiguity surrounds the process whereby organizational representatives are selected to serve on investigative commissions. What organizations should have representatives on any particular commissions, and why should the selection of these organizations be made solely by governmental officials? Does this not automatically exclude many other interested organizations from participation in the process — especially those that differ politically from the government? Moreover, as Elvander (1966:109) has pointed out, whereas the large labor-market organizations are usually permitted to select their own representatives for these commissions, the smaller organizations are often asked to submit several candidates to the sponsoring department, which then makes the final selection. These themes are reflected in the following statements:

> It is almost impossible for organizations like us to get representatives on investigative commissions. [SFS]

> Our point of view is often not listened to. We should be represented on more investigative commissions; sometimes we are not included when issues are directly relevant for us. [SHIO]

> Commissions will not try to get representation from all sides of questions. . . . Too often commissions don't include representatives of many points of view. This depends entirely on the top politicians and how they perceive the political situation in a particular case. The political climate determines the composition of commissions. [RMH]

Elvander's (1972b) study of tax issues also concluded that in many cases the government could and did exclude organizations from investigative commissions whenever it wished: "It appears that the parties . . . played major roles in the twelve royal commissions on tax policy which I investigated. The organizations were not represented on most of the commissions. The government—which in the Swedish system appoints all commissions of investigation—thus regarded tax policy as the domain of the political parties."

3. Other means of attempting to influence investigative commissions apart from having organizational representatives on the commission are relatively ineffective. Although any interested organization can send a written statement or other document to a commission, or may request (and normally be permitted) to testify orally before the commission, there is no way for the organization to ensure that its position will be given serious consideration by the commission. Another technique often used by organizations is to have one or more of their personnel appointed as technical experts for the commission. These experts do most of the actual investigative work of the commission and in this sense can have considerable indirect influence, but it is largely restricted to technical and scientific rather than policy issues; and these experts do not participate in the final decision making of the commission. Respondents who commented on this topic made remarks such as these:

> When investigations are made, it is difficult to have any influence through just consultation. [ABF]

> Every organization has the right to send a written statement to any commission. But it is difficult for organizations that do not have members on the commission to influence the discussion in the commissions, and this is when the most crucial compromises are often made. [TCO]

> We usually have experts working for commissions, but their advice is not necessarily followed or even listened to. [SKF]

4. Commission reports emphasize compromise and consensus and tend to avoid dissenting opinions or open conflict. Swedish political decision making is often described as "the politics of compromise," and it is within these investigative commissions that the compromise process begins. Most commissions will go to great lengths to present a unanimous report

to the public — no matter how "watered down" through compromise this document may be. As expressed by Nils Andrén (1968:185): "It is a recognized and appreciated ambition of most commissions to do their utmost to reach agreement and avoid minority reports or 'reservations.' This ambition cannot, of course, always be fulfilled. But it is a fact that a unanimous report stands a better chance of serving as a basis for future legislation than a report disclosing disagreement on important points." This push for consensus tends to choke off dissent and political conflict at a very early stage in the legislative process, before the general public, the Riksdag, or even most interest organizations have even had an opportunity to join in the debate. In the words of two of the respondents:

> These commissions are to a very great extent compromising bodies. But I wonder if compromises should be made at this early, formulative stage. [DPLN]

> The government is rarely faced with alternative solutions to problems, as political compromises are usually worked out in the commissions. It would be better for the government if several alternatives were recommended and documented in the commission reports. [DCOM]

5. The government often decides on at least the broad outlines of a solution to a problem before appointing a commission to investigate it and gives the commission little or no freedom to deviate from this previously established position. The role of the commission is then merely to work out the technical and applied details of the governmental solution. This strict governmental control over the work of the commissions is accomplished through the directions given the commission by the sponsoring department. These directives may be, in the words of Hans Meijer (1969:105, 114), "entirely free from preconceived notions of acceptable solutions and thus give the commission a broad frame of reference within which to operate, or they can directly indicate one or a few solutions that are to be considered. . . . As a rule the Departments leave the commissions relatively at liberty once the directives have been given, but if in some particular case it is feared that a commission is in the process of getting off the track and that it is proceeding contrary to the wishes of the Department, it is possible to intervene. New or complementary directives might be furnished the commission, or its membership might be augmented with a few new commissioners who can be expected to be more sympathetic to the wishes of the Government."

Frequent use of these control mechanisms by the government to dictate the main provisions, if not all the details, of commission reports was noted — often rather bitterly — by many of the respondents in this study:

> Investigative commissions have lost some of their importance in recent years. In many cases the position of the government is formulated before the commission is even appointed, and the directives given to the commission largely dictate the solution the government wants. [SFRF]

> In general, the government has already decided to make a policy change before a commission is appointed. They use the commissions only to work out technical details. The commissions can't alter basic political directions. This tendency, which reduces our role in the commissions to purely technical advisors, has been increasing during the past three years. The result is poorer quality reports; there is no opposition within the commissions, and not as much information is provided, especially contradictory information. [SIF]

> Investigative commissions were extremely important in the whole fabric of Swedish politics, but there has been a sharp decline in the influence of these bodies. The government has a tendency to ignore their advice. This is a rather slow procedure, and decision makers in the government tend to want instant solutions to problems. Moreover, commission reports may recommend things the government doesn't want. Consequently, there is a tendency for the government to tell the commission exactly what it wants, so as to tailor the work of the commission to the goals of the government. There are few unrestricted commissions any more. [SAEF]

6. Although the commissions may not actually formulate public policies or programs in most cases, they do perform many other valuable functions *for the government.* These include burying undesired issues, promoting compromises among conflicting organizations or otherwise controlling the policies and actions of interest organizations, providing useful information to governmental officials, coopting organizational leaders to support or at least not publicly criticize governmental policies and programs, and gaining broad-scale legitimacy for political decisions made by the government. A number of these "latent functions" of investigative commissions were recently listed by Meijer (1969:101): "Depending on how members of the commissions are recruited, they may serve as useful sources among various groups for policy decisions in specific questions. They may be used

as a means for putting off inconvenient decisions until a future date, or they can form the basis for creating consensus or compromise between parties, interest organizations, or experts prior to the time the government is forced to adopt an official position." Several of the respondents in this study were quite explicit in mentioning ways in which the government uses investigative commissions for its own purposes:

> When organizations have representatives on commissions, it is more useful to us. They then have to take more responsibility for the final proposal and to stand behind the decision. It is easier for us to handle the organizations in this way, and their specialized knowledge can be very useful to us. [DCMN]

> The departments can manipulate the commissions to give the decision that they want; the commissions are very useful to the departments in thus legitimizing departmental decisions. [DAGR]

> The government uses investigative commissions largely to prevent organizations from later complaining about the decisions taken; this is cooptation of the organizations by the government. [SKF]

7. Organizational representatives are steadily constituting a smaller and smaller proportion of commission members, and there is an increasing tendency toward appointing "departmental commissions" composed entirely of bureaucrats and technical experts from within the sponsoring department. A long-term decline in the number of commission members coming from interest organizations, and a corresponding rise in the number of civil servants, was documented by Elvander (1966:174–75), who showed that between 1945 and 1967 the proportion of organizational representatives dropped from 34 percent to 20 percent, while the proportion of governmental employees rose from 41 percent to 60 percent.[18] He commented that: "This trend can be interpreted as an indication of continued power centralization in the cabinet and the state bureaucracy, at the expense of . . . the organizations' influence in the investigative activities. The cabinet has acquired an extremely firm grip on the investigations, and these investigations have become increasingly integrated into the governmental administration." Nils Andrén (1968:186) described the trend in these words: "An alternative method of investigation, with the

18. Detailed figures on the trend since 1905 are given in both Elvander (1966:175) and Meijer (1969:109).

advantage of less built-in compromise procedures, has acquired increased importance in recent years. This method is investigations by experts in the departments themselves, carried out by their own staff or by experts employed for the purpose, who can make a concentrated effort over a brief period in order to produce the memorandum necessary for further action."[19]

This move toward increased reliance on expert "departmental commissions" — often called "task forces" to distinguish them from the usual type of commissions — was noted by most of the governmental officials in this study:

> If the government has a clear idea of a solution to a problem, it is much simpler and faster to simply make the investigation within the department. This is also done for political reasons, depending on which parties and organizations support a proposal. [DFIN]

> The government is getting tired of commissions; they take too much time and result only in political compromises. We get better results if we simply put two or three experts to work on a subject for a few months. There is a clear trend toward proposals being formulated entirely within the departments. [DCOM]

> We use scientific advisors more than organizations for consultation; we have about 130 such advisors, and they exercise great influence because of their professional status. [BWEL]

Surprisingly, however, only a handful of the organizational leaders were aware of this pervasive trend, and not all of them objected to it. Regardless of whether or not organizational leaders are aware of this trend, however, it is obviously leaving them outside the investigative process, thus increasingly shutting off this means of exerting influence on the government.

Taken together, these seven problems in the current use of investigative commissions rather overwhelmingly argue that this influence procedure is seen by its users as relatively worthless — for interest organizations — at the present time and is likely to become even less useful in the future. Although this influence procedure ideally allows any interest organization to have significant input into the early stages of public policy formation, the respondents in this study generally believed that, in practice, investi-

---

19. For another discussion of this trend, see Sjoberg, Hancock, and White (1967:9).

gative commissions are being used by the government to coopt and control the organizations and to legitimize its own decisions.

Commentaries.   As with investigative commissions, it is very easy to gain a superficial impression that written commentaries on commission reports — called *remiss* statements in Swedish — provide a highly viable channel through which interest organizations can have direct impacts on political decision making. Most published descriptions of this process credit it with great political weight. For instance, Andrén (1968:187) wrote that, "if the opinions submitted in the *remiss*-answers have been very critical, it is possible that the whole matter will be abandoned for some time until a new investigation can be made or the old report can be subjected to a major revision." Elvander (1966:180–81) also spoke rather positively about the effectiveness of these commentaries, although he did caution that their importance varied by types of questions and across various organizations:

> Organizational leaders consider, nearly without exception, that the *remiss*-procedure is of great importance, both for their own organization and from a more general point of view. Even if a *remiss*-statement is not taken into consideration in a governmental proposition, it can exert indirect, long-term influence on the state powers, especially as it attracts attention in debates in the Riksdag and the press. *Remiss*-answers become a kind of codification of an organization's policies, they force out attitudes on new questions, and they provide a basis for informing members and the general public. There is a general conception among the organizations that the direct effects of *remiss* statements are greatest in more specific, technical questions in which the organizations are immediately affected and in which they are considered to be experts, while the possibilities of affecting more general political questions are very small. This applies especially to business organizations. But with labor organizations it is more to the contrary; their statements on major issues, above all in the labor-market and social-policy areas, weigh heavily, while their statements on more detailed topics are seldom given sufficient consideration.

In his more recent research on tax issues, however, Elvander (1972b) expressed a somewhat more ambivalent stance, stating that "the parties often adopt views at the commission stage which coincide with their final standpoints on proposals, party motions, and parliamentary committee reports. In such cases the parties are but little influenced by the *remiss* answers of the organizations. The organizations' views serve to reinforce the opinions already adopted by the parties, rather than as a basis for their decisions."

In Table 9.1 we saw that this procedure had the highest average score among both organizational and governmental leaders (3.1 and 3.5, respectively). And in Table 9.2 commentaries ranked second among interest organizations and first among governmental units as the most effective influence procedure. Quite clearly, both organizational and political leaders think very highly of this practice of writing commentaries on the reports of investigative commissions. But again, we must probe beneath the surface to find out how the respondents evaluate the operational adequacy of this procedure.

1. One potential problem area explored in the interviews was the ease with which new and small organizations could become involved in the *remiss* process. Initially, copies of a commission report and requests for commentaries are sent by the originating department only to a selected list of the larger and more established organizations with which it has commonly worked in the past. Most of the governmental respondents were quick to point out, however, that any other interested organization could request a copy of the report and submit a commentary on it, and that these unsolicited statements were given as much attention as the solicited ones. For instance:

> We have a list of organizations for each question, depending on the topic. But any other organization can get a copy of a report and write a statement on it. All the organizations' commentaries are explicitly mentioned in the bill sent to the Riksdag. [DEDU]

> Any organization can write a statement. Getting on the list is only a result of showing interest over time. All organizations are given equal consideration. [DINT]

> Any organization can ask for the report and send in a statement. The organizations on the department's list get no special preference. [DCOM]

It does appear, then, that the departments make sincere efforts to include in the *remiss* process all organizations that wish to take part. Peripheral organizations of all kinds can write commentaries if they wish — as long as they keep abreast of commission reports being submitted and take the initiative to request copies of them from the departments.

2. Much more crucial is the question of whether all commentaries are given sufficient consideration. Commentaries by small associations such as the National Organization for Mental Health clearly do not carry as much weight with the government as do those by LO. As admitted by two governmental officials:

> All organizations can write to the board, but we do give most attention to larger organizations. [BEDU]

> Commentaries are used mainly for technical questions. The large organizations have much more weight than the smaller ones in this process. [DIND]

Such differential weighting may be justified in light of both size and scope of activities; but many respondents from smaller and weaker organizations felt that their *remiss* statements received scant attention from the government:

> The quality of reasoning in *remiss* statements is not as important as the standing of the organizations writing them. [RFHL]

The relative lack of influence of commentaries by organizations was attributed by some governmental leaders to the fact that many of these statements are essentially worthless:

> The *remiss* statements are often written primarily for the organization's members or the general public, rather than the government. They are often very general in nature, and lack specificity. [DIND]

> After a long and thorough investigation, it is not much use to get comments on minor details from organizations. They can't have much impact at that point. We do read all comments, and if there are really serious objections to a proposal, we take account of them. But most commentary is so trivial that it is not worth taking account of. [BEDU]

The answer of a number of organizational leaders to this charge, however, is that they are continually asked to respond to more reports than their resources permit. This is true of large organizations such as LO as well as smaller organizations:

> It often places a very heavy burden on LO to answer all the *remiss* requests that come to us. And we often don't get enough time to write adequate replies. [LO]

> *Remiss* writing is a very time consuming activity, . . . and recently we have been swamped by the increasing load of statements. [HGRF]

3. When respondents were pressed more directly about the adequacy of *remiss* statements as an influence procedure, an interesting split occurred between governmental and organizational leaders. All of the governmental respondents who offered detailed remarks about this procedure were rather favorable toward it, for a variety of reasons:

> The *remiss* procedure is the most effective means through which interest organizations exert influence on our agency, since if they turn down something we are suggesting there is no chance of getting it through. This is because of their heavy influence in the parties and the government. [BHOS]

> *Remiss* statements are more important than investigative commissions as a means of organizational influence because they represent the official policy of the entire organization, rather than just the opinions of one individual representative. [DJUS]

> Commentaries are usually concerned with minor issues in reports of a practical nature. These technical matters can be of great importance in the overall proposal, however, so that the organizations can have considerable influence in this manner. Within the formal system, *remiss* statements are the most important influence procedure; although they don't affect overall goals, they deal with the practical issues which are the crucial aspect of any proposal. [DCOM]

In sharp contrast, many of the organizational leaders were quite critical of the *remiss* procedure. They saw it as a largely or wholly inadequate influence channel, with the most frequent reason being that the government normally reaches its own decision concerning a proposal long before it is sent out for commentaries. Hence, the main function of the *remiss* procedure was seen as gaining support and legitimization from the organizations for governmental policies and proposals over which they had no control:

> When views differ on *remiss* statements, the government feels quite free to do whatever it wants. . . . The government doesn't always pay attention to statements it receives. . . . [DCMN]

> On a recent tax issue, 47 of 49 *remiss* statements were against it, but the government instituted it anyway. This is not unusual. We have serious questions about the value of the *remiss* process; it is too costly for us . . . and produces few results. [SGF]

> The government remits to organizations after a decision has already been made; it becomes just a formality most of the time. [SLF]

> It is extremely difficult to change proposals through *remiss* statements. Members of the government are already bound to the proposals they have formulated, especially when the investigative commission writing the initial report was composed entirely of officials from within the government. [SFF]

> In most cases, reports of research commissions cannot be significantly changed. Several years of work have already gone into formulating the reports, and their conclusions are based on much research. Nor are alternative sets of recommendations ever presented. The organizations can't say very much in *remiss* statements other than comment on small items, since there are no alternatives, and we can't ourselves work out alternatives. *Remiss* statements are used largely to ratify a *fait accompli* and to coopt organizations into supporting governmental decisions. [KRUM]

The bulk of the evidence clearly constitutes a severe condemnation of the adequacy of *remiss* statements to influence governmental decision making. Writing commentaries may give some organization members a feeling that they are participating in the political process, but it is evident that most leaders of these organizations hold a very different perception of the *remiss* process. Once more we encounter a procedure that was ostensibly established to encourage upward flow of influence from organizations to the government, but in practice it appears to have been largely usurped by the government as a means of acquiring organizational support for its own policies and goals.

Riksdag Membership. The first thing to remember when evaluating the Riksdag as an influence channel is that it exercises relatively little power in the Swedish political system, so that no matter how much influence organizations might have on the Riksdag, its ability to determine governmental policy is extremely limited. With a few exceptions, the Riksdag does not initiate legislation but, rather, simply debates and ratifies propositions formulated by the cabinet. These governmental proposals — including all fiscal matters — are vigorously debated in the Riksdag, but normally this discussion deals only with minor details and technical points, not the basic issue. Once the leaders of the Social Democratic party had endorsed a proposition, it was a foregone conclusion — considering the strong party discipline existing among most legislators — that it would be passed by the Riksdag with no major substantive changes. Speaking of political trends in Sweden since 1945, Nils Elvander (1966:290) wrote that "a shift in power has occurred, first and foremost to the cabinet, but also to the administrative agencies, and this shift has been at the expense of the Riksdag's influence."

"Under these circumstances," asks Roland Huntford (1971:108), "what functions remain to the Diet[20] and what remains for the members to talk about? After government and corporate organizations have agreed, the result of their deliberations is presented to the Diet for ratification. Debate is confined to empty oratory about generalities, designed to show the electorate that their representatives do, in fact, work. Whatever the question, the assembly is generally in agreement. Issue is rarely taken over principle, the permitted ration of criticism being concentrated on deatils, and intended to suggest that the government's opponents, while accepting its aims, could realize them better." A similar thought was also expressed by one of the LO respondents in this study: "With our present political system, we really don't need the Riksdag at all."

With this background in mind, we then ask whether or not organizations do attempt to get their representatives elected to Parliament, so as to acquire another influence channel. In a survey of members of the lower house of the Riksdag[21] in 1963, Elvander (1966:208–12) found that 94

---

20. Huntford translates the Swedish name *Riksdag* as "Diet" rather than as "Parliament."

21. At that time, the Swedish Riksdag consisted of two houses, of which only the lower one was popularly elected. Since then, the Riksdag has been changed to a single, popularly elected body.

percent of these people belonged to two or three organizations. But he immediately went on to point out that these membership figures gave no indication of the actual influence of the organizations in the Riksdag, since they did not indicate the extent to which members were actually serving as representatives or spokesmen for their organizations. When he counted only those persons who were either appointed functionaries or elected officials in their organizations, he found that only 32 percent of the 382 members of this house qualified as organizational representatives, and only half of these people — 16 percent of the total membership — actually considered themselves to be spokesmen for their organizations. Quite clearly, the organizations do not control the Riksdag through sheer weight of numbers.

At the same time, however, it is true that most of those members of the Riksdag who are spokesmen for the major organizations exercise additional influence in the Parliament because of their organizational connections. This was stated explicitly by one of the LO respondents in this study:

Many Riksdag members are of course also union members, but they don't speak for their unions at all. There are very few union leaders in the Riksdag; no more than four or five. But these few LO representatives in the Riksdag are quite influential.

Because of these LO representatives in the Riksdag, the LO respondents gave this procedure a score of 3 on the influence scale in Table 9.1. Most other organizational leaders gave this influence channel very low ratings, however, so that its average score among all economic organizations was only 1.3 and among noneconomic organizations 1.8, for an overall average of 1.5 — which is the lowest average score among all the eight procedures.[22] In addition, many respondents explicitly stated that Riksdag membership was totally worthless as an influence channel except for LO and other movement organizations (whose mean score on the influence scale was 2.7, compared with 1.2 for all other organizations).

From this analysis of Riksdag membership as an influence procedure, we conclude: (a) most organizations have few or no actual spokesmen in

22. Because all the governmental respondents were located in either departments or agencies and hence had no direct experience with the Riksdag, they were not asked to evaluate the adequacy of either of the two influence procedures involving the Riksdag.

the Riksdag, and (b) the Riksdag is by far the weakest link in the Swedish political system, but that (c) organizations within the movement are able to utilize this procedure with considerable effectiveness, primarily because of the political leverage their representatives can wield within the Social Democratic party.

Riksdag Committees. Given the relative powerlessness of the Riksdag in the Swedish political system, it is obvious that giving written or oral testimony to parliamentary committees cannot provide a very adequate means of exerting influence on the government. If the issues considered by the Riksdag are generally of only a minor or technical nature, then most testimony given to its committees is bound to be rather perfunctory. In fact, committee hearings in the Riksdag have traditionally been rather brief, with a minimum of testimony by persons or groups from outside the political parties, and with voting along strict party lines. Moreover, since most committee hearings are closed to the public, organizations have not even been able to use them as a platform for gaining press and public attention. As expressed by Elvander (1966:216–17): "From a broad perspective, it can be said that the organizations' insignificant activities in the important standing committees indicates that they do not attach any great meaning to the Riksdag as a way of directly influencing political decision formation. They don't expect the Riksdag committee hearings will lead to many important alterations in government propositions." And in his later research on tax issues (Elvander, 1972b), he concluded that "in important questions the organizations address themselves directly to the government by their *remiss* answers and informal contacts; they do not go via the parties in the Riksdag."

We saw in Table 9.1 that the influence scores of Riksdag committee hearings were almost as low as those of Riksdag membership: 1.8 for economic organizations and 1.6 for noneconomic organizations, for an overall average of just 1.7. Even the movement organizations did not evaluate this procedure very highly, although their average score (2.4) was significantly higher than that for nonmovement organizations (1.4).

During the past few years, there has been an effort in the Riksdag to utilize hearings more extensively, and some organizational leaders mentioned that they would like to make more use of this approach than they have in the past. But even so, they remained skeptical about the amount of influence that could be exerted in this manner. Typical of these remarks are the following:

We are making increasing use of testimony before Riksdag committees, but this is also a marginal procedure; it never concerns major political questions. [SBF]

Testifying before Riksdag committees is just window-dressing for our members, just a public ritual. The decision process has already gone too far by this time, and the decision is already largely made. [SLF]

In sum, if the total Swedish political system were to be altered toward giving more importance to parliamentary debate and voting, this procedure of testifying before Riksdag committees might become a significant influence channel. But under present circumstances, this is clearly not a viable route for organizations to follow in attempting to influence the government.

Agency Boards. Governing boards in the administrative agencies, containing representatives of interest organizations, are a rather new development in Sweden, so that there is considerable variation among the agencies in the composition and authority of their boards. Elvander's (1966:233) earlier research did not give much attention to this influence channel, partially because these boards were quite new at the time. Moreover, his evaluation of the effectiveness of various influence techniques did not distinguish between executive board representation and direct consultation at lower levels. The only generalization we can obtain from that work, consequently, is the broad statement that "the representation of interest organizations in the administration is of very broad scope in Sweden. One sign of this is that all of the examined top organizations . . . are represented in various administrative authorities, most in large numbers."

Two of the agency respondents in the present study were quite critical of this influence technique, and one of them said outright that "our executive board has extremely little influence" (BWEL). Four of the agency respondents, however, reported that their boards made basic policy decisions for the agency and that organizations played a highly influential role in this process:

For our agency, the administrative board is the major means through which organizations exert influence. We discuss all major policy decisions in this board. [BLBR]

> On any question of importance, there is always discussion with repre-
> sentatives of all the relevant organizations. The council . . . is con-
> tinually used. [BHOS]

Consequently, as seen in Table 9.1, the average influence score for this
procedure among the administrative agencies was relatively high, at 2.8.
And in Table 9.2 these agency respondents ranked it far above all other
procedures in terms of importance for their agencies.

Labor and business leaders, most of whose organizations are represented on one or more of these boards, also attributed considerable importance to agency governing boards, so that their mean score in Table 9.2
was 2.6. In particular, LO viewed this procedure as extremely valuable,
giving it a score of 5 on the influence scale:

> Most important for LO is the Labor Market Board. We have great
> influence there, as well as in several other boards dealing with matters
> of concern to LO.

The stance of most leaders from noneconomic organizations on
this question is strikingly different, however. Because few of these
organizations are represented on any of the agency boards, those respondents gave the procedure quite low scores: 1.6 among member-
serving organizations and just 0.7 among public-serving groups, for an
average score of 1.2. When questioned further about the importance of
agency board membership for their organizations, most of these respondents replied that the question was irrelevant for them — they didn't
have any representatives on agency boards and hence exercised no influence in this manner.

Our conclusion in this case is, therefore, that representation on governing boards of administrative agencies can be a highly effective influence
channel for the major economic organizations in those agencies in which
the board has real decision-making authority. But this influence procedure
is essentially worthless for noneconomic and other organizations not represented on any boards, and in those agencies in which the board has no
meaningful authority.

Agency Consultation. Lateral contacts and consultation between
operating bureaus and offices in the administrative agencies and their
counterparts in various interest organizations are extremely common in

Sweden and occur much more frequently than do lateral contacts between organizations and departments (Elvander, 1966:235). Although this consultation generally involves practical problems of program implementation rather than basic policy formation, the manner in which a public program is administered can be of crucial significance for organizations. As expressed by Elvander (1966:291): "The top executives in commercial organizations often say that the shift in power to the cabinet [from the Riksdag] means that their influence on political questions has decreased, but that this decrease has been compensated by the fact that the administration has gained in importance, since many issues are of a complicated and technical nature, and this gives commercial organizations a greater opportunity for exerting influence on technical, if not on political questions."

The business leaders in this study fully agreed with Elvander, giving this procedure a higher average influence score than any other procedure (Table 9.1 mean = 3.5). Similarly, administrative agency respondents also gave it the highest average score (3.1) of all the procedures pertaining to them. Labor leaders evaluated it much lower (2.3), however, as did leaders of noneconomic organizations (2.1). Part of this divergence is undoubtedly due to the fact that businessmen are primarily concerned with influencing technical and applied questions, which are also the primary concerns of agency personnel, whereas leaders of labor unions and noneconomic organizations are more concerned with input into basic political issues. Another reason for the divergency is probably that business organizations have more of the technical manpower and other resources needed for this kind of consultation than do most of the noneconomic organizations.

In any case, respondents in this study offered a variety of views concerning the usefulness of agency consultation as an influence technique. Leaders in both LO and TCO — the two largest labor organizations — saw it mainly as an information channel:

> We have many direct contacts with offices within the Labor Market Board, but not too much with most other agencies. But these are used primarily for exchange of information, not influence. [LO]

> These contacts are more for information exchange than for exerting influence. [TCO]

Business leaders, in contrast, stressed the importance of these contacts for them because of their technical nature:

> These contacts are the most effective influence procedure for us because our experts can be used in these circumstances. When political interests are more paramount, we have less influence. [SAF]

> This procedure is most important for us because it usually involves just technical questions, on which we can have some influence. [SFRF]

Another reason often cited — by both organizational and governmental respondents — for the usefulness of this procedure was the fact that it usually involves direct, day-to-day personal contacts, rather than written documents. For example:

> Of all the "formal" influence procedures, contacts with administrative agencies are the most important. In practice, these tend to be daily, informal, and personal interactions between experts of all kinds. [KF]

> The influence of administrative agency contacts is due to the similarity of opinions and interests between people in organizations and agencies at these levels, rather than because of any direct pressures. [BPLN]

> Direct contacts between agency personnel and organizations are quite frequent. Sometimes these are formal meetings to which only certain organizations are invited, but there are also frequent informal contacts between individuals. Sometimes we also set up joint committees with organizations for particular questions. [BWEL]

Finally, some of the respondents argued that sometimes these consultations led to policy formation as well as technical problem solving:

> Contacts with administrative agencies are the most effective means by which our organization exerts political influence, because it enables us to participate continuously in shaping operational policies and programs. When policy is formulated in the administrative agencies, it is put into effect, without the likelihood of being defeated the way a bill in Parliament might be. [RFHL]

> Use of this approach has recently been increasing, and on fairly im-
> portant, rather than just technical, questions. Our monthly meetings
> with the Riksbank [the national reserve bank] are crucial for setting
> financial policy. [SBF]

The divergency of views in this area prohibits a single overall evaluation, but we can observe that: (a) a fair amount of influence is exerted through agency consultation, primarily on technical questions but occasionally on policy issues; (b) this procedure is valued most by business organizations and least by the large labor organizations; and (c) to the extent that the focus of the Swedish political system continues to move away from political debate toward problems of program implementation, the importance of this influence channel could steadily increase in the future.

Informal Influence Techniques

Since this study was originally designed to deal only with the eight formal influence procedures, the interview schedule included no questions about such informal influence channels as private meetings, public opinion formation, or personal contacts. In the course of the interviews, however, respondents repeatedly kept mentioning these activities as being as important as any of the formal influence procedures if not more so.

Private Meetings. In addition to LO, which sponsors regular monthly meetings of its top executives and governmental and party leaders, five other respondents also mentioned that their organizations or governmental units did this kind of thing, though on a less-frequent basis. These respondents all considered private meetings to be an exceptionally useful influence channel — primarily because of the way in which they facilitated interpersonal contacts:

> Our second most effective way of exerting influence on the government
> [after personal contacts] is through the monthly meetings that are held
> between the LO board and governmental and party leaders. These meet-
> ings deal with both basic policies and smaller practical matters. [LO]

> We give a dinner for about 100 members of the Riksdag each year, and
> develop many informal contacts in this way. [HGRF]

> More effective for us than any of the formal procedures are the meetings
> we arrange periodically with members of the Riksdag, representing all
> the parties, at which we discuss current issues. [SKF]

On the basis of these comments, we might say that private meetings are merely one variant of the broader process of building interpersonal contacts between organizational and governmental personnel.

Public Opinion. Nine organizational (but no governmental) respondents mentioned public opinion creation as an important influence technique for their organizations. Five people ranked this activity ahead of all the formal procedures in terms of effectiveness for them, and the others all evaluated its usefulness quite highly. Especially interesting is the fact that four of the six public-serving noneconomic organizations ranked public opinion creation as most important for their groups. Typical comments on this topic were as follows:

> Building public opinion through the mass media and in other organizations is in the long run our most effective influence procedure. This indirect approach is much more important than direct approaches to the government. [RFHL]

> As important as all the formal procedures is building public opinion through education programs, mass media, etc. [CAN]

> The most effective influence procedure for our organization is public declarations in newspapers and articles, speeches, books, etc. The government must answer if we build up enough pressure through public opinion. [SIF]

> Another important procedure is influencing public opinion through the mass media. We try to do this as much as possible, on the local as well as the national level. If we have public opinion behind us, the government listens to us through all the other formal procedures. This is especially true in the case of initiatives; public opinion formation and taking initiatives work together and reinforce each other. [HGRF]

The last two statements bring out explicitly the main reason why many organizations — especially smaller and less powerful ones — rely so heavily on shaping public opinion. Without broad-based public opinion behind them, their proposals are often not given serious consideration by the government; but, with public opinion backing, they can go to the government with an initiative or to an administrative agency with a suggestion and have some hope of getting action on their request. In this way, formation of public opinion through the mass media acts as a "behind-the-scene" reinforcer of the formal influence procedures.

Personal Contacts.   Given the facts that the total population of top governmental and organizational leaders in Sweden numbers only a few hundred at the maximum, that almost all of them are located in Stockholm, that job mobility among various organizational and governmental positions is quite common, and that telephones are ubiquitous and constantly used, it is highly predictable that most of these leaders have large networks of personal friendships and many contacts with each other. Not quite so predictable, however, is the importance of these personal contacts as channels of political influence. Huntford (1971:105–6) has asserted that these contacts constitute the real government of Sweden: "The 'contact network' is discreet, informal, but elaborate. It exists at all levels, from village council to Cabinet. . . . In many ways, the network is the real, if invisible, government of Sweden. . . . The true political dialogue in Sweden takes place within the contact network, and public oratory, not to mention parliamentary debate, is mostly tactical verbiage." To what extent do the respondents in this study support his contention?

Quite conclusively, it would seem. Although none of the organizational leaders was specifically asked about personal contacts, a large majority of them — especially those in economic organizations — mentioned them on their own initiative. Specifically, such contacts were mentioned by respondents in all five of the labor organizations, in eight of the eleven business organizations, in four of the nine member-serving noneconomic organizations, but in only two of the six public-serving noneconomic organizations. Most of these respondents emphasized that the importance of personal contacts for their organization was equal to or greater than that of any of the eight formal procedures. For example:

Informal contacts with governmental officials are at least as important as any of these formal procedures. [TCO]

The most important procedure for us is direct, fairly informal negotiation with the departments and the administrative agencies. [LRF]

The director of our organization knows many people in the government, and these contacts are extremely important for the organization. [SGF]

By far the most important influence procedure is early, informal contact with departments, agencies, and investigative commissions. [SBF]

> By far the most effective procedure for us in influencing the government is direct, personal contact between our board and managers and government officials. We can meet with officials any time we need to. [KF]

> We have direct contacts with the Prime Minister and both of the ministers in the Education Department. These relationships are very close, and we talk and meet with them often. [ABF]

Governmental officials were specifically asked about the impact of personal contacts on their offices. Seven of the ten respondents in the departments and three of those in the administrative agencies answered that the influence exerted on them in this manner was critical, as seen in these statements:

> Informal personal contacts between organizations and the departments are the most effective means for exerting influence. These contacts are both initiated by the organizations and requested by the departments. This process works most easily for organizations with political views similar to those of the government; they can speak freely to the government in this manner since it is not public. [DSOC]

> Informal discussions are used by the organizations and by us quite fully. A key to the administration [of the Swedish government] is the continuing discussion among departments, parties, and organizations. We have continuous discussion with all organizations concerned with the problems with which we deal. The organizations also make extensive use of such discussions, and we each know where the other stands. This is a very effective procedure, as we can talk freely and openly, with great discretion. [DINT]

> Interpersonal contacts smooth out many ridges and waves in formulating programs. Often more influence is exerted this way than through formal procedures, depending largely on how well people know each other. [DAGR]

> Much of the influence process is informal, through personal contacts between individuals in organizations, the government, and the parties. These informal channels of communication are much more important than the formal procedures. Only through these contacts can one judge how strongly the organizations actually support their public statements, so that the government knows how much weight to attach to the views of the various organizations. [DIND]

The last two sets of comments appear to demonstrate fairly conclusively that informal personal contacts are of extreme importance to organizational leaders in their attempts to exert influence on the Swedish government. In relation to the formal procedures, such contacts are probably of greatest relevance to the two relatively unstructured techniques of initiatives and agency consultation. But personal contacts also accompany all of the other formal procedures, and many of them undoubtedly occur outside of the formal influence channels. Indeed, these interpersonal contacts apparently pervade most relationships between interest organizations and the government in Sweden.

It thus appears that our quest for the true dynamics of the Swedish influence system is finally ended. Although all eight of the formal procedures are used extensively, and some of them are seen as providing viable influence channels—especially for movement organizations—in actual practice, none of them appears to be as crucial as informal, personal contacts. If we add private meetings and public opinion formation together with personal contacts as additional means of circumventing the formal influence system, the functional inadequacy of that system becomes even more apparent. And finally, we have seen that initiatives and agency consultation, which received relatively high evaluations as formal procedures, also incorporate extensive personal contacts. In short, the respondents in this study believe that interest organizations in Sweden can effectively influence the government, to the extent that they supplement or circumvent the system of formal procedures through private meetings, public opinion creation via the media, and personal friendships and contacts, or else utilize personal interaction through initiatives and agency consultation.

Summary Generalizations

The findings of this study are in general agreement with the results of earlier studies of the Swedish organizational-governmental influence system, but they add considerable detail and refinement to those previous insights. This section reviews the main results from those previous works and then summarizes the major findings of this study in a series of fifteen generalizations.

Previous Conclusions

Nils Elvander (1966) summarized the major findings of his study of Swedish interest organizations in this manner:

In summary, one can say that the organizations' influence on the political decision-making process is greatest in the preparatory and execution stages — investigations, commentaries, and administration — and least in the decision-making stages, in the cabinet and the Riksdag. . . . It is through investigations and *remiss* statements that the organizations' influence on government is principally asserted. Administration also offers an important means for indirectly influencing the government. . . . The least effective and least used way of influencing political decisions is for most organizations the Riksdag — despite the fact that it does provide good opportunities for making contacts. But the Riksdag cannot be regarded as a center of power. Instead, the organizations generally go to the seat of power in the cabinet and attempt to influence it, primarily via the preparatory and execution stages in the decision-making process. [P. 257]

It seems to be a happy post-war development that informal discussions have replaced the negotiations between the state and the organizations. The consultative expert function of the organizations is now more important, but the power play from the organizations toward the state has diminished a little, and the formal supremacy of the state powers is now a fact. [Pp. 314–15]

As a result of Elvander's study, most subsequent descriptions of the Swedish influence system have reflected his main points: that the Riksdag is essentially powerless and ineffective as an influence channel; that involvement in investigations and commentaries, and to a lesser extent working with administrative agencies, are the most effective influence mechanisms for most organizations; and that, in many ways, informal contacts between organizational and governmental leaders are a vital part of this system. The resulting picture is less optimistic from the organizations' perspective than the ideal envisioned by the theory of sociopolitical pluralism, but it does leave interest organizations playing a vital — if somewhat reduced and indirect — role in the political system, primarily as a result of the special Swedish procedures of investigative commissions and *remiss* statements.

The results of this present research go beyond Elvander's work in questioning the functional adequacy of investigations and commentaries as well as most of the other formal procedures, with the result that the balance of political power in Sweden is now seen to be tilted severely in favor of the government. Elvander's (1972b) more recent work on tax issues also moved closer to this proposition that the government largely dominates the political system in Sweden, as seen in his final paragraph:

> The investigation of Sweden's tax policy provides extraordinarily clear evidence of the dominant role played by the government in the big and constantly topical questions of the extent of the state's resources, and the principles to be applied in the distribution of the burden of taxation over the different citizen groups. The roles of the parties and — even more so — of the organizations are largely confined to answering the proposals initiated or inspired by the government, and to trying to avert too unfavorable a distribution of the burden for their own groups.

What Elvander found to be true of recent tax issues, this present study has found to be applicable over the whole range of political topics, as perceived by the vast majority of organizational and governmental leaders interviewed for the study. In a few words, we have found that the Swedish system of formal influence procedures is seen as essentially inadequate as a means by which interest organizations can exert influence on the government, and that whatever political influence organizations have at the present time is wielded primarily through personal contacts and public opinion rather than through any of the formal procedures. At the same time, however, many of these procedures are used quite effectively by the government to manipulate or control the interest organizations for its own purposes.

With that proposition as a broad summary, we can state the main findings of this study in fifteen more detailed generalizations.

Research Generalizations

1. Overall, the majority of organizational and governmental leaders interviewed in this study are moderately satisfied with the Swedish influence system, primarily because of their ideological belief that this system promotes political democracy. Relatively few leaders want to see major changes made in this system, although most of them are aware of operational difficulties that could be improved.

2. Although most interest organizations would like to be able to influence decision making on basic political issues, many of them find it necessary to limit their actions to providing expert consultation on technical questions if they are to have any impact on the government. With the Social Democratic government in power at the time of this study, it was

primarily business organizations that emphasized this technical expert role, but under different political conditions the labor unions and other related organizations might also find it necessary to restrict themselves to technical consultations with the government. *Remiss* statements are increasingly being limited to these kinds of technical questions, as is also most consultation between interest organizations and administrative agencies.

3. In general, economic organizations are perceived to have more influence on the government than do noneconomic organizations, although in all cases these levels of influence are seen as quite low, with averages ranging only between "some" and "moderate" influence. Governmental leaders, however, tend to attribute significantly more influence to interest organizations than do organizational leaders themselves.

4. The Swedish Confederation of Trade Unions (LO) exerted considerably more influence on the government than did any other organization, because of its extremely close ties with the Social Democratic party and its enormous resources. Linked to LO and the party in various ways are a number of other organizations that together form what we have termed the Social Democratic Movement. The average influence scores for these movement organizations are noticeably higher than the corresponding scores for all nonmovement organizations. The government appeared to be listening much more intently to those organizations that shared its ideology and goals than to business and other organizations outside the dominant Establishment.

5. Small and new organizations can gain access to the influence system if they wish by sending written documents to investigative commissions, writing *remiss* statements, contacting administrative agencies, and by other similar methods, but it is highly questionable whether they can have meaningful impact on the government through any of these procedures. Their comments will be respectfully noted and recorded, but they may have little effect on basic governmental decision making.

6. The earlier in the legislative-administrative processing of any proposal that an organization becomes involved, the more likely it will be to have some impact on the final decision or program that emerges from this process. Hence, initiative taking can be a vital activity for interest organizations, and many organizations consider this to be one of their most useful channels for influencing the government. To a large extent, however, initiatives tend to be successful only if they are backed by strong public opinion or conveyed from organizations to the government via informal personal contacts.

7. Coupled with initiatives in terms of potential for influence exertion and reliance on interpersonal contacts, but at the opposite end of the legislative-administrative process, is consultation with administrative agencies concerning the implementation of public programs. Business organizations currently place great emphasis on this approach, and officials of the administrative agencies also see this procedure as highly effective. Other types of organizations place less reliance on agency consultation, although its usefulness could rise steadily in the future if Swedish politics continues to emphasize program administration over political debate.

8. Most organizational and governmental leaders in Sweden agree in principle with Elvander's earlier contention that the interlocking procedures of investigative commissions and *remiss* statements provide useful and effective influence channels. These two activities have higher average perceived influence scores than any other formal procedures, and they rank just below initiatives and agency consultation on relative usefulness to organizations. Economic organizations tend to favor investigative commissions, on which they often have representatives, whereas noneconomic organizations rely more on written commentaries. The governmental departments also see more influence being exerted on them from organizations through *remiss* statements than through investigations.

9. In actual practice, there are many serious limitations to both investigations and commentaries as influence procedures. In addition to the practical problems of (a) the time and resources required for these activities and (b) determining which organizations should be represented on commissions and invited to submit *remiss* statements, the most fundamental criticisms of these procedures are that (c) the directives given to commissions by the sponsoring departments often specify in advance at least the broad outlines of the proposals desired by the government, and the government can manipulate commission memberships to ensure that they will support the desired outcomes; (d) as a result of the pervasive drive in Swedish politics to achieve consensus through compromise, conflict and dissention are discouraged in the commissions, and the reports that are sent out for commentaries never offer alternative sets of recommendations to which organizations might respond; and (e) there is no way of ensuring that written statements submitted to investigative commissions or the *remiss* statements written in response to commission reports will be given serious consideration, let alone have any impact on the final deci-

sions. As a result of all these factors, many organizational leaders feel that basic governmental policy is often determined within the departments and the cabinet before the investigation-commentary process even begins, so that the organizations are limited to helping formulate program details and resolving minor technical problems.

10.   Investigative commissions are increasingly being composed entirely of technical experts from within the departments, with no outside representatives. This trend reflects a basic shift in current Swedish political thinking, with the primary function of government being redefined from decision making among conflicting segments of society to rational administration of established public policies and programs. Many government officials favor this trend toward departmental task forces on the grounds that it promotes greater operational efficiency. They justify the exclusion of organizational representatives from the commissions on the grounds that the organizations have plenty of opportunity to exert influence through *remiss* statements. To the extent that this trend is occurring, it further restricts organizations to the role of technical consultants — which is apparently the role that the government prefers to have them play — and removes them entirely from basic policy formation. Simultaneously, it also strengthens the role of the cabinet in the Swedish political system.

11. The effectiveness of policy councils in the departments and of governing boards in the administrative agencies depends largely on the amount of power exercised by these groups. Departmental councils tend to be relatively or totally powerless, so that their only function is exchanging information, rather than exerting influence. In contrast, most agency boards do exercise significant amounts of authority, so that representation on them can be a valuable influence device for some organizations. And the power of these boards appears to be expanding in several of the agencies. The usefulness of both these procedures is nevertheless quite limited by the fact that only a few of the major organizations are represented on either the councils or the boards. These influence channels are irrelevant for the rest of the interest organizations in Swedish society.

12.   Given the weakness of the Riksdag in the Swedish political system, neither membership nor committee consultation is a particularly useful influence procedure for interest organizations. Moreover, most organizations have few or no actual spokesmen in the Riksdag, and committee hearings are traditionally closed to the public and limited to relatively minor details of bills whose passage is already fully assured.

Consequently, only if the total Swedish political system were altered to give the Riksdag considerably more power than it presently wields — or perhaps if several parties held approximately similar strength in the Riksdag — would these two parliamentary influence channels become of any value to most interest organizations.

13. To the extent that interest organizations succeed in having any meaningful effects on political decision making in Sweden today, this process is seen as occurring primarily through practices that circumvent or supplement the system of formal procedures. By far the most important of these informal procedures — in the eyes of both organizational leaders and governmental officials — is personal contacts between individuals. Such contacts are especially helpful when an organization is trying to interest a department in a proposal it favors or is consulting with an administrative agency concerning program implementation. Considerable informal discussion also occurs between leaders of the major organizations and officials in various departments during the process of drafting legislation. In general, members of organizations whose political ideologies are similar to those of the then-ruling Social Democratic party and that form part of the Social Democratic Movement tended to have more extensive personal contacts with governmental officials than did persons in business or other organizations not sympathetic with the Social Democrats. However, almost all interest organizations apparently rely extensively on personal contacts as their major means of exerting influence on the government.

14. Another informal procedure employed by many interest organizations, especially smaller and less powerful groups and those outside the movement, is public opinion formation. Through newspapers (several of which have national circulations in Sweden), many other kinds of publications, public meetings and speeches, and similar techniques (but not through the state-controlled television networks), these organizations attempt to persuade the public to support its policies and proposals. The assumption underlying this process is that the government is more likely to listen to an organization if it is strongly supported by public opinion, although that supposition is at best tenuous and possibly often invalid.

15. Although Swedish interest organizations — with the possible exception of LO — are not often able to use the formal influence procedures as viable channels for exerting influence on the government, governmental departments and agencies do employ many of these mechanisms quite effectively to gain organizational support for their policies and programs,

to coopt organizational leaders into defending (or at least not openly criticizing) actions of the government, and to legitimize political decisions made by party or governmental leaders as resulting from a "democratic decision-making process." This subtle but pervasive control of the interest organizations by the government not only negates the whole idea of sociopolitical pluralism but also may fool much of the public into believing that their political system is operating democratically, which in turn pacifies whatever complaints they might have against the government and persuades them to accept willingly whatever policies the government chooses to implement.

Nearly a century and a half ago, Alexis de Tocqueville (1961) peered into the future and sketched the kind of society he foresaw developing in Western nations, as economic and political equality among the masses of people replaced traditional feudal patterns of rigid social classes and hierarchical political status. Although he formulated his prophesies in respect to the United States, the following paragraphs appear highly descriptive of the kind of society that Sweden might become if the government continues its present practice of inverting sociopolitical theory and using the various influence procedures as mechanisms for manipulating and controlling interest organizations:

> As the conditions of men become equal amongst a people, individuals seem of less importance, and society of greater dimensions; or rather, every citizen, being assimilated to all the rest, is lost in the crowd, and nothing stands conspicuous but the great and imposing image of the people at large. This naturally gives the men of democratic periods a lofty opinion of the privileges of society, and a very humble notion of the rights of individuals; they are ready to admit that the interests of the former are everything, and those of the latter nothing. They are willing to acknowledge that the power which represents the community has far more information and wisdom than any of the members of that community; and that it is the duty, as well as the right, of that power to guide as well as govern each private citizen. [P. 344]

Theoretical Reformulation

Sweden has undoubtedly made a greater effort than most other nations to implement sociopolitical pluralism, with private-interest organizations enacting a mediating role between individuals and the national government. However, if the procedures through which organizations attempt to exert political influence are not operating adequately, as the findings of this study suggest, then pluralism is failing in Sweden—no matter how fervidly political commentators praise it as an ideology.

The basic roots of this problem appear to lie in the fact that in Sweden—and all other modern societies—the political state has become far more powerful than any private organizations or networks of organizations within the society. Hence, when any interest organization attempts to influence the government, it is inevitably acting from a position of weakness in relation to the government. Rarely can such organizations exercise sufficient political power to ensure that governmental officials will give their interests serious consideration, let alone act in their favor. The theory of sociopolitical pluralism will be applicable to modern societies only if and when the relative balance of power between private organizations and the government is at least roughly equalized. How might this be accomplished?

Theoretical Argument

As numerous writers have repeatedly emphasized, the ability to exercise influence or power in social relationships rests primarily on functional dependence.[23] If A wants or needs something that B has or can provide, then B is in a position to exercise power over A in exchange for satisfying A's desires. In actual social situations, such dependence often expands into complex networks of mutual interdependence, in which each actor performs a specialized role and, in turn, is dependent on others for the satisfaction of all the rest of his or her needs. But the principle remains the same: To the extent that an actor performs activities or functions that benefit others, they become dependent on him or her, and this dependence in turn gives the actor the option of exercising power over them.

When we apply this principle to interest organizations at the national level, we find that private organizations can gain power vis-à-vis the state to the extent that they perform functions needed or wanted by the members of the society, so that the government becomes dependent on the organizations for these functions. Note that this is not a zero-sum process. Organizations are not necessarily taking power away from the state but rather are expanding their own power capabilities—often by performing functions that no one else had previously been doing.

The crucial factor in this argument is the requirement that private organizations shift their activities from merely promoting the particular

23. A number of papers stressing this point are reprinted in Olsen (1970: part 1). See especially the writings of Robert Dubin and Richard Emerson contained there.

interests of their members to performing important functions for the total society (or at least a significant portion of it). In effect, they change from special-interest to public-serving organizations — although they remain private, not public, entities.[24]

The Swedish Situation

Elvander (1972b) noted that many of the larger organizations in Sweden are now tending to take stands on political issues they see as being in the best interest of the total society, rather than just that of their own members:

> In almost all the tax questions investigated, the big mass organizations with heterogeneous memberships revealed a more-or-less strong tendency to formulate general interests. This was particularly true of the Swedish Cooperative Union's Wholesale Society (*Kooperative Förbundet,* KF), the organization with the most heterogeneous composition.... Even the big [labor] organizations, LO and TCO . . . have a tendency to consider the tax problems from the point of view of the general public; they do not usually relate their views to the group interests of their members, but have a more comprehensive, diffuse formulation of interests. On the other hand, the small and more homogeneous organizations of the wholesale trade, the retail trade, and small enterprises and agriculture . . . are clearly inclined to formulate purely group interests. [P. 71]

A similar theme was expressed by several of the respondents in this study. One of the LO officials said that "the goals of the LO are in general in congruence with those of the total society." And the respondent from the Swedish Federation of Industries (SIF) maintained that "industry must work within society for the good of society, not as partisans seeking their own goals." The idea that "what's good for General Motors is good for the United States" is quite foreign to contemporary Swedish economic leaders.

Nor is this merely political rhetoric, designed to give large organizations an altruistic public image. Several observers of Sweden have noted that it is quite common for private organizations to actually perform public functions which in other societies are usually done by the government. Three such comments, giving several concrete examples, are cited below:

---

24. Several papers discussing this organizational shift in modern societies are reprinted in Olsen (1970: part 7). See especially the writings of John Kenneth Galbraith and Daniel Bell contained there.

In innumerable ways, [organizational] activities are closely interwoven with those of government — so much so that it is at times difficult to tell where the organizations end and the government begins. Quite as a matter of course, functions which an outsider might regard as proper for official bodies are delegated to organizations dominated by private self-interest. For example, the General Export Association, whose membership consists of approximately 1,200 of Sweden's largest exporting companies, can practically be said to manage Sweden's foreign trade policy; and Sweden's bargaining position in international trade negotiations is largely the work of its experts. The National Association of Residential Tenants habitually negotiates the rents which are to be recognized as official in new apartment buildings. [Jenkins, 1968:81]

Organizations are often useful to the administration both by assuming, as in the case of agriculture, more-or-less direct administrative functions on behalf of the state and by lending their authoritative support to the administration in its relations with citizens. In these circumstances, it is very definitely in the interests of the administration to cooperate, and on the whole also in the interests of the organizations. [Heckscher, 1958a:168–69]

In a corporate State, nonofficial organizations carry out official duties. The Swedish trade unions provide a good example, unemployment insurance being entirely in their hands. They collect premiums, make payments, and administer the necessary public funds. The local trade-union branches serve as unemployment insurance offices and, in the exercise of this particular function, they do not require membership as a condition of service. They are, in fact, specifically prevented from doing so because, in this instance, they are acting as a government agency. [Huntford, 1971:95]

To explore this possibility further, organizational leaders in this study were asked, "Has there been any tendency lately for private interest organizations to be given direct responsibility for performing public service functions of various kinds, rather than assigning these functions to an administrative agency?" Some of the respondents replied in the negative, and others said they had seen no evidence one way or the other concerning such a trend, but fifteen of them agreed that such a process was occurring in Sweden today and mentioned examples of it. Several of these were the following:

The Board of Health and Welfare has delegated responsibility for the national program on health, food, and exercise to the Sports Federation. We handle all of this program. And the situation is similar with the Board of Education for physical education programs. We act almost as a governmental body. [SRIF]

We and the tenants' organization have the legal right to discuss the setting of rents that are not subject to rent controls. [SFF]

We participate with the Riksbank in developing national financial policies. In this role we try to act for the benefit of the total economy, not just our member banks. . . . There is a tendency to delegate to banks the responsibility for guaranteeing loans, which has been done by the Riksbank in the past. The government and private banks are sharing 50/50 ownership in many credit organizations that are making loans to small businesses. The tendency is to develop joint ventures between public and private organizations on policy problems in this area. [SBF]

We have taken some responsibilities from the Board of Education concerning vocational subsidies. [SHIO]

There is a tendency to increase the influence of employee organizations. They operate the unemployment funds, safety committees, and make actual decisions concerning hiring foreign labor. [SAF]

Most of the respondents who were aware of this trend saw it as desirable for organizations since it gives them greater leverage in their bargaining with the government. Two of them, however, saw in the trend a subtle attempt by the government to further coopt private organizations to support governmental policies — which is certainly a definite possibility:

There is a historical tendency in Sweden for cooperation between the government and private organizations. The government wants to "buy off" organizations. The organizations lose their room for maneuvering when they become too involved in the corporate state. [RFHL]

Delegation of governmental responsibility to organizations is not very common and is not real responsibility. We are rather wary of it, for it is sometimes done to gain support from the organizations for governmental policies and programs. [SIF]

It must certainly be granted that the dangers of governmental cooptation are always inherent in this process of shifting responsibilities for public functions to private organizations. But the primary argument still stands that, as they take on such public functions, organizations make the state dependent on them in at least limited areas, thus increasing their power capabilities vis-à-vis the state. And as they gain power through the creation of functional interdependence, private organizations are increasingly able to approach the state as equal bargainers rather than as powerless pleaders.

10. A Theory of
Participatory Pluralism

The theoretical discussions of participatory democracy and socio-political pluralism in chapter 2, as well as the empirical investigations of the theories in subsequent chapters, have revealed that both of these conceptions of contemporary democracy contain serious deficiencies.

The two major weaknesses of participatory democracy are that (a) it relies on a rather unreliable individual learning process to move people from participation in decision making within the workplace and other immediate settings into political involvement, without providing any social structural supports for this transference of concern and activity; and (b) it does not specify any procedures through which individuals are to expand their participation in public decision making, but merely assumes that people will become more involved in traditional political affairs.

The two major weaknesses of sociopolitical pluralism are that (a) although its mobilization version functions fairly effectively as a means of involving people in political activities, both of the above weaknesses of participatory democracy — reliance on an individual learning process and absence of any specified participation procedures — also apply to this thesis; and (b) its mediation version is limited by the fact that so few people take part in political activities within intermediate associations, and it becomes meaningless if these organizations lack adequate resources and processes for exerting influence on government.

Fortunately, however, the ideas of participatory democracy and socio-political pluralism complement each other in several vital ways, thus

274 PARTICIPATORY PLURALISM

compensating for one another's weaknesses. This final chapter outlines a proposed synthesis of these two conceptions of contemporary democracy, which I term *participatory pluralism*. The five principal characteristics of this thesis, which are discussed in the following sections of this chapter, are (a) power decentralization, (b) functional organization, (c) governmental constriction, (d) participatory involvement, and (e) societal activism.

Power Decentralization

For most citizens of the contemporary world, complex organization automatically means a hierarchical power structure in which decisions are made by those at the top and imposed upon the rest of the organization. This process of hierarchical control may be exercised through either legitimatized authority or coercive force, but in either case the power structure of the organization is highly centralized, and few members of the organization have any opportunity to take part in collective decision making.

Hierarchical Organization

Political democracy supposedly reverses this process, vesting ultimate political power in the hands of the people rather than political leaders. As proponents of the elitist theory of democracy have forcefully argued, however, popular elections are often nothing more than a procedure for legitimizing the de facto positions of ruling elites and for pacifying the masses of citizens into believing that public leaders are responsive to them. Hierarchical power structures pervade contemporary "democratic" governmental processes, so that we can scarcely conceive of government that is not hierarchically organized. In the words of Frederick Thayer (1973:63), "The mainstream of contemporary 'democratic' thought begins with an assumption that all social organizations . . . are and should be hierarchically structured, and that governmental structures must be consistent with all the others." And hierarchy inevitably involves gross power inequality between those at the top and the bottom of the structure.

Theoretical support for this virtually blind assumption that complex organizations — both private and public — must be based on a hierarchical power structure is commonly derived from the early-20th-century writings of Max Weber (1947) and Robert Michels (1962). Weber's bureaucratic model, which pervades most current thinking on complex organizations, holds that organizations function most rationally (effectively and efficiently) when both administrative and decision-making activities are centralized at the top of a hierarchical authority structure. Occupants of those positions, who are presumably the most highly qualified individuals in the organization, will provide the overall coordination and control believed to be necessary for rational organization functioning. Michels, meanwhile, argued that, even if an organization intentionally seeks to democratize its decision making, for a variety of reasons it will almost inevitably drift toward oligarchy, so that "who says organization says oligarchy."

Decentralized Organization

In recent years, however, several writers have questioned the necessity of hierarchy in complex organizations and have offered alternative models for structuring authority. One of the earliest of these was Rensis Likert's (1961) concept of "group decision making," which pushed decision making down the hierarchy but did not eliminate that structure. In the same year, Eugene Litwak (1961) introduced a model for professional organizations in which groups of professionals working on similar or common tasks are loosely clustered together into work teams with considerable autonomy. Peter Blau (1970) is another proponent of organizational decentralization, arguing that most of the control processes normally performed by managers and supervisors can be accomplished through impersonal operational mechanisms. More recently, Bengt Abrahamsson (1977) and others have given considerable attention to experiments in "organizational democracy" being conducted in several Swedish factories.

Decentralization can also occur on the societal level, and it is a fairly common theme in writings about current and future trends in the United States and other industrial societies. The following three statements are typical of these observations:

> When society is complex and advanced, when it faces a multiplicity of alternatives for development, the need for information becomes urgent. But centralized planning and decision making are not vehicles for adequate information. A complex society cannot develop and use the necessary information unless social and political control, decision-making, and productive units are dispersed. This quest for information may require a movement away from the traditional representative and mass political institutions, and the multiplication of functional and local political organizations. [Palma, 1970:211]

Modern philosophers of freedom have tended to emphasize . . . either the individual's *release* from power of every kind — generally through an appeal to natural rights — or the individual's *participation* in some single structure of authority like General Will, which replaces all other structures. But from the point of view . . . of liberal democracy, freedom has rested neither upon release nor upon collectivization, but upon the *diversification* and the *decentralization* of power in society. In the division of authority and the multiplication of its sources lie the most enduring conditions of freedom. [Nisbet, 1962:269–70]

The variety of new kinds of organizations that are emerging (particularly ones with a high component of technical and research personnel) indicates that the older models, patterned on pyramidical structures, may no longer be applicable, and that in the coming decades the "traditional" bureaucratic form will have given way to organizational modes more adaptive to the needs for initiative, free time, joint consultation, and the like. The emergence of new structural forms of nonbureaucratic organization is one more item on the long agenda of new problems for the postindustrial society. [Bell, 1968:150]

New Bases of Power

One of the major forces promoting power decentralization — whether in business, government, or elsewhere — is the emergence of new resources in modern societies. Social power accrues to those actors who possess and utilize vitally needed resources. In an agricultural society, the most crucial resource is arable land. In a handicraft society, skilled labor becomes the major resource. In an industrial society, investment capital is the dominant resource. However, as a society moves into what Daniel Bell (1973) calls a "post-industrial" phase based on complex technology and extensive human service functions, it becomes increasingly dependent on scientific knowledge, specialized technical and administrative abilities, information storage and processing systems, and communication and education skills. Knowledge and the ability to use it become the scarcest and most important resource in these societies.

Because knowledge and expert skills are almost infinitely expandable, this emerging resource base promotes the continual growth and diversification of social power throughout society. Business and industry continue to enact vital roles in such a society, but they are supplemented with many new power centers such as scientific laboratories, schools and universities, public and private service agencies, the mass media, consulting firms, and data-processing organizations. Because knowledge is so widely dispersed throughout "post-industrial" society, power becomes increasingly decentralized, and no single organization or sector of society can exercise dominant power outside its sphere of expertise.

Another crucial resource base for exerting social power in modern societies is control of energy. In broad perspective, energy has always been a fundamental resource for human societies (Cottrell, 1955), but it has generally been readily available in the form of wood, wind, moving water, domestic animals, or slaves. With the advent of industrial, transport, and heating technologies utilizing first coal and later petroleum and natural gas, however, control of energy supplies became increasingly concentrated in the hands of a few large corporations. Their functional dominance in the energy marketplace has enabled these corporations to exert enormous economic and social power throughout society.

With the impending exhaustion of these fossil fuels, contemporary societies have recently begun exploring a wide array of potential alternative energy sources. Some of these possibilities, such as solar energy satellites or nuclear energy centers, would concentrate the flow of energy even more than at present. But many other new energy technologies — such as solar heating panels, district heating projects, and wind generators — would disperse our energy sources (O'Toole, 1976). As a direct result of such a diverse and dispersed energy system, social power would also be increasingly decentralized throughout society.

Attaining Power Decentralization

The more extensively power structures are decentralized — within both private organizations and governments — the greater the opportunities for individuals and groups to participate in collective decision making. Hence power decentralization is a fundamental first necessity for participatory pluralism.

As a minimal step toward power decentralization within bureaucratic organizations, their authority structures could be somewhat flattened by reducing the number of structural levels between top officials and ordinary members, by introducing organizationwide referenda on crucial policy questions affecting all members, by establishing elected decision-making councils with significant spheres of authority, and by granting more functional autonomy to all subunits of the organization. On the basis of experience gained through these procedures, organizations might then experiment with more radical forms of nonhierarchical structure. For instance, although a central administrative unit is absolutely necessary in any complex organization to perform overall communication and co-ordination functions, it is not mandatory that this unit also perform decision-making and control functions. Overall decision making for the organization could be lodged in an elected body representing all seg-ments of the organization, while social control could be the responsibility of semiautonomous small work groups. The administrative unit of the organization would then become merely one of many coequal functional units within the organization, and all members would be able to exercise meaningful influence on those policies and programs that directly affect-ed them.

On the national level, meanwhile, participatory pluralism would carry power decentralization much further than does the current pluralistic mod-el. In the prevailing conception of sociopolitical pluralism, the power of the national government is limited by an array of intermediate special-interest associations, but the polity remains the dominant arena of activity on the national level. In practice, this has meant that intermediate associations must compete with each other in their attempts to influence governmental decision making, but they do not compete directly with the government. They act only as pleaders for their special interests before the all-ecompassing power of the state. With fully developed participatory pluralism, in contrast, political power is decentralized to the point where the polity becomes only one among many equally powerful sectors of society, so that neither it nor any other sector can dominate the entire society. The ability of all these component units of society to exercise meaningful power in the public arena is derived from the prin-ciple of functional organization, with resulting countervailing power processes, to which we turn in the next section.

Functional Organization

Sociopolitical pluralism attempts to decentralize the structure of power in society and promote greater involvement in collective decision making by utilizing private interest associations as channels through which indi-viduals can exert influence on the government. But in practice, as we have seen, this ideal is rarely attained. Approximately one-third of the popu-lation in most modern nations belongs to no such organizations, and only a small fraction of those who are members actually participate in their organizations. Most large interest associations tend to become highly centralized and oligarchical, so that ordinary members often have little or no effect on the actions and goals of the total organizations. And most private interest organizations, no matter how large and important within their own sphere of activity, are relatively powerless in relation to the national government and have no effective means of exerting influence on political leaders. Even in Sweden, where consultation between interest associations and the government is built into the formal legislative process, the flow of influence is typically downward from the government to the organizations, with governmental agencies using this procedure to coopt organizations and gain their support and cooperation.

In reality, consequently, the theory of sociopolitical pluralism has frequently served primarily to legitimize a system of "pluralistic elites" who compete with one another for power within the political system, but which excludes most citizens from these political processes. Pluralism's problems of individual apathy and organizational elitism are surmounted, however, by the idea of functional social organization, as first developed by G. D. H. Cole (1920) in his writings on guild socialism and social theory.

Proponents of Functional Organization

G. D. H. Cole saw functional organization as the fundamental characteristic of all social organizations: "The underlying principle of social organization, a principle which must be distinct from the principle of community . . . is the principle of Function" (1920:48). His main concern, however, was with functional organization as a remedy for the deficiencies of representative democracy:

> There can be only one escape from the futility of our present methods of parliamentary government; and that is to find an association and method of representation for each function, and a function for each association and body of representatives. In other words, real democracy is to be found, not in a single omnicompetent representative assembly, but in a system of coordinate functional representative bodies . . . . Democracy, then, must be conceived in the first place as a coordinated system of functional representation. [1920:108–9]

More specifically, extensive functional organization would involve people directly in public decision making within their own spheres of daily activity:

It should be the aim of those who strive to direct the course of social organisation to promote the fullest participation of everybody in the work of government. This alone is true democracy, and this can only be secured by the fullest development of functional organisation. The current theory of representative government is a denial of this principle; for, having chosen his representative, the ordinary man has, according to that theory, nothing left to do except to let other people govern him. Functional organisation and representation, on the other hand, imply the constant participation of the ordinary man in the conduct of those parts of the structure of Society with which he is directly concerned, and which he has therefore the best chance of understanding. . . . Functional organisation gives everyone the chance of being, in the measure of his competence and interest, an active citizen. [Cole, 1920:114]

Carole Pateman's work on *Participation and Democratic Theory* (1970) draws extensively and approvingly on Cole's writings as a theoretical foundation for participatory democracy. She views functional organization primarily as an effective means of facilitating the political education process that was emphasized by Mill and Rousseau and that is so prominent in her own conception of participatory democracy. As a result, she largely misses the radical consequences that functional organization could have for the overall structure of a society and its political system, which are examined below.

Peter Drucker (1968) does recognize the significance of functional organization as an emergent structural trend in modern societies, although he focuses largely on the national level. For him, a major feature of this emerging trend is the substitution of function for territory as a basis for social and political organization, resulting in a new conception of pluralism:

Pluralist power centers of yesterday — the duke, the count, the abbot, even the yeoman — differed from each other only in titles and revenues. One was the superior and overlord of the other. Each center was limited in territory, but each was a total community and embraced whatever organized social activity and political life there was. Each center was concerned with the same basic activity, above all, wresting a livelihood from the land. The federalism of the American system still assumes this traditional pluralism. The federal government, state governments, and municipalities all have their own distinct geographic limitations and stand to each other in a position of higher and lower. But each has essentially the same function. Each is a territorial government with police powers and tax powers, charged with traditional governmental tasks, whether defense or justice or public order.

This is simply not true of the new institutions. Each of them is a special-purpose institution. The hospital exists for the sake of health care, the business to produce economic goods and services, the university for the advancement and teaching of knowledge, each government agency for its own specific purpose, the armed services for defense, and so on. Not one of them can be considered "superior" or "inferior" to the other, for only a fool would consider the advancement of knowledge superior to health care or to the provision of economic goods and services. But at the same time, not one of them can be defined territorially. [1968:176]*

From these writings we can extract the essence of functional organization as a crucial aspect of our theory of participatory pluralism.

Principles of Functional Organization

This thesis argues that all social organization should be based on the principle of function determining structure — following the architectural dictum of "form follows function." Units performing similar functions would be grouped together into larger organizations and functional networks, regardless of their geographical location. Each unit of each organization within each network would have its own specific function to perform, but no one unit or organization or network would attempt to perform all social functions.

A society organized on functional principles would be composed of a series of highly complex but functionally specialized social networks, each consisting of numerous limited-purpose organizations, each of which in turn contained many specialized units and subunits. Each network — and all the organizations and units within it — would be concerned only with a particular type of social activity. Thus there might be separate networks and component organizations for economic production, economic distribution, communication, transportation, education, health care, law, science, religion, recreation, and numerous other activities. A functionally specialized network or organization need not be a monolithic or hierarchical body that authoritatively controls all its constituent parts. Rather,

---

*Reprinted by permission of Harper & Row, Publishers, Inc. from *The Age of Discontinuity* by Peter F. Drucker. Copyright © 1968, 1969 by Peter F. Drucker.

it could be essentially an administrative process for promoting communication, coordination, regulation, and planning among all its parts. Operating power and responsibility could remain largely in the hands of small units, so that each organization, each network, and the total society would all be relatively decentralized along functional lines.

Graphically, each functional network might be pictured as a large circle. Any individual or organization with an interest in its activities could voluntarily enter the network through participation in activities at its periphery. As this social actor increased its participation in network functions, gained necessary knowledge and skills, assumed broadening responsibilities, and exercised greater authority, it would in effect move closer to the middle of the circle. Such "inward" movement of actors within the network would be determined by the extent of their expertise in this area, by their willingness to assume more duties and social responsibilities, and by their commitment to the professional norms guiding network activities. Those actors occupying positions at the center — who together might perhaps constitute an executive council — would have primary responsibility and authority for coordinating the entire network. Their power would be severely checked, nevertheless, by the diverse influences exerted on them by all the partially autonomous organizations comprising the network. Each of these component subunits might in turn constitute a smaller circle, with individual members entering at its periphery and moving inward toward its center positions of organizational responsibility.

In this model of society, the state loses its predominance over other sectors of society and becomes merely another network of functionally specialized organizations. Governments at all levels would no longer become engaged in highway construction, old-age pension programs, urban renewal, mail delivery, public health programs, or any of the hundreds of other activities that governments presently perform. Governments could then concentrate on their unique function of governing: political planning, policy formation, decision making, conflict resolution, and coordination.

Countervailing Power

Functional organization differs from traditional pluralism in much the same way that John Kenneth Galbraith's (1952) idea of countervailing power in an organized economy differs from the traditional model of a competitive marketplace.

In the competitive-market scheme, as in the usual pluralistic model, power is controlled by competition among a large number of relatively small and independent units — such as producers of a certain commodity — all of which operate on the same side of the market. For example, if one manufacturer of shoes attempts to increase his profits by raising his price, he will be brought back into line by other shoe manufacturers who will undersell him. In the pluralistic model of society, if one voluntary association seeks to gain more than its fair share of benefits from the government, it will be undercut by other competing associations that demand less and offer more in return.

The countervailing-power model was specifically devised to fit the contemporary United States, in which many spheres of economic activity are largely dominated by a few huge corporations. The power of such organizations tends to be limited, not by their few competitors, but rather by organized forces operating on the opposite side of the market, such as labor unions, consumer-oriented chain stores (or consumer cooperatives in some societies), and governmental regulatory agencies. Functional organization generalizes this theme beyond the economy to all parts of society, so that each sphere of activity — whether it be education or religion or communication or medicine or the economy or government — is principally controlled by other organized functional networks exercising countervailing power against it, rather than by a proliferation of relatively small organizations operating within the same area.

Unlike the relatively weak special-interest associations emphasized by traditional pluralistic theory, networks of specialized functional organizations could exercise considerable countervailing power vis-à-vis each other and government. This power would be derived from the fact that each network and every organization within it performed a functionally necessary service for the society or the community. Effective performance of these functional responsibilities would in turn give each network and organization legitimate authority based on its particular functional expertise, but only within the bounds of that special competence.

At the same time, functional organization diffuses social power throughout society along functional lines. Because of the functional specialization and interdependence among all parts of society, no single entity — government, corporation, or the military, for instance — could wield overwhelming social power. Each network and organization would control a leverage point for exerting power in the form of functional dominance, and any indiscriminate or irresponsible use of this power would be held in check by the fact that many other parts could exert countervailing power against it if needed. Hence such a society would be quite unlike the traditional laissez-faire model, in which the exercise of power is minimized. Functional organization maximizes the exercise of power in society in order to control the pervasive tendency toward power centralization in modern nations.

Functional Organization and Pluralism

Extensive functional organization would fundamentally alter our conception of sociopolitical pluralism. In the traditional pluralistic model, special-interest associations located between the people and the government attempt — often vainly — to bring pressures to bear on the government in pursuit of their special goals. In practice, these organizations compete vigorously with one another in their efforts to exert political influence, but only rarely do they directly affect policies of the national government, which remains the dominant seat of power in society.

Functional organization expands the power-wielding capabilities of these organizations tremendously, however, as they assume responsibility for performing necessary social functions. Concurrently, government becomes only one of several equally powerful functional networks in a society. Governmental units would still exercise considerable power within many realms of action, but they would be functionally interdependent with numerous other organizations performing interrelated activities. All of these organizations would therefore be able to interact with the government as equals in the pursuit of the public interest.

Governmental Constriction

Both of the preceding themes of power decentralization and functional organization imply a relatively constricted role for government. Let us now explicitly examine this third characteristic of participatory pluralism.

Privatization of Governmental Functions

If a society were organized along functional lines, as described above, government would no longer perform any functional activities. All such responsibilities would be turned over to specialized nongovernmental organizations, leaving government free to deal with basic problems of collective goal setting, policy formation, internetwork coordination, and long-range planning.

Daniel Bell (1968) views this trend as part of a broader process of decentralization of national government to local government, as well as to functional organizations:

> Clearly what is necessary in the next several decades is a comprehensive overhaul and modernization of governmental structures to find the appropriate size and scope of units which can handle the appropriate tasks.... All sorts of functions can be "detached" and lodged in multistate or regional "compacts" which can take over such functions.... If a single principle can be established it would be this: that the function of the federal government should be primarily in the areas of policy and funding, and that operative functions be in the hands of regions, metropolises, and nonprofit corporations whose size and scope would be appropriate to the function that had to be performed. [1968:147]

A more extensive and explicit analysis of this trend is provided by Peter Drucker (1968),* however. He calls it "reprivatization," but this assumes that all of these functions were once performed by private organizations, and are now slowly being given back to them. In fact, many of these activities are relatively recent social innovations, and have never been performed by anyone but government — usually because no other organization would or could undertake them. Hence the term *privatization* provides a more realistic description of Drucker's thesis. His argument can be summarized in three generalizations.

1. Contemporary national governments are becoming too large and complex to govern adequately; they can no longer control their own bureaucratic empires or give policy leadership to the nation:

> Modern government has become ungovernable. There is no government today that can still claim control of its bureaucracy and of its various agencies. Government agencies are all becoming autonomous, ends in themselves, and directed by their own desire for power, their own rationale, their own narrow vision rather than by national policy and by their own boss, the national government.
>
> This is a threat to the basic capacity of government to give direction and leadership. Increasingly policy is fragmented, and policy direction becomes divorced from execution. Execution is governed by the inertia of the large bureaucratic empires, rather than by policy. [1968:220]

---

*Excerpts reprinted by permission of Harper & Row, Publishers, Inc., from *The Age of Discontinuity* by Peter F. Drucker. Copyright © 1968, 1969 by Peter F. Drucker.

2.   Meanwhile, a vast system of large, functionally specialized private organizations has developed throughout society, each of which performs a vital social function:

> Historians two hundred years hence may see as central to the twentieth century what we ourselves have been paying almost no attention to: the emergence of a society of organizations in which every single social task of importance is entrusted to a large institution. To us, the contemporaries, one of these institutions — government or big business, the university or the labor union — often looks like *the* institution. To the future historian, however, the most impressive fact may be the emergence of a new and distinct pluralism, that is, of a society of institutional diversity and diffusion of power [1968:171]

> What makes the real difference is that all our major social functions are today being discharged in and through these large, organized institutions. Every single social task of major impact — defense and education, government and the production and distribution of goods, health care and the search for knowledge — is increasingly entrusted to institutions which are organized for perpetuity and which are managed by professionals, whether they are called "managers," "administrators," or "executives." [1968:175]

3.   In light of the above conditions, if modern societies are to survive and meet the needs of their members in a satisfactory manner, government must entrust all functional activities to specialized nongovernmental organizations that can operate with much greater effectiveness and efficiency than can governmental agencies, while focusing its own efforts exclusively on the process of governing:

> The purpose of government is to make fundamental decisions, and to make them effectively. The purpose of government is to focus the political energies of society. It is to dramatize issues. It is to present fundamental choices.

> The purpose of government, in other words, is to govern.

> This, as we have learned in other institutions, is incompatible with "doing." Any attempt to combine governing with "doing" on a large scale, paralyzes the decision-making capacity. Any attempt to have

decision-making organs actually "do," also means very poor "doing." They are not equipped for it. They are not fundamentally concerned with it.

If this lesson were applied to government, the other institutions of society would then rightly become the "doers." "Decentralization" applied to government would not be just another form of "federalism" in which local rather than central government discharges the "doing" tasks. It would rather be a systematic policy of using the other, the nongovernmental institutions of the society of organizations, for the actual "doing," i.e., for performance, operations, execution.

Such a policy might be called "reprivatization." The tasks which flowed to government in the last century because the original private institution of society, the family, could not discharge them, would be turned over to the new, nongovernmental institutions that have sprung up and grown these last sixty to seventy years. [1968:233-34]

The opposite side of this "governmental privatization" coin might be called "organizational publicization." In the traditional conception of pluralism, all intermediate organizations are entirely privately controlled and are concerned only with their own particular interests and goals. The purpose of government is to represent the broader public interests of the entire community or society, which it does by coordinating, regulating, and controlling the activities of the competing private organizations.

With functional organization and governmental privatization, however, the line between public and private interests would become blurred or nonexistent. Most of the functional organizations and networks comprising the society would be simultaneously public and private in nature. They would be public in that their prime responsibility would be to serve public needs and interests, and they would be accountable to the government for meeting this responsibility. At the same time, they would remain private in the sense that they would operate with considerable autonomy and be expected to provide financial self-support (although not a profit).

If such a fusion of public goals with private control sounds utopian, consider such organizations as the United States Postal Service or the Tennessee Valley Authority (which are legally public bodies but which operate independently of the government except for overall policy reviews). Conversely, consider Harvard University or many hospitals (which are legally private organizations but which operate to serve the public welfare). This eradication of the distinction between public and private organizations would be a fundamental feature of participatory pluralism, for it would enable all individuals and organizations to participate in public decision making within the contexts of their private activities.

The Governmental Network

To the extent that all "public" functions were performed by "private" organizations, what would remain of government? Like all other networks in a society, government would have its own unique functions, which Peter Drucker describes as "governing." How might they be carried out?

Responsibility for societywide goal setting, decision making, and policy formation might be lodged in a supreme council or congress — perhaps called the "societal policy council" — composed of elected representatives from each of the major functional networks. Each network, in turn, might have its own council composed of elected representatives from its constituent organizations; each of these organizations would have its own council of elected representatives from its major units; and so on down to the smallest work group.

This form of governmental structure was a key feature of G. D. H. Cole's conception of functional organization, for it incorporates all sectors of society directly within the government: "The co-ordinating agency can only be a . . . Joint Council or Congress of the supreme bodies representing each of the main functions in Society. Each functional association will see to the execution of its own function, and for the co-ordination of the activities of the various associations there must be a joint body representative of them" (1920:135–36). An additional benefit of this type of governmental structure was noted by Terrence Cook and Patrick Morgan (1971:18–19): "A hierarchy of assemblies instead of one national legislature would have the merits of permitting amateurs at the basic level to directly participate in deliberating on issues of national importance. Since the ultimate decision would not be made entirely by a potentially selfish local unit, the system would preserve accountability to the whole nation."

The form of any such political order would not be as important, however, as the functions performed by the political elites. A distinction must be drawn at this point between technical and valuative decisions. To the extent that any program or problem was purely technical in nature, it would be handled by the members of the network or networks concerned with that special area, on the basis of the best available technical knowledge and according to rational operational criteria. Political elites would deal only with matters that went beyond technical details, such as setting overall societal goals, formulating long-range policies, evaluating the desirability of various social programs, setting priorities and allocating resources among competing activities, resolving nontechnical conflicts among social networks, or suggesting guidelines for future societal development.

In short, the incompatibility between "official" and "expert" authority that plagues many contemporary organizations would be resolved by assigning all technical operations to specialized experts, insofar as possible, and reserving for political officials only those questions that involved social values and hence required a nonspecialized, societal orientation and concern.

Participatory Involvement

One of the basic principles of functional organization, as noted above, is completely open access for all individuals to at least peripheral positions within all organizations in the society. Individual social participation would therefore be determined solely by personal interest and ability, without restrictions based on any ascribed characteristics. Access to the periphery positions in any organizations would be open to all interested persons, regardless of previous experience or training, although most such positions would involve only minor or routine activities and would often be done on a voluntary basis in order to gain experience in that kind of activity. Thus every person could associate with any area of activity of his or her choosing, to the degree that one wished. Advancement to more central positions of increasing responsibility within organizations or networks would then be based on the individual's experience, knowledge, skills, and performance.

Each individual would normally participate in several different organizations and/or networks, either simultaneously or successively, though probably in varying degrees at different times. Thus a person's total pattern of social involvement could become as diversified and involved as he or she wished. At the same time, organizations and networks would have extensive overlapping memberships, which would give the society overall social cohesion and stability. Most crucial for our present concern, however, is the fact that such patterns of involved social participation would have direct consequences for promoting greater political involvement through both the mobilization and mediation processes.

Mobilization and Political Involvement

The central theme of participatory democracy is that all citizens must have the opportunity to participate as extensively as they wish in political affairs and public decision making. This process is to be extended beyond the formal political arena to encompass all spheres of organized life, and is to go beyond voting to include a wide array of participatory procedures. People are to be mobilized for full participation through both (a) a political education process, as stressed by Rousseau, Mill, and Pateman, and (b) an organizational involvement process, as depicted by the mobilization version of pluralist theory and demonstrated in chapter 4 of this book.

Participatory pluralism, incorporating decentralized power structures, functional social organization, and constricted governmental activities, would strengthen both of these political mobilization processes.

The political education process would become more immanent in people's daily lives since they would have numerous opportunities to participate in decentralized decision making in many spheres of daily activities. Functional organization would ensure that the resulting decisions were relevant and meaningful, since each unit within each functional organization would exercise enough power to carry out its own decisions. And Government would not be able to thwart or control the resulting organizational actions through petty bureaucratic rules and requirements. In short, all aspects of peoples' social lives would continually teach them to be politically involved citizens. As expressed by Carole Pateman:

> The argument of the participatory theory of democracy is that participation in the alternative areas would enable the individual better to appreciate the connection between the public and the private spheres. The ordinary man might still be more interested in things nearer home, but the existence of a participatory society would mean that he was better able to assess the performance of representatives at the national level, better equipped to make decisions of national scope when the opportunity arose to do so, and better able to weigh up the impact of decisions taken by national representatives on his own life and immediate surroundings. In the context of a participatory society the significance of his vote to the individual would have changed; as well as being a private

individual he would have multiple opportunities to become an educated, public citizen. [1970:110]*

At the same time, the organizational mobilization process would be expanded in scope and impact. As we saw in chapter 4, this process does occur within voluntary associations and community affairs, but it is hampered by the relatively low rates of participation in these activities, and the process does not appear to occur within most work settings. Hence its effectiveness is at present severely limited. With functional organization and concurrent power decentralization and restricted governmental control, however, most people should become more deeply and personally involved in organized activities of various kinds. Particularly crucial here would be a diminution of the distinction between vocational and avocational activities, as people became involved in a variety of groups and organizations that all performed socially necessary and meaningful functions. Consequently, the organizational mobilization process could involve all individuals in numerous aspects of their daily living. The heightened commitment to organizations resulting from functional organizations was noted by G. D. H. Cole in these terms:

> A functional association . . . is concerned with doing a definite job . . . .
> The member is connected with the association because its business is his business, and he is therefore able far more intelligently to initiate and criticize action in relation to it than in relation to an *amnium gatherum* miscalled "politics." Functional organisation gives every one the chance of being, in the measure of his competence and interest, an active citizen. [1920:114–15]

Mediation and Political Involvement

The principal goal of the mediation version of sociopolitical pluralism is to provide channels, via special-interest associations, through which individuals can communicate with and exert influence on government. As we saw in chapters 8 and 9, however, this ideal is rarely realized because of such problems as (a) low membership and participation rates in such organizations, (b) tendencies toward oligarchy in these organizations, (c) lack of adequate influence resources and procedures among most organizations, and (d) the ability of government to coopt these organizations to

---

*Reprinted by permission of Cambridge University Press from *Participation and Democratic Theory* (Cambridge: Cambridge University Press, 1970).

serve the goals of the state. These kinds of problems are undoubtedly endemic in all forms of social organization, but to the extent that a society incorporated power decentralization, functional organization, and governmental constriction, the mediation process should operate much more effectively than at present.

Under those conditions, the mediation process would occur within all organizations throughout society. Each unit within every organization would be able to act in a relatively autonomous manner but would also be linked into broad communication/influence networks. And functional organizations of all kinds would command the resources necessary to interact with one another and with government on a relatively equal power basis. All the organizations comprising a community or functional network, from the smallest and most informal activity group to the largest and most complex business corporation, could participate as political actors in public decision-making processes, serving such functions as articulating the interests of their members, aggregating resources and concentrating influence on specific targets, providing communication and influence channels between their members and public officials, and acting as countervailing checks on each other's power wielding. Thus organizations of all kinds would be much more highly politicized than in the traditional pluralist model, and the mediation process would pervade the entire organizational structure of society.

For individuals, meanwhile, political involvement through the mediation process would be greatly enhanced. Political participation would no longer be a special, set-aside kind of activity that one undertook in addition to all one's other roles, but rather would become an integral part of virtually all daily activities. Each individual would have opportunities to participate meaningfully and effectively in the political mediation process through the everyday performance of each of his or her normal vocational and avocational roles. The amount of influence wielded by any individual in this process would depend on his or her interests, roles, and relationships, but every role within every organization would be part of the total societal decision-making process. Hence everyone would participate to some degree in all political processes that affected his or her life. And to the extent that one chose to increase one's participation in any kind of organized social activity, this would also mean greater political involvement. In G. D. H. Cole's words:

> The essence of functional democracy is that a man should count as many times over as there are functions in which he is interested. To count once

is to count about nothing in particular: what men want is to count on the particular issues in which they are interested. Instead of "One man, one vote," we must say "One man as many votes as interests, but only one vote in relation to each interest." [1920:115]

Participatory Pluralism and Political Involvement

Most writings on the role of citizens in a political democracy have used the term participation, and the phrase citizen participation is almost sacrosanct among many political activists. Unfortunately, however, the word *participate* implies that one is an outsider coming into an activity that is not part of one's usual life activities. This semantic connotation was clearly evident in many early citizen participation efforts, in which the citizens were included only at the invitation of public officials and were restricted to the rather passive role of commenting on or responding to proposals and plans made by the officials.

With participatory pluralism, in contrast, political decision-making processes would pervade the entire society, and every individual would be personally involved in these processes whenever he or she engaged in any kind of social activity. Each person could exert influence on public decision making in at least three different ways: (a) through the performance of one's normal roles within all kinds of functional organizations; (b) through one's representatives on policy-making councils at each level of organization within each functional area in which one was involved; and (c) through voting and all other traditional forms of political activity, but in relation to valuative issues within one's sphere of concern rather than to elect individual public officials. In short, participatory pluralism would reverse the current process of political involvement. Instead of "taking people to decision making," this kind of society would "take decision making to the people" in the sense that all public decision-making processes would be brought directly into the social roles and organizations of people's daily lives. Social living would become political involvement.

Societal Activism

Amitai Etzioni (1968:466–67) has suggested that contemporary societies can be classified into one of four types: (a) passive societies, characterized by little overall control or consensus; (b) overmanaged societies, characterized by effective societal control capacities but inadequate consensus-building processes; (c) drifting societies, characterized by inadequate societal control capacities but extensive consensus; and (d) active societies, characterized by viable "societal guidance" that maximizes both effective societal control by public leaders and authentic value consensus among all the people. His central point is that most societies are relatively incapable of acting decisively and effectively through democratic political processes to achieve the national goals they seek. To the extent that participatory pluralism would strengthen a society's democratic political processes, it should enhance its societal activism.

Dynamic Leadership

Translating that potential into actual societal accomplishments would require an additional ingredient, however. As expressed by Etzioni (1968:430), "to the degree that a society is able to act in unison at all, it has some mechanisms for converting the aggregate demands of its members into collective directives . . . ." And the effectiveness of those collective action mechanisms will depend largely on the quality of leadership exercised by societal leaders.

The key feature in Etzioni's conception of societal guidance is the ability of leaders in all realms of social life to exert dynamic and responsible leadership through a two-pronged process. On the one hand, they must be able to exercise the social control necessary to direct collective activities toward common goals through judicious employment of cybernetic information flows, efficient mobilization of resources for effective power exertion, and establishment of responsive decision-making procedures. On the other hand, they must be continuously sensitive to the need to maintain adequate consensus on basic values and goals among all the component segments of society, so as to avoid alienating the population and losing public support. In short, effective societal guidance by public leaders is "a combination of downward control and upward consensus-formation processes" (1968:670).

Etzioni's model of an active society is rather elitist, with little provision for involvement by citizens in societal guidance activities. Even consensus formation occurs within a hierarchical structure, following an averaging principle. Hence his particular conception of societal activism is incompatible with our concern in this book for power equity and political involvement. But the basic idea of societal activism can be incorporated within our conception of participatory pluralism without also adopting Etzioni's elitist version of this thesis.

Conflict Activism

Societies are not monolithic structures that can move as a single unit toward collective goals on the basis of effective control and extensive consensus. All societies beyond primitive tribes — even the most thoroughly totalitarian ones — are composed of countless semiautonomous organized entities of all kinds. Each of these social entities will normally have its own interests and goals, some of which will be unique to it and some of which will be shared with other entities in the society.

To the extent that the groups, organizations, and networks comprising a society choose to seek their own unique goals and can exert sufficient social power to act on these choices, they will invariably come into conflict with one another. Most of the time, that is, collective goal attainment processes are characterized much more by social conflict and power exertion than by common consensus and unified control. And trends toward power decentralization, functional organization, and governmental constriction within a society would greatly exacerbate the appearance of social conflict and power exertion.

If most contemporary societies lack activism and are more passive, drifting, or overmanaged than desired by their members, it is not generally because they have insufficient control or consensus procedures. Rather it is because such small proportions of the population are at all involved in any publicly oriented collective activities and decision making, and because we do not know how to deal creatively with social conflict to facilitate collective goal attainment. If societal leaders would concentrate less on promoting control and consensus, and give more attention to maximizing citizen involvement in public decision making in all realms of social life and creatively managing social conflict, then collective goals would certainly be attained — although they might not be the goals desired by the leaders. In short, give the people real power and enable them to engage in creative conflict, and there will be plenty of political activism in society.

Conclusion

The ultimate ideal of political democracy is that all people should participate in public affairs as equitably as possible and should govern their own lives as fully as possible. A fundamental requirement for the attainment of democracy is therefore full involvement by all citizens in the decision-making processes through which their society and all its component parts are governed.

The model of sociopolitical pluralism sketched in this chapter is designed to maximize and equalize citizen involvement in political processes throughout all realms of social life. It incorporates the current themes of both participatory democracy and sociopolitical pluralism, synthesizing them into a new conception of political processes that eliminates the weaknesses inherent in both of its predecessors. The five main characteristics of sociopolitical pluralism discussed in this chapter are power decentralization, functional organization, governmental constriction, participatory involvement, and societal activism.

Taken together, those principles of participatory pluralism describe the kind of society in which political democracy might eventually be achieved. All of them are vital, for "government of the people, by the people, and for the people" depends ultimately on the way in which the total society — not just its political system — is organized and operated. Democracy is not just a form of politics, but a total way of organized social life. Sociopolitical pluralism provides the necessary blueprint for constructing a fully democratic society in the future. The rest is up to us all!

References

Chapter One

Bell, Daniel. "The Rediscovery of Alienation: Some Notes Along the Quest for the Historical Marx." *Journal of Philosophy* 56 (November 1959):933–52.

Dahrendorf, Ralf. *Class and Class Conflict in Industrial Societies.* Stanford, Cal.: Stanford University Press, 1959.

Erbe, William. "Social Involvement and Political Activity: A Replication and Elaboration." *American Sociological Review* 29 (April 1964):198–215.

Fromm, Erich. *Marx's Concept of Man.* New York: Ungar, 1961.

Keller, Suzanne. *Beyond the Ruling Class.* New York: Random House, 1963.

Keniston, Kenneth, "Alienation and the Decline of Utopia." *American Scholar* 29 (Spring 1960):161–200.

Levine, Murray B. *The Alienated Voter.* New York: Holt, Rinehart & Winston, 1960.

Litt, Edgar. "Political Cynicism and Political Futility." *Journal of Politics* 25 (May 1963):312–23.

Marx, Karl. *Economic and Philosophical Manuscripts,* trans. by T. B. Bottomore. In Erich Fromm, *Marx's Concept of Man.* New York: Ungar, 1963.

McDill, Edward L., and Jeanne C. Ridley. "Status, Anomie, Political Alienation, and Political Participation." *American Journal of Sociology* 63 (September 1962):205–13.

Mills, C. Wright. *The Power Elite.* New York: Oxford University Press, 1956.

Nisbet, Robert. *Community and Power.* New York: Oxford University Press, 1962.

Olsen, Marvin E. Political Assimilation, Social Opportunities, and Political Alienation. Unpublished Ph. D. dissertation, Department of Sociology, University of Michigan, 1965.

Olsen, Marvin E. "Two Categories of Political Alienation," *Social Forces* 47 (March 1969):288–99.

Olsen, Marvin E. "A Model of Political Participation Stratification." *Journal of Political and Military Sociology* 1 (Fall 1973):183–200.

Olsen, Marvin E. "Interest Association Participation and Political Activity in the United States and Sweden." *Journal of Voluntary Action Research* 4 (Fall 1974):17–33.

Oppenheimer, Martin. "The Limitations of Socialism: Some Sociological Observations on Participatory Democracy." In C. George Benello and Dimitrios Roussopoulos, eds., *The Case for Participatory Democracy*, New York: Viking Press, 1971. Pp. 271–82.

Pateman, Carole. *Participation and Democratic Theory*. Cambridge, Eng.: Cambridge University Press, 1970.

Pranger, Robert. *The Eclipse of Citizenship: Power and Participation in Contemporary Politics*. New York: Holt, Rinehart and Winston, 1968.

Sayre, Wallace, S., and Herbert Kaufman. *Governing New York City*. New York: Russell Sage Foundation, 1960.

Seeman, Melvin, "On the Meaning of Alienation." *American Sociological Review* 24 (December 1959):783–91.

Thompson, Wayne E., and John E. Horton. "Political Alienation as a Force in Political Action." *Social Forces* 38 (March 1960):190–95.

Verba, Sidney, and Norman H. Nie. *Participation in America: Political Democracy and Social Equality*. New York: Harper and Row, 1972.

Chapter Two

Almond, Gabriel, and Sidney Verba. *The Civic Culture*. Princeton, N. J.: Princeton University Press, 1963.

Altschuler, Alan A. *Community Control*. Indianapolis: Bobbs-Merrill Co., 1970.

Bachrach, Peter. *The Theory of Democratic Elitism: A Critique*. Boston: Little, Brown and Co., 1967.

Banfield, Edward C. *Political Influence*. New York: Free Press, 1961.

Benello, C. George, and Dimitrios Roussopoulos, eds. *The Case for Participatory Democracy: Some Prospects for a Radical Society*. New York: The Viking Press, 1971.

Bentley, Arthur F. *The Process of Government*. Chicago: University of Chicago Press, 1908.

Berelson, Bernard R., Paul F. Lazarsfeld, and William N. McPhee. *Voting*. Chicago: University of Chicago Press, 1954.

Berry, David. *The Sociology of Grass Roots Politics*. London: Macmillan & Co., 1970.

Blumberg, Paul. *Industrial Democracy: The Sociology of Participation*. New York: Schocken Books, 1969.

Bottomore, T. B. *Elites and Society*. New York: Basic Books, 1964.

Cahn, Edgar S., and Barry A. Passett. *Citizen Participation: Effecting Community Change*. New York: Praeger Publishers, 1971.

Cook, Terrence E., and Patrick M. Morgan, eds. *Participatory Democracy*. San Francisco: Canfield Press, 1971.

Dahl, Robert. *A Preface to Democratic Theory*. Chicago: University of Chicago Press, 1956.

Dahl, Robert. *Who Governs?* New Haven, Conn.: Yale University Press, 1961.

Dahl, Robert A., and Charles E. Lindblom. *Politics, Economics, and Welfare*. New York: Harper and Row, 1953.

Dahrendorf, Ralf. *Class and Class Conflict in Industrial Society*. Stanford, Cal.: Stanford University Press, 1959.

Deutsch, Karl. "Social Mobilization and Political Development." *American Political Science Review* 55 (September 1961):493–514.

Domhoff, G. William. *The Higher Circles*. New York: Random House, 1970.

Galbraith, John Kenneth. *Economics and the Public Purpose*. Boston: Houghton Mifflin, 1973.

Gans, Herbert J. *More Equality*. New York: Random House, 1968.

Howard, John R. *The Cutting Edge*. Philadelphia: J. P. Lippincott, 1974.

Keller, Suzanne. *Beyond the Ruling Class*. New York: Random House, 1963.

Killian, Lewis M. *The Impossible Revolution?* New York: Random House, 1968.

Kornhauser, William. *The Politics of Mass Society*. Glencoe, Ill.: Free Press, 1959.

Leggett, John C. *Taking State Power*. New York: Harper and Row, 1973.

Lenski, Gerhard. *Power and Privilege*. New York: McGraw-Hill, 1966.

Lind, Alden. "The Future of Citizen Participation." *The Futurist* 9 (1975):316–28.

Lipset, Seymour Martin, Martin Trow, and James Coleman. *Union Democracy*. Garden City, N. Y.: Anchor Books, 1956.

Marshall, T. H. *Class, Citizenship, and Social Development*. New York: Doubleday, 1964.

Michels, Robert. *Political Parties*. New York: Free Press, 1966. (Originally published in 1915.)

Milbrath, Lester W. *Political Participation*. Chicago: Rand McNally, 1965.

Miliband, Ralph. *The State in Capitalist Society*. New York: Basic Books, 1969.

Miller, S. M., and Pamela A. Roby. *The Future of Inequality*. New York: Basic Books, 1970.

Moore, Barrington, Jr. *Social Origins of Dictatorship and Democracy*. Boston: Beacon Press, 1966.

Nisbet, Robert. *Community and Power*. New York: Oxford University Press, 1962.

O'Brien, David J. *Neighborhood Organization and Interest-Group Processes*. Princeton, N. J.: Princeton University Press, 1975.

Olsen, Marvin E. *The Process of Social Organization: Power in Social Systems*, 2nd ed. New York: Holt, Rinehart and Winston, 1978.

Pateman, Carole. *Participation and Democratic Theory*. Cambridge, Eng.: Cambridge University Press, 1970.

Pranger, Robert J. *The Eclipse of Citizenship*. New York: Holt, Rinehart and Winston, 1968.

Presthus, Robert. *Men at the Top*. New York: Oxford University Press, 1964.

Redford, Emmette S. *Democracy in the Administrative State*. New York: Oxford University Press, 1969.

Ricci, David. *Community Power and Democratic Theory: The Logic of Political Analysis*. New York: Random House, 1971.

Riesman, David, et al. *The Lonely Crowd*. New York: Doubleday, 1954.

Sartori, Giovanni. *Democratic Theory*. Detroit: Wayne State University Press, 1962.

Schumpeter, Joseph. *Capitalism, Socialism, and Democracy*. London: George Allen & Unwin, 1943.

Thayer, Frederick C. *An End to Hierarchy! An End to Competition!* New York: New Viewpoints, 1973.

Tocqueville, Alexis de. *Democracy in America*, Vol. 2, trans. by Henry Reeve. New York: Schocken Books, 1961. (Originally published in French in 1840).

Truman, David E. *The Governmental Process*. New York: Alfred A. Knopf, 1951.

Verba, Sidney, and Norman H. Nie. *Participation in America: Political Democracy and Social Equality*. New York: Harper and Row, 1972.

Walker, J. Malcolm. "Organizational Change, Citizen Participation, and Voluntary Action," *Journal of Voluntary Action Research* 4 (Fall 1975):4–22.

Walker, Jack. "A Critique of the Elitist Theory of Democracy." *American Political Science Review* 60 (June 1966):285–95.

Chapter Three

Agger, Robert E., and Vincent Ostrom. "The Political Structure of a Small Community."
    Public Opinion Quarterly 20 (Spring 1956):81–89.
Alford, Robert R., and Eugene C. Lee. "Voting Turnout in American Cities," *American
    Political Science Review* 62 (December 1968):796–813.
Alford, Robert R. *Bureaucracy and Participation: Political Cultures in Four Wisconsin
    Cities.* Chicago: Rand McNally and Co., 1969.
Aron, Raymond. "Social Class, Political Class, Ruling Class." *European Journal of
    Sociology* 1 (March 1960):260–81. Trans. by Reinhard Bendix and Seymour M.
    Lipset.
Berelson, Bernard, Paul F. Lazarsfeld, and William McPhee. *Voting.* Chicago: University
    of Chicago Press, 1954.
Berry David. *The Sociology of Grass Roots Politics.* London: Macmillan & Co., 1970.
Campbell, Angus, Gerald Gurin, and Warren Miller. *The Voter Decides.* Evanston, Ill.:
    Row, Peterson, 1954.
Dahl, Robert. *Who Governs?* New Haven, Conn.: Yale University Press, 1961.
Erbe, William. "Social Involvement and Political Activity: A Replication and Elabo-
    ration." *American Sociological Review* 29 (April 1964):198–215.
Freeman, Linton, Thomas J. Fararo, Warner Bloomberg, Jr., and Morris H. Sunshine.
    "Locating Leaders in Local Communities: A Comparison of Some Alternative Ap-
    proaches." *American Sociological Review* 28 (October 1963):791–98.
Hunter, Floyd. *Community Power Structure.* Chapel Hill, N. C.: University of North
    Carolina Press, 1953.
Jones, W. H. Morris. "In Defense of Apathy: Some Doubts on the Duty to Vote." *Political
    Studies* 2 (1954):25–37.
Katz, Daniel, and Fern Piret. "Circuitous Participation in Politics." *American Journal of
    Sociology* 69 (January 1964):367–73.
Katz, Elihu, and Paul F. Lazarsfeld. *Personal Influence.* New York: Free Press, 1955.
Katz, Fred E. and Fern U. Piret. "Circuitous Participation in Politics." *American Journal
    of Sociology* 69 (January 1964):367–73.
Key, V. O., Jr. *Public Opinion and American Democracy.* New York: Alfred A. Knopf,
    1963.
Kornhauser, William. *The Politics of Mass Society.* Glencoe, Ill: Free Press, 1959.
Lane, Robert E. *Political Life.* Glencoe, Ill: Free Press, 1959.
Lenski, Gerhard E. *Power and Privilege: A Theory of Social Stratification.* New York:
    McGraw-Hill, 1966.
Lipset, Seymour Martin. *Political Man.* New York: Doubleday, 1960.
Marshall, T. H. *Class, Citizenship, and Social Development.* Garden City, N. Y.: Anchor
    Books, 1965.
Merriam, Charles, and Harold F. Gosnell. *Non-Voting.* Chicago: University of Chicago
    Press, 1924.
Milbrath, Lester W. *Political Participation.* Chicago: Rand McNally, 1965.
Mills, C. Wright. *The Power Elite.* New York: Oxford University Press, 1956.
Mosca, Gaetano. *The Ruling Class,* trans. by Hannah D. Kahn, ed. and revised by Arthur
    Livingston. New York: McGraw-Hill Book Co., 1939.
Nie, Norman H. G., Bingham Power, Jr., and Kenneth Prewitt. "Social Structure and
    Political Participation: Developmental Relationships." *The American Political Sci-
    ence Review* 63 (June 1969):361–78, and (September 1969):808–32.
Nisbet, Robert. *Community and Power.* New York: Oxford University Press, 1962.
Olsen, Marvin E. "Social and Political Participation of Blacks." *American Sociological
    Review* 35 (August 1970):682–97.

Olsen, Marvin E. "Social Participation and Voting Turnout." *American Sociological Review* 37 (June 1972):317–33.

Palma, Giuseppe di. *Apathy and Participation: Mass Politics in Western Societies*. New York: Free Press, 1970.

Pareto, Vilfredo. *The Mind and Society,* trans. by Bongiorno and A. Livingston, ed. by A. Livingston. New York: Harcourt, Brace, 1935.

Pateman, Carole. *Participation and Democratic Theory*. Cambridge: Eng. Cambridge University Press, 1970.

Pranger, Robert J. *The Eclipse of Citizenship: Power and Participation in Contemporary Politics*. New York: Holt, Rinehart, and Winston, 1968.

Robinson, W. S. "The Motivational Structure of Political Participation." *American Sociological Review* 17 (April 1952):151–56.

Rose, Arnold. *The Power Structure: Political Process in American Society*. New York: Oxford University Press, 1967.

Sudman, Seymour. "Probability Sampling with Quotas." *Journal of the American Statistical Association* 61 (September 1966):749–71.

Tocqueville, Alexis de. *Democracy in America,* vol. 2. Trans. by Henry Reeve. New York: Schocken Books, 1961. (Originally published in 1840).

Verba, Sidney, and Norman H. Nie. *Participation in America: Political Democracy and Social Equality*. New York: Harper and Row, 1972.

Verba, Sidney, Norman H. Nie, and Jeo-on Kim. *The Modes of Democratic Participation: A Cross-National Comparison*. Beverly Hills, Cal.: Sage Publications, 1971.

Weber, Max. *From Max Weber,* trans. by H. H. Gerth and C. Wright Mills. New York: Oxford University Press, 1946.

Woodward, Julian L., and Elmo Roper. "Political Activity of American Citizens." *American Political Science Review* 44 (December 1950):872–85.

Chapter Four

Alford, Robert R. *Bureaucracy and Participation*. Chicago: Rand McNally and Co., 1969.

Alford, Robert R., and Eugene C. Lee. "Voting Turnout in American Cities." *American Political Science Review* 62 (September 1968):796–813.

Alford, Robert R., and Harry M. Scoble. "Sources of Local Political Involvement." *American Political Science Review* 62 (December 1968):1192–206.

Almond, Gabriel, and Sidney Verba. *The Civic Culture*. Princeton, N. J.: Princeton University Press, 1963.

Ambrecht, Biliana C. S. *Politicizing the Poor: The Legacy of the War on Poverty in a Mexican American Community*. New York: Praeger, 1975.

Andrews, Frank, James Morgan, and John Sonquist. *Multiple Classification Analysis* Ann Arbor, Mich.: Institute of Social Research, 1967.

Andrews, William G. "American Voting Participation." *Western Political Quarterly* 19 (December 1966):639–52.

Berelson, Bernard, Paul F. Lazarsfeld, and William McPhee. *Voting*. Chicago: University of Chicago Press, 1954. Pp. 50–53.

Berry, David. *The Sociology of Grass Roots Politics*. London: Macmillan & Co., 1970.

Campbell, Angus, Philip E. Converse, Warren E. Miller, and Donald E. Stokes. *The American Voter*. New York: John Wiley and Sons, 1960.

Campbell, Angus, Gerald Gurin, and Warren E. Miller. *The Voter Decides*. Evanston, Ill.: Row, Peterson and Co.

Dahl, Robert. *Who Governs?* New Haven, Conn.: Yale University Press, 1961.

David, James C. "The Family's Role in Political Socialization." *The Annals of the American Academy of Political and Social Science* 361 (September 1965):10–19.

Duncan, Otis Dudley. "A Socioeconomic Index for All Occupations." and Appendix B. In Albert J. Reiss, Jr., *Occupations and Social Status.* New York: The Free Press of Glencoe, 1961. Pp. 109–38, 263–75.

Erbe, William. "Social Involvement and Political Activity: A Replication and Elaboration." *American Sociological Review* 29 (April 1964), pp. 198–215.

Glenn, Norval D., and Michael Grimes. "Aging, Voting, and Political Interest." *The American Sociological Review* 33 (August, 1968):563–75.

Greenstein, Fred. *Children and Politics.* New Haven, Conn.: Yale University Press, 1965.

Hall, Nason E., and Kent P. Schwirian. "Occupational Status, Community Structure and Local Political Participation." *Sociological Focus* 1 (Spring 1968):17–30.

Hunter, Floyd. *Community Power Structure.* Chapel Hill, N. C.: University of North Carolina Press, 1953.

Hyman, Herbert. *Political Socialization.* Glencoe, Ill.: Free Press, 1959.

Hyman, Herbert, and Charles R. Wright. "Trends in Voluntary Association Memberships of American Adults." *American Sociological Review* 36 (April 1971):191–206.

Inkeles, Alex. "Participant Citizenship in Six Developing Countries." *American Political Science Review* 63 (December 1969):1120–41.

Lane, Robert E. *Political Life.* Glencoe, Ill.: Free Press, 1959.

Langton, Kenneth P. *Political Socialization.* New·York: Oxford University Press, 1969.

Lipset, Seymour Martin. *Political Man.* New York: Doubleday, 1960.

Marvick, Dwaine, and Charles Nixon. *Political Decision-Makers.* New York: Free Press, 1961.

McDill, Edward L., and Jeanne C. Ridley. "Status, Anomie, Political Alienation, and Political Participation." *American Journal of Sociology* 68 (September 1962):205–13.

Milbrath, Lester W. *Political Participation.* Chicago: Rand McNally and Co., 1965.

Nie, Norman H., G. Bingham Powell, Jr., and Kenneth Prewitt. "Social Structure and Political Participation: Developmental Relationships, Part I." *The American Political Science Review* 63 (June 1969):361–78; Part II, 63 (September 1969):808–32.

Olsen, Marvin E. "Two Categories of Political Alienation." *Social Forces* 47 (March 1969):288–99.

Olsen, Marvin E. 1970 "Social and Political Participation of Blacks." *American Sociological Review* 35 (August 1970):682–97.

Olsen, Marvin E. "Social Participation and Voting Turnout: A Multivariate Analysis." *American Sociological Review* 37 (June 1972):317–33.

Orum, Anthony M. "A Reappraisal of the Social and Political Participation of Negroes." *American Journal of Sociology* 72 (July 1966):32–46.

Palma, Giuseppe di. *Apathy and Participation: Mass Politics in Western Societies.* New York: Free Press, 1970.

Pateman, Carole. *Participation and Democratic Theory.* Cambridge, Eng.: Cambridge University Press, 1970.

Tocqueville, Alexis de. *Democracy in America*, vol. 2. Trans. by Henry Reeve. New York: Schocken Books, 1961. (Originally published in 1840.)

Verba, Sidney, and Norman H. Nie. *Participation in America: Political Democracy and Social Equality.* New York: Harper and Row, 1972.

Woodward, Julian L., and Elmo Roper. "Political Activity of American Citizens." *American Political Science Review* 44 (1950):872–85.

Chapter Five

Almond, Gabriel and Sidney Verba. *The Civic Culture*. Princeton, N. J.: Princeton University Press, 1963.

Berry, David. *The Sociology of Grass Roots Politics*. London: Macmillan & Co., 1970.

Curtis, James. "Voluntary Association Joining: A Cross-National Comparative Note." *American Sociological Review* 36 (October 1971):872–80.

Erbe, William. "Social Involvement and Political Activity: A Replication and Elaboration." *American Sociological Review* 29 (April 1964):198–215.

Fisk, Margaret, ed. *Encyclopedia of Associations*, 8th ed., vol. 1. Detroit: Gale Research Co., 1973.

Hausknecht, Murray. *The Joiners*. New York: Bedminster Press, 1962.

Hyman, Herbert H. and Charles R. Wright. "Trends in Voluntary Association Memberships of American Adults." *American Sociological Review* 36 (April 1971):191–206.

Jenkins, David. *Sweden and the Price of Progress*. New York: Coward-McCann Co., 1968.

Johansson, Sten. *Politiska Resurser*. Stockholm: Allmänna Förlaget, 1971.

Maccoby, Herbert. "The Differential Political Activity of Participants in Voluntary Associations." *American Sociological Review* 23 (October 1958):524–32.

Milbrath, Lester W. *Political Participation: How and Why Do People Get Involved in Politics?* Chicago: Rand McNally, 1965.

Nie, Norman H., G. Bingham Powell, Jr., and Kenneth Prewitt. "Social Structure and Political Participation: Developmental Relationships, part I." *The American Political Science Review* 63 (June 1969):361–78.

Nisbet, Robert. *Community and Power*. New York: Oxford University Press, 1962.·

Olsen, Marvin E. *Power in Societies*. New York: Macmillan, 1970.

Olsen, Marvin E. "Social Participation and Voting Turnout: A Multivariate Analysis." *American Sociological Review* 37 (June 1972):317–33.

Palma, Guiseppe di. *Apathy and Participation: Mass Politics in Western Societies*. New York: Free Press, 1970.

Tocqueville, Alexis de. *Democracy in America*, vol. 2, trans. by Henry Reeve. New York: Schocken Books, 1961. (Originally published in French in 1840).

Tomasson, Richard F. *Sweden: Prototype of Modern Society*. New York: Random House, 1970.

Verba, Sidney, and Norman H. Nie. *Participation in America: Political Democracy and Social Equality*. New York: Harper and Row, 1972.

Wright, Charles R., and Herbert H. Human. "Voluntary Association Memberships of American Adults: Evidence from National Sample Surveys." *American Sociological Review* 23 (June 1958):284–94.

Zetterberg, Hans L. "Voluntary Associations and Organized Power in Sweden." Columbia University Bureau of Applied Social Research, mimeograph, 1959.

Chapter Six

Alford, Robert R. and Eugene C. Lee. "Voting Turnout in American Cities." *American Political Science Review* 62 (September 1968):796–813.

Alford, Robert and Harry Scoble. "Sources of Local Political Involvement." *American Political Science Review* 62 (December 1968):1192–1206.

Berelson, Bernard, Paul F. Lazarsfeld, and William McPhee. *Voting*. Chicago: University of Chicago Press, 1954. Pp. 336–337.

Buchanan, William. "An Inquiry into Purposive Voting." *Journal of Politics* 18 (May 1956):281–296.

Campbell, Angus, Philip E. Converse, Warren E. Miller, and Donald E. Stokes. *The American Voter*. New York: John Wiley and Sons, 1960. Pp. 49–64, 250 ff.

Campbell, Angus, Gerald Gurin, and Warren E. Miller. *The Voter Decides*. Evanston, Ill.: Row, Peterson, 1954. Pp. 187–194.

Campbell, Angus and Robert L. Kahn. *The People Elect a President*. Ann Arbor: Survey Research Center, 1952. P. 29.

Connelly, Gordon M. and Harry H. Field. "The Non-Voter: Who He Is, What He Thinks." *Public Opinion Quarterly* 8 (Summer 1944):175–87.

Dahl, Robert A. *A Preface to Democratic Theory*. Chicago: University of Chicago Press, 1956.

Dahl, Robert A. *Who Governs?* New Haven, Conn.: Yale University Press, 1956. Pp. 276–78.

Deutsch, Karl. "Social Mobilization and Political Development." *American Political Science Review* 55 (September 1961):493–514.

Erbe, William. "Social Involvement and Political Activity: A Replication and Elaboration." *American Sociological Review* 29 (April 1964):198–215.

Glaser, William A. "Intention and Voting Turnout." *American Political Science Review* 52 (December 1958):1030–40.

Glaser, William A. "The Family and Voting Turnout." *Public Opinion Quarterly* 24 (Winter 1960):563–70.

Glaser, William A. "Television and Voting Turnout." *Public Opinion Quarterly* 29 (Spring 1965):74–86.

Glenn, Norval D. and Michael Grimes. "Aging, Voting, and Political Interest." *American Sociological Review* 33 (August 1968):563–75.

Hastings, Philip K. "The Voter and the Non-Voter." *American Journal of Sociology* 62 (November 1956):302–7.

Janowitz, Morris and Dwaine Marvick. *Competitive Pressure and Democratic Consent*. Ann Arbor, Mich.: University of Michigan Press, 1956. P. 26.

Karlsson, Georg. "Voting Participation among Male Swedish Youth." *Acta Sociologica* 3 (1958):98–111.

Key, V. O., Jr. *Political Parties and Pressure Groups*. New York: Thomas Y. Crowell, 1958. Pp. 622 ff.

Kornhauser, William. *The Politics of Mass Society*. Glencoe, Ill.: Free Press, 1959.

Lane, Robert. *Political Life*. Glencoe, Ill.: Free Press, 1959.

Lazarsfeld, Paul F., Bernard Berelson, and Hazel Gaudet. *The People's Choice*. New York: Duell, Sloan, and Pearce, 1944. Pp. 40–51, 121–25, 145–47.

Lipset, Seymour Martin. *Political Man*. New York: Doubleday and Co., 1960.

Lipset, Seymour Martin, Paul Lazarsfeld, A. H. Barton, and J. Linz. "The Psychology of Voting: An Analysis of Political Behavior." In *Handbook of Social Psychology*, vol. 2, ed. by Gardner Lindzey. Cambridge, Mass.: Addison-Wesley Co., 1954. Pp. 1124–75.

Lipset, Seymour Martin, Martin Trow, and James Coleman. *Union Democracy*. Glencoe, Ill.: Free Press, 1956.

Maccoby, Herbert. "The Differential Political Activity of Participants in Voluntary Associations." *American Sociological Review* 23 (October 1958): 524–32.

Merriam, Charles and Harold F. Gosnell. *Non-Voting*. Chicago: University of Chicago Press, 1924.

Milbrath, Lester W. *Political Participation*. Chicago: Rand McNally, 1965.

Miller, Mungo. "The Waukegan Study of Voter Turnout Prediction." *Public Opinion Quarterly* 16 (Fall 1952):381–98.

Nie, Norman H., G. Bingham Powell, Jr., and Kenneth Prewitt. "Social Structure and Political Participation: Developmental Relationships." *American Political Science Review* 63 (June and September 1969):361–78 and 808–32.

Nisbet, Robert. *Community and Power*. New York: Oxford University Press, 1962.

Olsen, Marvin E. "Social and Political Participation of Blacks." *American Sociological Review* 35 (August 1970):682–97.

Orum, Anthony M. "A Reappraisal of the Social and Political Participation of Negroes." *American Journal of Sociology* 72 (July 1966):32–46.

Pinard, Maurice. "Mass Society and Political Movements: A New Formulation." *American Journal of Sociology* 78 (May 1968):682–90.

Ranney, Austin, and Leon D. Epstein. "The Two Electorates: Voters and Non-Voters in a Wisconsin Primary." *Journal of Politics* 28 (August 1966):598–616.

Sudman, Seymour. "Probability Sampling with Quotas." *Journal of the American Statistical Association* 61 (September 1966):749–71.

Tocqueville, Alexis de. *Democracy in America*, trans. by Henry Reeve. New York: Schocken Books, 1961. (Originally published in French in 1840.)

Truman, David B. *The Governmental Process*. New York: Alfred A. Knopf, 1951.

Zimmer, Basil G. and Amos H. Hawley. "The Significance of Membership in Voluntary Associations." *American Journal of Sociology* 65 (1959):196–201.

Chapter Seven

Alford, Robert R., and Harry Scoble. "Sources of Local Political Involvement." *American Political Science Review* 62 (December 1962):1192–1206.

Berry, David. *The Sociology of Grass Roots Politics*. London: Macmillan & Co., 1970.

Blau, Peter M., and Otis Dudley Duncan. *The American Occupational Structure*. New York: John Wiley, 1967.

Bowman, Lewis, and G. R. Boynton. "Recruitment Patterns among Local Party Officials." *American Political Science Review* 60 (September 1966):667–76.

Bowman, Lewis, Dennis Ippolito, and William Donaldson. "Incentives for the Maintenance of Grass Roots Political Activism." *Midwest Journal of Political Science* 13 (February 1969):126–39.

Campbell, Angus, Gerald Burin, and Warren E. Miller. *The Voter Decides*. Evanston, Ill.: Row, Peterson, 1954.

Conway, Margaret, and Frank B. Feigert. "Motivation, Incentive Systems, and the Political Party Organization." *American Political Science Review* 62 (December 1968):1159–73.

Deutsch, Karl W. "Social Mobilization and Political Development." *American Political Science Review* 55 (September 1961):493–514.

Duverger, Maurice. *Political Parties: Their Organization and Activities in the Modern State*, trans. by B. North and R. North. New York: John Wiley, 1963.

Eldersveld, Samuel J. *Political Parties: A Behavioral Analysis*. Chicago: Rand McNally, 1964.

Erbe, William. "Social Involvement and Political Activity: A Replication and Elaboration." *American Sociological Review* 29 (April 1964):198–215.

Hirschfield, Robert S., Bert E. Swanson, and Blanche D. Blank. "A Profile of Political Activists in Manhattan." *Western Political Quarterly* 15 (1962):489–506.

Holt, Robert T., and John E. Turner. *Political Parties in Action: The Battle of Barons Court*. New York: Free Press. 1968.

Ippolito, Dennis. "Motivational Reorientation and Change among Party Activists." *Journal of Politics* 31 (November 1969):1098–1101.

Keefe, William J., and William C. Seyler. "Precinct Politicians in Pittsburg." *Social Science* 35 (Winter 1960):31.

Key, V. O., Jr. *Politics, Parties, and Pressure Groups,* 5th ed. New York: Thomas Y. Crowell, 1964.

Knoke, David. "A Causal Model for the Political Party Preferences of American Men." *American Sociological Review* 37 (December 1972):679–89.

Lane, Robert E. *Political Life: Why and How People Get Involved in Politics.* New York: Free Press, 1959.

Marvick, Dwaine, and Charles Nixon. *Political Decision-Makers.* New York: Free Press, 1961.

Milbrath, Lester W. *Political Participation: How and Why Do People Get Involved in Politics?* Chicago: Rand McNally, 1965.

Monroe, Alan D. "Political Party Activism: Causes and Consequences." Ph.D. dissertation, Department of Political Science, Indiana University, 1971.

Nie, Norman H., G. Bingham Powell, Jr., and Kenneth Prewitt. "Social Structure and Political Participation: Developmental Relationships." *American Political Science Review* 63 (June and September 1961):361–78, 682–97.

Olsen, Marvin E. "Social and Political Participation of Blacks." *American Sociological Review* 35 (August):682–97.

Palma, Giuseppe di. *Apathy and Participation: Mass Politics in Western Societies.* New York: Free Press, 1970.

Patterson, Samuel C. "Characteristics of Party Leaders." *Western Political Quarterly* 16 (June 1963):332–52.

Reiss, Albert J., Jr. *Occupations and Social Status.* New York: The Free Press, 1961. pp. 109–38, 263–75.

Rokkan, Stein. *Citizens, Elections, Parties.* New York: David McKay Co., 1970.

Verba, Sidney, and Norman H. Nie. *Participation in America: Political Democracy and Social Equality.* New York: Harper and Row, 1972.

Chapter Eight

Andrén, Nils. *Modern Swedish Government.* Stockholm: Almqvist & Wiksell, 1968. Chs. 2, 10.

Baskin, Darryl. *American Pluralist Democracy: A Critique.* New York: Van Nostrand and Reinhold, 1971.

Dahl, Robert A. *A Preface to Democratic Theory.* Chicago: University of Chicago Press, 1956.

Domhoff, G. William, *The Higher Circles.* New York: Random House, 1970.

Elvander, Nils. *Intresseorganisationerna i Dagens Sverige.* Lund: CWK Gleerup Bokförlag, 1966.

Elvander, Nils. "Democracy and Large Organizations." in M. Donald Hancock and Gideon Sjoberg, eds., *Politics in the Post-Welfare State* New York: Columbia University Press, 1972a. Pp. 302–24.

Elvander, Nils. "The Politics of Taxation in Sweden 1945–1970: A Study of the Functions of Parties and Organisations." *Scandinavian Political Studies,* 7 (1972b):63–82.

Fleisher, Frederic. *The New Sweden: The Challenge of a Disciplined Democracy.* New York: David McKay Co., 1967. Chs. 4, 8.

Fleisher, Wilfred. *Sweden: The Welfare State.* New York: J. Day Co. 1956.

Garinger, Gail. "The Consumers' Cooperative Movement: A Study in the 'Iron Law of Oligarchy.'" Research paper, Department of Sociology, Indiana University, 1968.

Gusfield, Joseph R. "Mass Society and Extremist Politics." *The American Sociological Review* 27 (February 1962):19–30.

Heckscher, Gunnar. "Interest Groups in Sweden." In Henry W. Ehrmann, ed., *Interest Groups in Four Continents*. Pittsburgh: University of Pittsburgh Press, 1958a. Pp. 154–72.

Heckscher, Gunnar. "The Role of the Voluntary Organization in Swedish Democracy." In Joseph A. Lauwerys, ed., *Scandinavian Democracy*. Copenhagen: Danish Institute, 1958b. Pp. 126–39.

Huntford, Roland. *The New Totalitarians*. London: Allen Lane, Penguin Press, 1971. Chs. 5, 7.

Jenkins, David. *Sweden and the Price of Progress*. New York: Coward-McCann, 1968. Ch. 5.

Key, V. O., Jr. *Public Opinion and American Democracy*. New York: Alfred A. Knopf, 1963.

Kornhauser, William. *The Politics of Mass Society*. Glencoe, Ill.: Free Press, 1959.

Lipset, Seymour Martin. *Political Man*. Garden City, N. Y.: Doubleday, 1959.

Lundqvist, Lennart. "Crisis, Change, and Public Policy: Considerations for a Comparative Analysis of Environmental Policies." *European Journal of Political Research* 1 (June 1973):133–62.

Meijer, Hans. "Bureaucracy and Policy Formulation in Sweden." In Olof Ruin, ed., *Scandinavian Political Studies,* vol. 4/69. Oslo: Universitetsförlaget, 1969. Pp. 103–16.

Michels, Robert. *Political Parties,* trans. by Eden and Cedar Paul. New York: Free Press, 1966. (Originally published in Italian in 1911.)

Miliband, Ralph. *The State in Capitalist Society*. New York: Basic Books, 1969.

Mills, C. Wright. *The Power Elite*. New York: Oxford University Press, 1956.

Nisbet, Robert. *Community and Power*. New York: Oxford University Press, 1962. Ch. 11.

Presthus, Robert. *Men at the Top: A Study in Community Power*. New York: Oxford University Press, 1964.

Riesman, David, Nathan Glazer, and Reuel Denny. *The Lonely Crowd*. New Haven, Conn.: Yale University Press, 1951.

Rustow, Dankwart A. *The Politics of Compromise: A Study of Parties and Cabinet Government in Sweden*. Princeton, N. J.: Princeton University Press, 1955. Ch. 6.

The Swedish Institute, *Fact Sheets on Sweden: Law and Justice in Sweden* Stockholm: Swedish Institute, 1970a.

The Swedish Institute. *Fact Sheets on Sweden: Swedish Government in Action*. Stockholm: Swedish Institute, 1970b.

Tomasson, Richard F., *Sweden: Prototype of Modern Society*. New York: Random House, 1970, Chs. 2 & 8.

Vinde, Pierre. *Swedish Government Administration*. Stockholm: Swedish Institute, 1971.

Wheeler, Christopher. *White Collar Power: Changing Patterns of Interest Behavior in Sweden*. Urbana: University of Illinois Press, 1975.

Chapter Nine

Andrén, Nils. *Modern Swedish Government*. Stockholm: Almqvist & Wiksell, 1968. Chs. 2, 10.

Carey, Jane Perry, and Andrew Galbraith Carey. "Swedish Politics in the Late Nineteen-Sixties: Dynamic Stability." *Political Science Quarterly* 84 (September 1969):461–85.

Carlson, Bo. *Trade Unions in Sweden.* Stockholm: Tidens Förlag, 1969. Pp. 101–33.

Elvander, Nils. *Intresseorganisationerna i Dagens Sverige.* Lund: CWK Gleerup Bokförlag.

Elvander, Nils. "Democracy and Large Organizations." In M. Donald Hancock and Gideon Sjoberg, eds., *Politics in the Post-Welfare State.* New York: Columbia University Press, 1972a. Pp. 302–24.

Elvander, Nils. "The Politics of Taxation in Sweden: 1945-1970: A Study of the Functions of Parties and Organisations." *Scandinavian Political Studies,* (1972b)63–82.

Fleisher, Frederic. *The New Sweden: The Challenge of a Disciplined Democracy.* New York: David McKay Co., 1967.

Hammar, Thomas. "Government." In *Facts about Sweden.* Stockholm: Swedish Institute, 1969.

Heckscher, Gunnar. "Interest Groups in Sweden." In Henry W. Ehrmann, ed., *Interest Groups in Four Continents.* Pittsburgh: University of Pittsburgh Press, 1958a. Pp. 154–72.

Heckscher, Gunnar. "The Role of the Voluntary Organization in Swedish Democracy." In Joseph A. Lauwerys, ed., *Scandinavian Democracy,* Copenhagen: Danish Institute, 1958b. Pp. 126–39.

Huntford, Roland. *The New Totalitarians.* London: Allen Lane, Penguin Press, 1971. Chs. 5, 7.

Jenkins, David. *Sweden and the Price of Progress.* New York: Coward-McCann Co., 1968. Ch. 5.

Lundqvist, Lennart. "Crisis, Change, and Public Policy: Considerations for a Comparative Analysis of Environmental Policies." *European Journal of Political Research* 1 (June 1973):133–62.

Meijer, Hans. "Bureaucracy and Policy Formulation in Sweden." In Olof Ruin, ed., *Scandinavian Political Studies,* vol. 4/69. Oslo: Universitetsförlaget. 1969. Pp. 103–16.

Nisbet, Robert. *Community and Power.* New York: Oxford University Press, 1962.

Olsen, Marvin E. *Power in Societies.* New York: Macmillan, 1970.

Rustow, Dankwart A. *The Politics of Compromise: A Study of Parties and Cabinet Government in Sweden.* Princeton, N. J.: Princeton University Press, 1955.

Sjoberg, Gideon, M. Donald Hancock, and Orion White, Jr. *Politics in the Post-Welfare State: A Comparison of the United States and Sweden.* Bloomington: Indiana University, 1967.

Stjernquist, Nils. "Sweden: Stability or Deadlock." In Robert Dahl, ed., *Political Opposition in Western Democracies.* New Haven, Conn.: Yale University Press, 1966. Pp. 118–46.

The Swedish Institute. *Fact Sheets on Sweden: Law and Justice in Sweden.* Stockholm: Swedish Institute, 1970a.

The Swedish Institute. *Fact Sheets on Sweden: Swedish Government in Action.* Stockholm: Swedish Institute, 1970b.

Tocqueville, Alexis de. *Democracy in America,* vol. 2, book 4. Trans. by Henry Reeve. New York: Schocken Books, 1961. (Originally published in French in 1840.)

Tomasson, Richard F. *Sweden: Prototype of Modern Society.* New York: Random House, 1970.

Vinde, Pierre. *Swedish Government Administration*. Stockholm: The Swedish Institute, 1971.

Wheeler, Christopher. *White Collar Power: Changing Patterns of Interest Behavior in Sweden*. Urbana: University of Illinois Press, 1975.

Chapter Ten

Abrahamsson, Bengt. *Bureaucracy or Participation*. Beverly Hills, Cal.: Sage Publications, 1977.

Bell, Daniel. "The Adequacy of Our Concepts." In Bertram M. Gross, ed., *A Great Society*. New York: Basic Books, 1968. Ch. 6.

Bell, Daniel. *The Coming of Post-Industrial Society*. New York: Basic Books, 1972.

Blau, Peter M. "Decentralization in Bureaucracies." in Mayer N. Zald, ed., *Power in Organizations*. Nashville, Tenn.: Vanderbilt University Press, 1970. Ch. 4.

Cole, G. D. H. *Social Theory*. London: Methuen, 1920.

Cook, Terrence E., and Patrick M. Morgan. *Participatory Democracy*. San Francisco: Canfield Press, 1971.

Cottrell, Fred. *Energy and Society*. New York: McGraw-Hill, 1955.

Drucker, Peter. *The Age of Discontinuity: Guidelines to Our Changing Society*. New York: Harper and Row, 1968.

Etzioni, Amitai. *The Active Society*. New York: Free Press, 1968.

Galbraith, John Kenneth. *American Capitalism*. Boston: Houghton Mifflin, 1952.

Likert, Rensis. *New Patterns of Management*. New York: McGraw-Hill, 1961.

Litwak, Eugene. "Models of Bureaucracy That Permit Conflict." *American Journal of Sociology* 67 (September 1961):177–84.

Michels, Robert. *Political Parties*. New York: Free Press, 1962. (Originally published in Italian in 1911.)

Nisbet, Robert. *Community and Power*. New York: Oxford University Press, 1962.

O'Toole, James. *Energy and Social Change*. Cambridge, Mass.: MIT Press, 1976.

Palma, Giuseppe di. *Apathy and Participation: Mass Politics in Western Societies*. New York: Free Press, 1970.

Pateman, Carole. *Participation and Democratic Theory*. Cambridge, Eng.: Cambridge University Press, 1970.

Thayer, Frederick C. *An End to Hierarchy! An End to Competition!* New York: Franklin Watts, 1973.

Weber, Max. *The Theory of Social and Economic Organization*. Glencoe, Ill.: Free Press, 1947.

Index

311